SOUTHAMPTON AND HAVRE STATION.

SEASON, 1829.

Will Start from Southampton.

AUGUST.

Saturday, - 15th, at 7 morn.
Thursday, - 20th, at 6 even.
Tuesday, - 25th, at 4 aftern.
Monday, - 31st, at 7 even.

SEPTEMBER.

Saturday, - 5th, at 6 aftern.
Thursday, - 10th, at 4 aftern.
Tuesday, - 15th, at 7 morn.

SEPTEMBER.

Monday, - 21st, at 6 even.
Friday, - 25th, at 5 aftern.
Wednesday, 30th, at 6 even.

OCTOBER.

Tuesday, - 6th, at 5 aftern.
Tuesday, - 13th, at 5 aftern.
Tuesday, - 20th, at 5 aftern.
Tuesday, - 27th, at 5 aftern.

Will Start from Havre.

AUGUST.

Wednesday, 12th, at 6 even.
Monday, - 17th, at 9 even.
Saturday, - 22nd, at 2 aftern.
Friday, - 28th, at 7 morn.

SEPTEMBER.

Wednesday, 2nd, at 11 morn.
Tuesday, - 8th, at 3 aftern.
Saturday, - 12th, at 6 morn.
Friday, - 18th, at 1 aftern.

SEPTEMBER.

Wednesday, 23rd, at 5 aftern.
Monday, - 28th, at 8 morn.

OCTOBER.

Friday, - 2nd, at 12 noon.
Friday, - 9th, at 5 aftern.
Friday, - 16th, at 12 noon.
Friday, - 23rd, at 5 aftern.
Friday, - 30th, at 12 noon.

GEORGE IV. calls at Portsmouth for Passengers about an Hour and a Half after Starting.

FARES:

Each Passenger	-	£2 2 0	Carriages	- - -	£4 4 0
Servants and Children	-	1 1 0	Horses	- - -	4 4 0

A STEWARDESS WILL ATTEND ON THE LADIES.

EARLY SOLENT STEAMERS

For: John & Margaret —
Hope it's readeble — love,
cousin
Fred
5/93

EARLY SOLENT
STEAMERS

A History of Local Steam Navigation

CAPTAIN F. T. O'BRIEN

Glasgow
PROWN, SON & FERGUSON, LTD., NAUTICAL PUBLISHERS,
52 Darnley Street

For my daughter, Caroline

First printed in 1973 by David & Charles (Holdings) Ltd.

2nd Edition 1981

ISBN 0 85174 417 6

© Brown, Son & Ferguson, Ltd.,
52, Darnley Street,
Glasgow G41 2SL

CONTENTS

LIST OF ILLUSTRATIONS

LINE DRAWINGS IN THE TEXT

8

9

FOREWORD

By Admiral of the Fleet the Earl MOUNTBATTEN OF BURMA, KG, PC, GCB, OM, GSSI, GCIE, GCVO, DSO, Governor of the Isle of Wight.

JUST AS the era of the sail ship has proved such a fascination for so many people, so too has the era of the steam ship, and I am sure all who read Captain O'Brien's book about the early Solent steamers will find it an excellent account of the early days of steam navigation in the Solent. He has evidently done very careful and extensive research, not only into the facts, but has succeeded in reproducing some very interesting pictures and photographs.

It is almost sixty years ago, in fact on 8 May 1913, that I did my first trip from the mainland to the Isle of Wight in a steamer. I was then seven weeks short of my 13th birthday and was on my way to join the Royal Naval College at Osborne as a naval cadet.

Since then I have made countless trips to the Island, not only while I was at the college and later when my parents lived at Kent House in East Cowes, but latterly I have been a fairly regular passenger in the Red Funnel steamers when visiting the Isle of Wight in my capacity as Governor.

Many of the early steamers were called after members of my family: the *Princess Victoria*, the *Duchess of Kent*, the *Princess of Wales*, the *Prince Albert*, the *Prince of Wales*, the *Princess Royal*, the *Duke of Edinburgh*, the *Princess Alice*, the *Princess Louise*, the *Princess Beatrice*, the *Duchess of Edinburgh*, and the *Duchess of Connaught*. One of the very latest, the *Cowes Castle*, was launched by my elder daughter Patricia, Lady Brabourne, so our family have a continuing interest in them.

The Solent steamers have played a vital part in the development of the Isle of Wight, and particularly in making the island one of the great tourist attractions in the British Isles, and Captain O'Brien is to be congratulated for his efforts in putting on record this important part of British maritime history.

Mountbatten of Burma

A. F.

INTRODUCTION

THIS BOOK sets out to tell the story of the early days of steam navigation in the Solent—a small but important chapter of maritime history which has hitherto gone unrecorded.

Since few records concerning these early steamers and their service have survived the years, much of the initial research was devoted to consultation of numerous local newspapers and extraction of the names of steamers and the dates on which they were placed in service. This information and other newspaper reports provided the basis of the work and made possible subsequent reference to the few remaining official records relating to these vessels. The names and dates of the principal newspapers consulted will be found on page 236.

No attempt has been made to interpret 'advertised' or claimed tonnage or to alter 'burthen' or other forms of tonnage, the interpretation of which changed frequently during the nineteenth century. Masters' names, where known, have been quoted and may, it is hoped, help to identify some of the many strange sail to be found in this book, particularly among the cross-Channel and coasting vessels. Ship registrations, where quoted in full, are taken from records held at HM Customs and Excise Offices and by the Registrar-General of Shipping and Seamen, at Cardiff.

Because this is the first such history of local steam navigation in the Solent, and despite the several years of research devoted to its compilation, it lays no claim to be fully comprehensive and the author would welcome any new information or illustrations which might help to supplement this record or to fill in such gaps as there may be.

F. T. O'BRIEN

Cowes, Isle of Wight

CHAPTER ONE

SOUTHAMPTON AND COWES STEAMERS: 1815-39

> Boatman, shove in, and take me up
>   for I'm in haste to cross.
> If I'm not ferried o'er tonight
>   I shall sustain great loss.
>
> Well, lose or gain, Sir, sink or swim,
>   t'is more than I dare do.
> My bark's now off, is quite choke full
>   and I've no room for you.
>
> <div align="right">THE FERRY BOAT—<i>Nautical Magazine</i> 1835,
but of earlier origin</div>

THE SOLENT, which forms the background to this story of early local steam navigation, divides the Isle of Wight from the mainland and is approximately twenty miles in length measuring from the Nab entrance to the Needles. For centuries it has been an important highway for coastal and foreign-going vessels, encompassing within its limits the medieval port of Southampton at the head of the six mile-long Southampton Water, the later naval arsenal of Portsmouth and the shipbuilding rivers of Hamble, Beaulieu and Lymington. The Solent is sheltered, well-piloted and offers good holding-ground in Cowes Roads and at Motherbank. It also has the considerable advantage of a double high-water twice in every twenty-four hours—a phenomenon mentioned as long ago as the seventh century by the Venerable Bede and traditionally associated with the celebrated but unsuccessful tidal demonstration credited to King Canute.

The story of steam vessels in the Solent begins in Cowes, for it was here, in 1820, that the principal owner of the first local steam boat, George Ward of Northwood House, Cowes, lord of the manor of Debourne, established a steam-packet service to operate between Cowes and Southampton. And it was from Cowes that the first masters and crews came.

Then, as now, trade to the Isle of Wight depended upon sea routes to and from the mainland and Cowes, strategically situated at the mouth of the Medina river, which is navigable to Newport, the capital of the island, gradually developed until, by the eighteenth century, it was overtaking Newport as the island's principal port. Although the population of Cowes at the turn of the nineteenth century was little more than 2,000, many craft were based there including fishing and pilot boats and coastal and cross-Channel vessels. The wooden shipbuilding yards, particularly those of Thomas White (1773-1859) and Lynn Ratsey (1764-1830), were kept busy and their services were also in frequent demand for repairs and maintenance to vessels in the Roads.

A major factor in the prosperity of Cowes, and one that was to make her name famous throughout the world, was the sport of yachting. Yacht racing began at Cowes in the late eighteenth century, the races taking place principally during the summer months and mainly under the supervision of the local sub-commissioners of pilotage of Trinity House. The influence of these activities further increased after 1815, when a group of distinguished yachtsmen formed the Yacht Club. The Prince Regent—later, in 1820, George IV—became a member in 1817, as did the King's brothers, the Dukes of Clarence and Gloucester in the following year. This royal patronage led to the new

16

Page 17 (*above*) Southampton's first steamer, the *Prince of Cobourg*, hulked on Woolston shore, opposite the tidal dock, c 1843; (*below*) the *Thames*, Southampton's second steam packet, 1821, from an anonymous watercolour

Page 18 (above) The Royal Pier, Southampton, c 1840. The Island steamer is dwarfed by the large P&O or R.W.I. mail steamer; (below) the *Ruby* (ex-*Pride of The Waters*) at Ryde Pier Head, October 1846

title in 1820 of the Royal Yacht Club, to be changed again in 1833 to that of the Royal Yacht Squadron, as it is still known today. The first Commodore, in 1833, was Charles Pelham, 1st Earl of Yarborough (1781-1846) of Appledurcombe, whose yacht *Falcon* was a full-rigged, three-masted ship of some 183 tons, 87ft in length, with a beam of 22ft 3in and a depth of 6ft 5in[1]. Such yachts, large even by present-day standards, were then not uncommon and the *Falcon* was later sold, in 1836, to London owners for use in the South Seas trade. At this time, the Royal Yacht Squadron fleet comprised more than a hundred vessels aggregating well over 9,000 tons and employing over a thousand seamen. The Squadron clubhouse still dominates Cowes seafront.[2]

Cowes provided yet another interest during the early years of the nineteenth century for it had become extremely fashionable as a spa—seaside holidays having been popularised by George III's partiality for Weymouth and the Prince Regent's liking for Brighton. And the bathing machine, that very necessary apparatus in a far from permissive society, was available in considerable numbers at Cowes, where it was hauled up and down the beach and kept level with the tide by means of capstans, instead of the horses employed at most other resorts for this purpose. Thus, the wealthy and fashionable would flock to Cowes in the summer months, bringing variety and prosperity to an increasingly thriving little community of merchants, shipowners, tradesmen and seamen. Then, as now, walks taken along Cowes Parade, rebuilt in 1824 and claimed as the finest promenade in England, were extremely popular.

The principal landing at Cowes, as is the case today, was the Fountain Quay, West Cowes, situated opposite the old Fountain Inn, which was extensively rebuilt in 1810, though the exterior remains virtually unchanged. The Quay, built in 1816, was considerably enlarged in 1824 by George Ward. A 70-ft-long wooden jetty was added in 1836 which was replaced in 1846 by a stone pier, 100ft in length and 24ft wide. The pier was extensively repaired some nine years later and finally, in 1861, most of it was removed and a 'cottage loaf'-shaped pontoon secured in place to facilitate the embarkation and landing of passengers, a forerunner of those in use today. The old quay at East Cowes was rebuilt in 1834, partly with stones from the ruins of Antwerp Cathedral, brought to Cowes in the form of ships' ballast.

The sailing vessels which maintained the passage between Cowes and the mainland, and which were soon to be replaced by steam boats, were well built and fast. Indeed, one Cowes-built ship, the 40-ton pilot-cutter *Lively* (Capt Avery) was bought by the London whaling-ship owners, Messrs Enderby, in 1831-32 for use as a tender to their whalers in the South Seas and sailed out to Port Phillip, Australia, via the Falkland Islands and Cape Horn, in five months. Nearer home, most Cowes-built passage vessels could make the crossing from Cowes to Southampton, under favourable conditions, in $2\frac{1}{2}$ hours. These included such ships as the 30-ton *Mermaid* (built 1810: 40ft 8in x 14ft 6in x 7ft 6in) and the 42-ton *Frederick* (built 1802: 48ft 2in x 15ft $5\frac{1}{2}$in x 7ft 11in). The Cowes to Portsmouth passage was maintained by the 32-ton *Sons of Commerce* (built 1812: 41ft x 14ft 4in x 7ft 11in) and the 31-ton *Fox* (built 1806: 40ft 10in x 14ft $4\frac{1}{2}$in x 7ft $5\frac{1}{2}$in). But sometimes, under adverse wind and tidal conditions, the passage could prove extremely tedious; as Hessle complained in 1790 when his trip from Portsmouth to Cowes took all of seven hours.[3]

On windless days it was a case of 'Down sail and out oars', as Capt James Windover found on one occasion when he was obliged to forsake the *Mermaid* for a rowing-boat. This was in 1827 and the *Hants Chronicle* of 1 January reported:

> In consequence of the dead calm on Saturday afternoon, Mr Windover was obliged to proceed with the mail from Cowes in an open boat. Fog came on and after rowing till seven o'clock in the evening and thinking they were near Southampton, they re-

entered Cowes Harbour, fortunately without meeting any accident.

Southampton at the turn of the nineteenth century was a small but thriving port numbering some 8,000 inhabitants.[4] The great days of its medieval wool and wine trade with the Mediterranean had long ceased but the coastal and cross-Channel trade continued and shipbuilding was extensively carried out in the small yards along the banks of the river Itchen. Like other coastal towns, Southampton was also deemed a spa and though much of the town was contained within the old walls, new buildings were erected to provide accommodation for the visitor. The celebrated Assembly Rooms have long since gone, but the 'Dolphin' and 'Star' inns in the High Street remain as examples of this period.

At the waterfront, however, only at the town quay, situated by the Water Gate, could vessels come alongside. It was not until 1833 that the Royal Pier was built by William Betts, a Kent building contractor who had settled in Southampton, to the design of John Doswell (1782-1856), surveyor and engineer to the Southampton Harbour commissioners for more than fifty years. The pier was erected over the site of the old breakwater on which building had started in 1804 when the old sailing vessel *Snow Queen* was sunk close in to the shore at a point later to be protected by an embankment, built in 1820. The pier, 246ft in length and 36ft wide, comprised a roadway bounded on each side by a footpath, 8ft wide. It was opened on 10 July 1833 by Princess Victoria, accompanied by her mother, the Duchess of Kent.[5] In August 1843, after she had ascended the throne, Victoria visited the pier again to embark in the royal yacht but, to the consternation of officialdom, it was found that the traditional red carpet laid out on the pier did not reach far enough, whereupon the mayor and aldermen placed their crimson robes upon the bare area, the Queen taking care not to tread upon the fur collars.

The development of Southampton in the Victoria era resulted

21

from the introduction of the steam engine, on both land and sea. The construction of extensive docks in Southampton had been proposed in an Act of Parliament of 1803 but it was not until 1836, in anticipation of the coming of the railway, that the Southampton Dock Company was formed under the chairmanship of Joseph Liggins, a West India merchant and shipowner who remained chairman of the company until the mid-1850s. '220 acres of muddied land' were then acquired at the mouth of the Itchen and work on the dock commenced in 1838, the foundation stone being laid by Rear-Admiral Sir Lucius Curtis, KCB. This dock, now known as the Princess Alexandra Dock, was opened in August 1842 and was followed in November 1851 by the opening of the inner or close dock which was filled-in during 1965.

By the time the open dock had been completed in 1842, the London & Southampton Railway was already in operation, the terminus station having been built on marshlands at the eastern end of the town. But the railway had also taken a long time to come to fruition. Proposed in 1825, the necessary Act of Parliament was not obtained until 1833 and the building of the railway line occupied six years—1834 to 1840. By 1843, with both railway and dock in operation, Southampton was known as the 'Premier mail and passenger port of the United Kingdom', accommodating the large steam vessels of the Peninsular & Oriental Line and those of the Royal West India Mail S.P. Co. As a further measure of the town's development, the population, which in 1841 was 27,103, had by 1861 increased to 46,960.

Until the advent of steam boats, travellers and holidaymakers bound for the Isle of Wight were obliged to make the passage to Cowes by sailing craft. Rates for passengers and the carriage of goods on all routes to the I.O.W. were (By Private Act of Parliament of 1784) fixed annually by Hampshire Justices of the Peace at Quarter Sessions who also tried offenders. This Act was in force until 1939. A mail packet left Southampton for Cowes every morning at seven o'clock and returned in time for the London mail coach. Southampton-based packets of the early nineteenth century included the *Earl St Vincent*, the *Bee* and the *Mary Ann*.[6] Strong winds could mean the postponement of departure times, while very light winds or calms must have made such trips exceedingly wearisome, even though travellers of those days were hardy creatures who took the delays, discomforts and inconveniences, if not without complaint, at least in their stride. Yet, no doubt, then as now, there was much pleasure to be had from a passage on a good sailing day, such as *Skelton's Southampton Guide* of 1819 describes:

> The sail from Southampton to the island is replete with amusement. The river presents to the eye a broad extensive sheet of water, not unlike the noble estuaries of the New World; the banks of which, sloping gradually to the river side, are covered with noble woods and afford much sylvan scenery.

The introduction of local steam navigation was announced in December 1815, when the *Hants Chronicle* reported that 'the projectors of steam boats are contemplating an Isle of Wight service'. But five years were to elapse before these 'contemplations' had any result, by which time the rapid development of the steam vessel had lead to many improvements. The history of steam navigation had, of course, begun long before, this method of propulsion having been proposed as early as 1543, though its practical application had had to await Newcomen's atmospheric engine of 1712, which was used by the accepted pioneer of the steam boat, the Marquis Jouffroy d'Abbans[7], for his first experiments in 1778. The atmospheric engine of this time, however, was too heavy and too low powered for use afloat and further development in this direction was delayed until the introduction of Watt's condenser and Trevithick's high-pressure engine.

Steam boat services in Europe were pioneered by Henry Bell, Scottish engineer and inventor (1767-1830), with the 51ft-long wooden paddle-boat, the *Comet*, which had a low-pressure engine fired by a simple boiler set in brickwork. In August 1812 the *Comet*, capable of a speed of almost seven knots, maintained a passenger service between Glasgow, Greenock and Helensburgh —thirteen years before the world's first passenger rail service was to be inaugurated between Stockton and Darlington.

The *Comet* carried a sail set upon a yard mounted on her funnel, and even up to the end of the nineteenth century many steamships continued to carry and use sails. Indeed, many of the early steamers were provided with up to three masts with sails. Most of these were designed as steamships, and were not converted sailing vessels, although they came from the yards of builders of sailing vessels and the methods of constructing their wooden hulls were the same. These were usually of pine planking on oak frames, secured by means of 'treenails' or wooden pegs, or copper bolts. Such hulls would often 'work' in a seaway or during heavy weather, often to such an extent as to fracture the paddle-wheel shaft. In the early steamers, the paddle-wheel axis or shaft was sited just forward of amidships so that the weight of engine,[8] boiler and tall funnel, usually some two feet in diameter, could be located directly amidships in the interests of trim and stability.

The first steam vessel to appear in the Solent was the 49-ton steam yacht *Thames* (Capt Dodd), which put into Portsmouth on 9 June 1815, while on passage from the Clyde to London. The *Thames* was built on the Clyde by J. & C. Wood of Glasgow in 1814 and originally named the *Duke of Argyle*. Carvel-built of wood (76ft 6in x 14ft 6in [over paddle boxes, 25ft] x 6ft 6in), her 9ft diameter and 4ft wide paddle wheels, with six floats to each wheel, were driven by a 14hp single-cylinder, side-lever engine built by James Cook of Tradeston and, at 30 rpm, gave the *Thames* a speed of just over six knots. She carried 15 tons of coal, which gave her a range of about 1,500 miles.[9] In the course of her passage from the Clyde—the first open-sea voyage undertaken by a British steam vessel—she put into both Dublin and

Plymouth, having somewhat spectacularly demonstrated her command over wind and tide by taking a turn around the Waterford packet off Milford Haven before heaving-to and passing over some mail. Later, off Hayle, in Cornwall, she stopped and rescued the only two survivors of a party of ten young men and women whose boat had capsized during a squall while they were celebrating 'Not wisely but too well'.

The *Thames* gave another impressive demonstration on the day following her arrival at Portsmouth, when she made a three-hour cruise around the harbour and to and from Spithead. Among the naval officers on board as guests were Admiral Sir Edward Thornborough, KCB, and Rear-Admiral Halkett. It was reported that a speed of six knots had been attained 'against a strong flood tide 'and that 'She will make 10 knots with a favourable wind and tide'. On her 758-mile voyage from the Clyde, the *Thames* averaged 6·2 knots and on arrival in London she was employed on the London to Margate service until 1816, when she replaced the steam boat *Margery*, sailing between London and Gravesend.

The first steamer to operate in the Solent was the *Britannia* of 70 tons burthen, which maintained the passage between Portsmouth and Ryde for a brief period during May and June of 1817. Her arrival, and the earlier success of the *Comet*, further stimulated interest in steam navigation in the Solent area, and this culminated in 1820 with the introduction of a steam packet, the *Prince of Cobourg*, on the passage between Southampton and Cowes. The pioneering local shipowners responsible were George Ward and William Fitzhugh acting, it is recorded, upon the suggestion of Capt James Hoskins Knight. (See Chapter 9, Owners and Masters.)

The *Prince of Cobourg* was built at Gainsborough, Lincolnshire, in 1817. The builder was Henry Smith of Gainsborough, joint owner together with the famous Aaron Manby, iron founder of Horsley, Staffs. It was named after the husband of Charlotte

25

Augusta, daughter of the Prince Regent, who had been married the previous year. The *Cobourg* was a wooden, carvel-built paddle-wheel steam vessel with three masts and a bowsprit, and was typical of the early steamers as regards her size, 52 tons (71 burthen), and dimensions: length 76ft 11in, beam 14ft 4½in, and depth of hold, 5ft 10in. (Picture, p17.) Vessels of this time were often ornamented, and the *Cobourg* had a 'scroll' head and a square stern adorned with genuine quarter galleries as distinct from those which were merely painted on the stern and quarters and known as mock or sham galleries. The *Cobourg*'s paddle wheels were driven by a 24 hp low-pressure engine, a type which, despite some reduction in efficiency, afforded passengers and crew a not inconsiderable peace of mind because boiler explosions, resulting in damage to vessels and injury or death to passengers or crew, were by no means uncommon at this time. Indeed, the proprietors of the *Cobourg* took pains to assure their passengers:

> The public are respectfully informed that this steam vessel is fitted with the lower-pressure engine and safety valve, as enacted by Act of Parliament, and that from such fitting and construction, the danger that existed in steam vessels originally fitted without this improvement and security, is entirely removed, as will be clearly and satisfactorily explained by the Engineer on board, if required.—James Hoskins Knight, Master.

The *Prince of Cobourg* arrived in the Solent from Sheerness one week before going into service on Monday, 24 July 1820, and on 31 July the *Hants Telegraph* reported:

> The long-expected steam vessel, *Prince of Cobourg*, began to run between Southampton and Cowes as a regular post-office packet. She performed the voyage to Cowes and back, three times in a day, being a distance of nearly nine miles (sic), part of which was necessarily against the wind and tide. This fine vessel must be a great convenience to passengers, particularly in calms when only open boats may be used. Her velocity in a calm sea, even against the tide, is about 8 knots.

Her passage time would be about one and a half hours and the fares charged were 2s 6d in the state cabin and 1s 6d in the fore cabin, single. Until 1824 at Cowes, when the Fountain Quay was rebuilt, and 1833 at Southampton, when the Royal Pier was opened and then subject to tidal conditions, all passengers were obliged to board and disembark from the steamer by means of boats.

Burst boilers were apparently not the only hazard faced by passengers in the *Cobourg* for it was recorded on 8 November 1820: 'Last Saturday, the steam packet was returning from Cowes when one of the chains which support the ponderous iron funnel gave way, fell over the side, and sank. Providentially, no other mischief was done.' The passengers, however, appear to have remained undaunted because when the steamer was laid up for the winter, the usual practice on this station during the early years, the owners thought fit to announce:

> The proprietors of the *Cobourg* beg to return their thanks for the liberal encouragement they have met with during the past season and also inform the public in general, that she has ceased running until the Spring. That fast sailing packet *Frederick* (Capt J. H. Knight) will start from Southampton at precisely 8 o'clock in the morning and will leave Cowes at half past 4 o'clock in the afternoon. Fares: after cabin 1s 6d; fore cabin 1s.

In 1821 there came news of two other local steamers. The first report was in April, when it was stated that a steam boat built to tow barges on the Portsmouth & Arundel Canal was undergoing trials; the second was in May, when an announcement was made that the *Thames* was to operate on the Southampton to Cowes passage:

> The public are respectfully informed that the *Thames* steam yacht will leave Cowes every morning at half-past 8 o'clock and in the afternoon at 2 o'clock and will leave Southampton at 10 o'clock and 6 o'clock in the evening. Children under the age of three—free. Chief cabin 2s 6d, fore cabin 1s. It was by invitation of the members of the inhabitants and visitors of the Isle

MAIL *PACKET*

TO *COWES.*

CAPTAIN KNIGHT begs leave to inform the Public in general, that he has commenced running that fast-sailing Packet the FREDERICK to Cowes, for the Winter Season.— She will start from Southampton precisely at Eight in the morning, and leave Cowes at Half-past Four in the afternoon.—Fares, After Cabin, 1s. 6d.—Fore Cabin, 1s.

Southampton, Nov 6th, 1824.,

Sailing-packet notice of November 1824

of Wight and Southampton that this yacht was established in her present employ; and not in any spirit of opposition, but fully to accommodate the public the necessity of which is evident, from the impossibility of one packet being at two places at the same time. Those of the nobility, gentry and public in general, who may wish to leave the island late, will find this a desirable opportunity where the most obliging and obedient attention will be rendered to their comfort by the Captain and crew of the steam yacht. N.B. This yacht is abundantly supplied with masts, sails and maritime stores.

The *Thames*, a 49-ton three-master, was registered at Cowes and her owners were a consortium of John Burden and James Webb of Cowes; William Cape, a tea dealer, of Lombard Street, London; George Leyburn of Stamford Hill, Middlesex; and William Townsend of Brick Lane, St Luke, Middlesex. (Picture,

28

p17.) Her London agents were Messrs Gregory & Burden of 59 Snowhill and she was advertised modestly:

> The steam yacht *Thames*. A fine and lively, seaworthy vessel in any weather and has navigated from Scotland to Dublin and around Land's End to London and is particularly strong built.

During the latter part of her one and only season maintaining the Isle of Wight passage, under the command of Capt Samuel Summers, the *Thames* sailed between Cowes and Portsmouth.

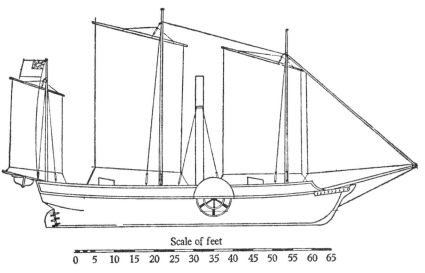

Scale of feet

0   5   10   15   20   25   30   35   40   45   50   55   60   65

Conjectural drawing of the steam packet *Thames*

In May 1822 another steamer maintained a brief service between Southampton and the island, although she was primarily a cross-Channel vessel. This was the *Swift* (Capt MacGregor), driven by an 80 hp engine, which left Brighton for Southampton on Mondays at 8.0 am, calling at Ryde, and left Southampton for Brighton at 10.0 am on Tuesday, calling at Ryde. Single fares were: Brighton to Southampton 15s and 10s; Brighton to Ryde 10s and 7s; and Ryde to Southampton 4s and 3s.

29

The third steamer to be placed on the Southampton to Cowes passage, and the first to be built expressly for the island service, was launched from the yard of Lynn Ratsey[10] on 8 June 1822. This was the *Medina*, an 84-ton wooden paddle steamer with two masts, schooner-rigged, a 'running' bowsprit, 'woman' head and mock quarter galleries. Launched in 1822, her dimensions were 85ft 9in x 18ft 9in x 9ft 10½in, and she was driven by a 36 hp engine.

The *Medina* maintained the passage from Southampton to Cowes together with the *Cobourg* when she was not off on her travels, for in June 1823 the *Medina* was the first steam vessel into Guernsey and Jersey, and in May 1824 she made several

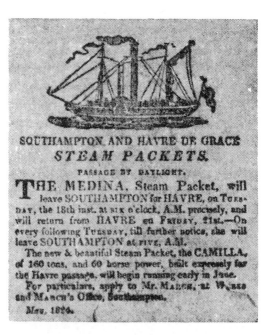

SOUTHAMPTON AND HAVRE DE GRACE
STEAM PACKETS.
PASSAGE BY DAYLIGHT.

THE MEDINA, Steam Packet, will leave SOUTHAMPTON for HAVRE, on TUESDAY, the 18th inst. at six o'clock, A.M. precisely, and will return from HAVRE on FRIDAY, 21st.—On every following TUESDAY, till further notice, she will leave SOUTHAMPTON at FIVE, A.M.

The new & beautiful Steam Packet, the CAMILLA, of 160 tons, and 60 horse power, built expressly for the Havre passage, will begin running early in June.

For particulars, apply to Mr. MARCH, at Wyatt and March's Office, Southampton.

May, 1824.

Advertisement for the steam packet *Medina*

crossings to Le Havre. She had the further distinction in September 1823 of being the first steam vessel to make an excursion around the Isle of Wight.

Sail was, nevertheless, still represented for in October 1823 Capt Edward Stephens of the *Sons of Commerce* was fined £5 for 'neglecting to convey some horses, belonging to Mr Bloxham, Surgeon, from Portsmouth to Cowes'.

During the summer of 1824, the *Cobourg* and the *Medina* maintained the passage to Cowes, sailing from Southampton at 8.0 am and 3.0 pm and returning from Cowes at 1.30 am and 5.0 pm. But as the Fountain Quay had been extensively rebuilt by the proprietors of the steam packets 'for the purpose of landing and embarking passengers without the inconvenience of using boats, and as the earnings, hitherto, have proved very inadequate to the expenditure . . .' it became necessary to alter the fares. These were now 3s single on the quarterdeck and 4s 6d if 'to and from Cowes on the same day'; and 1s 6d foredeck and 2s 6d, again if 'to and from Cowes on the same day'. And as a concession, 'a moderate quantity of luggage in one or two packages' was allowed free.

At the same time, the local press commented upon the popularity of Capt Knight, '. . . who has deservedly, for many years, been a favourite of the passengers and no passenger will ever have reason to complain of the treatment which might be experienced in the course of so short an acquatic excursion . . .'. Reference was also made to his diplomacy in refusing to discriminate between the different inns of East and West Cowes, which implies that the masters of these vessels were easily approachable and, in consequence, personally involved with their passengers while under way.

By 1824 sea excursions had become popular. The cross-Channel steamer *Ariadne* made an excursion around the Isle of Wight on 17 July with a 'full military band' on board, the passenger fare being 5s (Picture, p53). In the following week, the

Notice of a *Medina* excursion in 1824

Medina made a similar excursion—'In consequence of the sailing match between Mr Weld's fine yacht *Julia* and Mr Talbot's *Gulie*'. The two owners, James Weld and C.R.M. Talbot were both founder members, in 1815, of the Royal Yacht Squadron, and the *Julie* won the match despite giving the *Gulie* a mile start. For the remainder of the summer season, the *Ariadne* and the *Medina* each made a weekly excursion around the island, the *Ariadne* on one occasion closing the yacht *Fairy*, belonging to William Chamberlayne, MP for Southampton, and giving him three cheers.

The *Medina* took between 6½ and 9 hours to steam around the Isle of Wight, a time equalled by three coastguard cutters, the *Mermaid*, 145 tons, the *Stag*, 107 tons, and the *Vigilant*, 91 tons, of Yarmouth, which sailed around the island in under 7 hours in April 1824. In 1873, a 27ft long whaler, manned by two teams of five oarsmen (Southampton firemen), rowed around the Island in 12 hours, 34 minutes.

In July 1824 the *Medina* made a special trip from Southampton to Portsmouth, taking visitors to Portsdown Fair, leaving Southampton at 9.0 am and Portsmouth at 6.0 pm. Fares were 5s return, and 3s 'if only going or returning'. A more venturesome excursion was advertised by the same steamer the following month, to attend the Torquay and Baby comb (sic) Regatta on 29 and 30 August, provided '. . . a sufficient number of passengers make it answer, namely, 50 passengers at 2 guineas'. As an inducement, it was added: 'The voyage will be made by daylight' as at this time coastlines were inadequately lighted. The *Medina* was to sail at 6.0 am from Southampton and return on the following Saturday, calling at Cowes out and home.

Additional excursions were frequently made by the *Ariadne* from Southampton to Brighton, calling at Cowes, charging '7s each way or 12s out and home'. Passengers were landed at the Chain Pier, the steamer returning the following day.

The daily routine of these steamers was not without incident, as when a Hythe wherry carrying passengers had the effrontery to impede the *Cobourg*

> . . . by sailing across her hawse, when Mr Wiltshire, a respectable clothier of Frome, was precipitated into the water. The engine of the *Cobourg* was immediately stopped and neither Mr Wiltshire or the other passengers, several of whom were females, were injured beyond the alarm experienced from the incident. . . .

Yet another steamer, the second to be built expressly for the island passage, was launched in the spring of 1825 from the yard of Lynn Ratsey, at Cowes, for Ward and Fitzhugh. This was the 64-ton *Earl of Malmesbury*. Carvel-built of wood, she was single-masted and smack-rigged, with a 'running' bowsprit; a 'male' figurehead—presumably a likeness of the Earl, who was Gover-

33

nor of the Isle of Wight and a former Lord of the Treasury—and had a square stern ornamented with quarter galleries.[11]

The *Earl of Malmesbury* went into service on 2 May 1825 and, with the *Cobourg* and *Medina*, implemented '... an improved facility of conveyance', sailing from Southampton for Cowes at 8.0 am and 3.0 pm and from Cowes at 9.0 am and 5.0 pm. In addition, a steamer left Cowes for Portsmouth at 10 am, leaving the latter place for Cowes at 3.0 pm. (The Southampton to Portsmouth summer service was to continue, with some modification, until 1968.) The fares from Southampton to Cowes were 4s 6d and 3s return, the through fare to Portsmouth being 5s and 3s 6d return.

The island passage to Portsmouth was also not without incident. On one occasion a deserter from HMS *Rodney*, who had been arrested in Jersey, was being escorted from Southampton to Portsmouth in the *Medina* when, in an attempt to escape, he jumped over the side as the vessel was steaming down Southampton Water. A boat nearby picked him up and made for the packet, which had meanwhile stopped, but on coming alongside he produced a large clasp knife and threatened to use it should he be compelled to go on board, stating he would die rather than return to the *Rodney*. In view of his threat and to avoid detaining the packet, the master of the *Medina* '... deemed it prudent to let him take his own course and he was suffered to go where he pleased.'

Soon afterwards, passengers in the *Ariadne* had their share of excitement while on an excursion around the island. There were 200 passengers on board when a man and a boy in a boat attempted to board the steamer off Cowes while she was still under way. Their boat caught under a paddle wheel and was capsized. The man managed to cling to the upturned boat but the boy was drawn in under the paddle box, and but for the promptness of the engineer in stopping the engine would have been killed. Both were got on board safely and the appreciative passengers pre-

Page 35 (above) The *Gem* steam packet entering Cowes Harbour, c 1853; (below) the *Emerald* of 1857, moored in Yarmouth, Isle of Wight

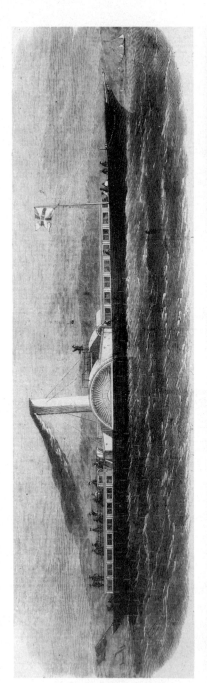

Page 36 (above) The Southampton & Isle of Wight Improved Steam Boat Co's packet *Lord of the Isles*, 1861, the first Island steamer with deckhouse saloons; *(below)* a contemporary model of the 1861 packet *Lady of the Lake*

sented the engineer with the sum of £5. A similar incident occurred in October 1825, when a boat went alongside the *Medina*, fouled a paddle wheel and sank. The occupants, however, were again saved.

The cross-Channel steamer *Camilla*, also made excursions around the Isle of Wight during the latter part of the 1825 summer season, charging '... From Southampton, 7s, servants and children 3s 6d'; and '... From Cowes, 5s, servants and children 2s 6d'. The *Camilla*, at this time, was sailing from Southampton for Havre every Tuesday, returning on Friday. (Picture, p53.)

One of the most spectacular incidents witnessed by excursionists occurred in September 1825, when the *Medina* visited Portsmouth to see the launching of the 104-gun 1st Rate *Princess Charlotte*. During the ceremony, the lock gates burst open, causing considerable damage to many small craft and injuring more than forty people.

The Southampton steamers ceased running for the season on 26 November 1825, and it was back to sail for those travelling to Cowes.[12] But during the preceding months, Sotonians, perhaps envious of the success of the island steamers owned by Ward and Fitzhugh, decided to enter into opposition with a steam packet of their own. A new steam navigation company was formed, shares of '£100 at 6s premium' were quickly taken up, a lease of the breakwater acquired and, civic pride being at its peak, it was announced that the new vessel was to be called the *Southampton* of Southampton. However, the name finally chosen was the more patriotic *George IV* and her arrival was so long delayed that it was rumoured she was merely a hoax until a local pressman enlightened his readers with a soothing review:

> I have not seen any to rival her in model, workmanship and accommodation, and should she prove afloat what she appeared on the stocks, no one in Southampton Water will keep pace with her. The engine is from one of the finest manufactories in the Kingdom, on the latest and most improved principles, of the

C

enormous force of 56 hp which, together with a copper bottom and other things not usual in vessels of her tonnage, render her the most complete.

Before her arrival at Southampton, a gas light was erected on the Town Quay as an aid to mariners; and George Ward and William Gibbs, Recipient of Pier Dues, Coastwise, were battling with the Crown over the payment of port dues levied on luggage

THE PUBLIC ARE RESPECTFULLY INFORMED, THAT

The GEORGE IV.

SAFETY STEAM-PACKET,

LEAVES Southampton for COWES, RYDE & PORTSMOUTH, at NINE o'clock every Morning ; COWES for RYDE and PORTS-MOUTH at Half-past Ten ; returns from PORTS-MOUTH at Two every Afternoon, for RYDE and COWES ; and COWES for SOUTHAMPTON at Four o'clock.

T. BULLMORE, *Commander,*
May be spoken with at the principal Inns.

FARES AS USUAL.

N.B.—Passengers by the GEORGE THE FOURTH, have the advantage of embarking and disembarking at Cowes, free of Expense, AT ALL TIMES OF TIDE.

Advertisement for the steam packet *George IV*

passing through Southampton and Cowes. And the *Medina* and the *Earl of Malmesbury* made an excursion to Wootton Bridge with sightseers to witness the launching of Lord Yarborough's 351-ton yacht *Falcon* from Daniel List's yard.

At long last, in June 1826, the *George IV* arrived at Southampton and was received in rapture as 'a remarkable, powerful, elegant and commodious vessel, presenting a great width of deck and exceedingly handsome chine.' Built by William Evans at Rotherhithe, the 60-ton *George IV* was single-masted and smack-rigged, with a bowsprit, 'man bust' head (possibly a likeness of the reigning monarch), and an unadorned square stern. Her dimensions were 95ft x 16ft x 8ft 3in and she was driven by a 56 hp engine.[13]

No sooner had she gone into service—she made an excursion around the island on 29 June 1826, the fares being 6s and 4s—than she was nearly lost, being discovered on fire at her moorings off the Town Quay on 2 July. It appears that the deck facing 'the furnaces and copper had not been sheeted with iron, in consequence of which, the ignited cinders communicated to the floor and completely burnt through the lining on one side.' She was taken out of service for repairs and her advertised excursion was undertaken by the *Ariadne*, 135 passengers being embarked at Southampton and a further 40 at Cowes.

Repairs were completed within a week and the *George IV* then began her passage work, leaving Southampton at 9.00 am and 2.30 pm for Cowes and returning at 11.0 am and 5.0 pm. The time allowed for her passage, $1\frac{1}{4}$ hours, was considered 'truly astonishing', but she faced formidable competition from her rivals. The *Medina* left Southampton for Cowes and Portsmouth at 8.0 am, returning from Portsmouth at 3.0 pm with mails for Cowes and Southampton; the *Cobourg* left Cowes for Southampton at 9.0 am and 4.0 pm, returning from Southampton at 12.30 pm and 6.0 pm; while the *Earl of Malmesbury*, which was based at Portsmouth, left the latter place at 9.0 am

bound for Cowes and Southampton, and returned from Southampton at 3.0 pm and from Cowes at 5.30 pm.

All these steamers incidentally received some useful publicity
as the result of a newspaper report in July 1826 which drew
attention to the dangers of making the passage under sail. A
Newport solicitor, Edward Kirkpatrick, missed the steamer to
Cowes and so took passage in the sailing boat *The Hero*, which
capsized off Calshot during a squall, spilling the occupants into
the water. He was drowned and his body was later recovered and
buried at Whippingham churchyard.

The rivalry which now developed among local steamers is
mentioned in a Sotonian's contemporary description of an outing
to Cowes in 1826 during that then, as now, celebrated occasion—
Cowes Week:

> The rivalry between the steam boats of our townsmen and
> those of the 'Island King' [George Ward], contributed in no
> trifling degree to impart something of the lively, animated scene
> to Southampton, where the High Street and Quay presented a
> most unusual bustle from an early period of the morning. Rustics
> pouring in from their land situations, foresters and farmers,
> mounted and dismounted yeomen, nobility and gentry from
> their adjacent residences and above half the population of
> Southampton ... having come to board the steam boats to enjoy
> a day's recreation and to commit the heinious offence of making
> merry to the lascivious melodies of a full band of music and
> joining the antimethodistical supporters of good eating and
> drinking and harmless amusements. On Southampton Quay, the
> acute observer of human nature might find much to interest him.
> The excitement and bustle among the touters on the Pier and the
> most innocent and praiseworthy exertions of the porters, cads,
> boatmen and stewards, proprietors and Captains of the various
> steam boats, who having placed their scouts half way up the
> High Street, assailed every passenger with 'For *George IV*!',
> 'the *Prince of Cobourg*!', 'the *Earl of Malmesbury*!'. In short,
> Captain Tobias Young [*George IV*] and Captain J. H. Knight,
> with their gentlemen, stewards and retainers, fought a hard battle
> for superiority in numbers, and we, as loyal men, are delighted to

find that the majority decided in favour of *George IV*. In addition to the usual passage vessels, the *Camilla* and *Lord Beresford* [cross-Channel] were also put to requisition, and such clouds of smoke and steam issued therefrom when they were all in motion, as completely obscured all distant objects. Calshot Castle and the New Forest were scarcely visible and the murky vomitings of the furnaces covered the surface of the Southampton Water from side to side. The first glimpse of Cowes Harbour, after rounding the point of Calshot Castle, presented a forest of masts and streamers, gaily floating in the winds, whilst the brilliancy of the day and the flags and the congregate groups which lined the shore, made the scene one of unusual animation. Nearly 300 sail of yachts, pleasure vessels, pilot boats, including every variety of build, rig and tonnage, were to be seen at anchor in the Roads or tacking about in view of the Harbour.[14]

Despite local support of the *George IV*, it was apparent to Sotonians that she could be better employed and the proprietors were urged to provide a service between Southampton and Portsmouth, especially in view of the fact that the profits made by Ward and Fitzhugh during the preceding twelve months were estimated to be in the region of £3,000, a not inconsiderable sum in those days. Whereupon, for the remainder of the 1826 season, until 18 October, the *George IV* left Southampton for Cowes and Portsmouth every morning at 9.0 o'clock, returning at 3.0 pm for Cowes and Southampton.

The *Prince of Cobourg*, after six years on passage, was taken out of service in October 1826 and, in the absence of contemporary records, was temporarily lost to sight. A letter of 1833 now in the possession of the Fitzhugh family refers to the *Cobourg* having been 'broken up some years previously', but a pencilled note on records held by the Registrar-General of Shipping and Seamen, Cardiff, states that she was: 'On the mud in the port of Southampton, used as a depot for stores etc. per letter from Customs dated 21 September 1840.' The latter statement is confirmed by an undated print by T. G. Hart (see p 17) which shows the *Cobourg* hulked on the Woolston shore

41

opposite Cross House and to the north-east of Southampton dock which was opened in 1842. Her final end or 'breaking up' appears to have gone unrecorded.

The *George IV* opened her 1827 season in April with a special trip to Weymouth, after which she returned to join the *Medina* (Capt J. H. Knight) and the *Earl of Malmesbury* (Capt J. H. Knight Jnr) on the island passage—'Now forming a line of communication with the Ryde steam packets.' But within a few weeks a war of attrition broke out when the sailing times of the *Malmesbury* were altered to coincide with those of the *George IV*, this resulting in a blunt newspaper announcement: 'Owing to Mr Ward having altered the time of running of his steam packet, the *George IV* will now leave Southampton a half hour earlier'. But the *Malmesbury*'s sailing time was likewise put forward and this 'leap frogging', which might have led to a night service had it continued, finally ended in compromise in July 1827, after which the three steamers worked together in tolerance for the remainder of the season. The *George IV* rounded off her year's work with a special trip to Torquay, carrying the dowager Marchioness of Bute and her suite, after which the winter passage was maintained by sailing vessels 'at the usual hour'.

The 1828 season opened with the news that the *Medina* and the *Malmesbury* had been refitted during the winter lay-up with new boilers and cylinders and completely re-embellished. Fares were unaltered; Southampton to Cowes, 3s and 1s 6d; Southampton to Portsmouth, 3s 6d and 2s; Cowes to Portsmouth, 2s 6d and 1s 6d, but a warning of renewed competition now appeared in local papers:

> The proprietors, in sincerely thanking the inhabitants of Southampton and its vicinity for the great preference they have given to the *George IV*, beg to assure them that neither pains nor expense shall be spared to afford them every accommodation, and that in accordance with the many solicitations of their numerous friends, they intend with all possible despatch to have another vessel for the midday passage.

SOUTHAMPTON, ISLE OF WIGHT, AND PORTSMOUTH STEAM-PACKETS.

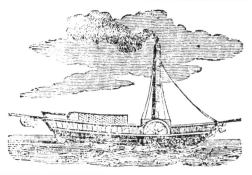

THE MEDINA.

JAMES KNIGHT, Commander.

THE GEORGE IV.

DAVID CORKE, Commander.

THE MALMESBURY.

JAMES KNIGHT, Jun, Commander.

One of the above Packets LEAVES SOUTHAMPTON every day, at Half-past Eight, Three, and Five o'Clock, for COWES, RYDE, & PORTSMOUTH, and PORTSMOUTH for RYDE, COWES, and SOUTHAMPTON, at the same hours. The 5 o'Clock Packet proceeding to COWES, only, & returning thence at 9 on the following morning.

For Particulars enquire of CAPTAIN KNIGHT, Gloucester Square; or of JOSEPH CLARK, Junior, 18, High Street.

The rival companies share a timetable in 1828

43

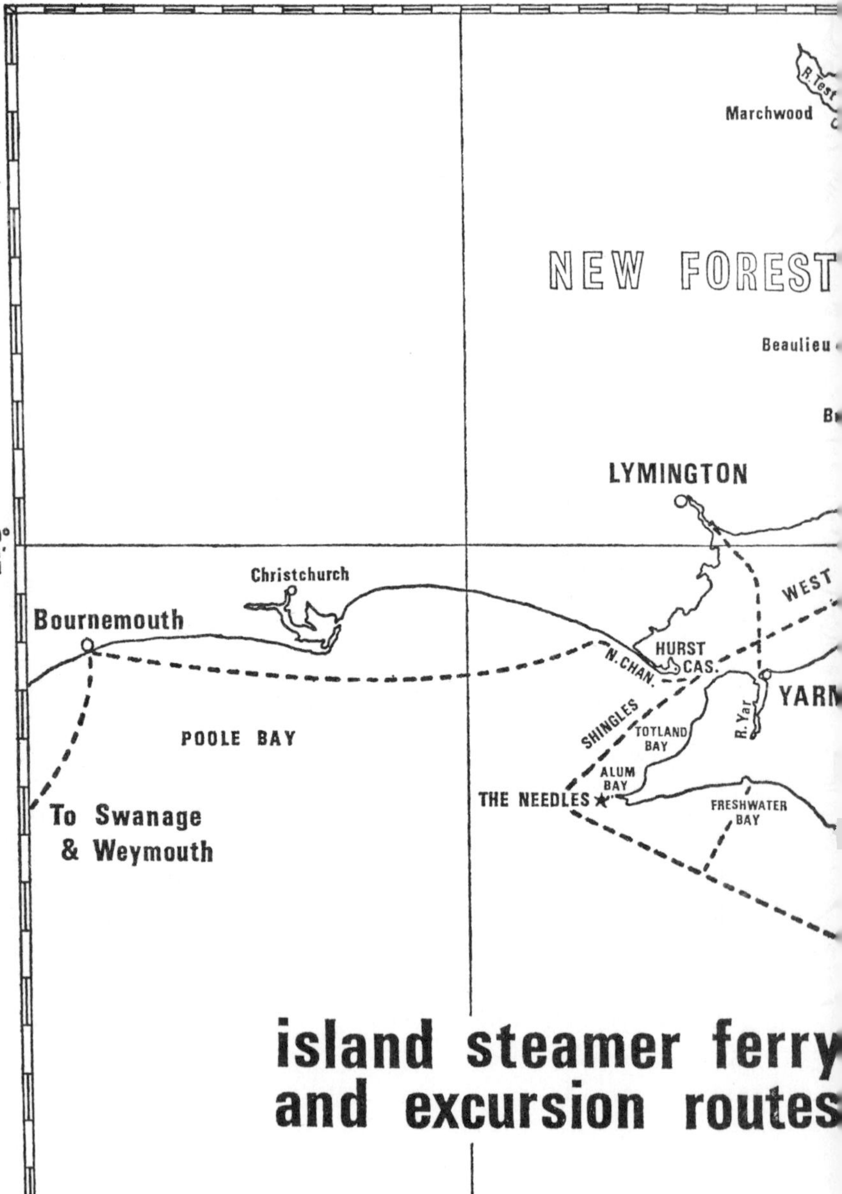

40'

Marchwood

R. Test

NEW FOREST

Beaulieu

B

LYMINGTON

50° 45' N

Christchurch

WEST

Bournemouth

N. CHAN.

HURST CAS.

YARM

POOLE BAY

SHINGLES

R. Yar

TOTLAND BAY

To Swanage & Weymouth

ALUM BAY

THE NEEDLES ★

FRESHWATER BAY

island steamer ferry
and excursion routes

This threat was repeated over a period of weeks and then, as suddenly as the advertisement had appeared, its place was taken by a common timetable, carrying the names of the masters of all three steamers, indicating that they had at last joined forces. As a local newspaper commented at the time: 'A union of interest!' And so the two companies began what was to prove a long and close association until their merger in 1861, when the present Southampton Company was formed. Their frequent calls off Ryde drew the observation: 'The passengers embarking and disembarking the whole of the day, added much to the beauty of the scene.' The steamer service season for that year, 1828, ended on 18 November.

In February 1829 George Ward, pioneering owner of the first island steamers, died and control of his vessels passed to his partner, William Fitzhugh. (Pictures, p54.) The steamers began the service in March and the following months were not without incident. In May the *Medina* (Capt J. H. Knight) made a special crossing to Le Havre and for the remainder of the summer made a weekly excursion around the island. Together with the *George IV*, she also attended the Southampton Regatta, 'accompanying the yachts', at 3s 6d per head. In May 1829 the first passenger to die as a result of an accident in a local steamer met his end in a steamer at Portsmouth. The man, 74-year-old T. C. Morgan, of East Cowes, had fallen down the hold. He was later buried in Whippingham churchyard.

The *Malmesbury* came into the news in August 1829 when, while returning from Southampton to Portsmouth, a Southampton boatman named Blandford was seen struggling in the water off Calshot. He had taken a party to Cowes and was returning to Southampton when a sudden squall capsized his boat. A Cowes seaman in the *Malmesbury*, named Harris, immediately jumped into the stern boat and was preparing it for lowering when the stern fall parted and he was thrown over the side, striking his head as he fell. His body was later dragged up and buried in

Cowes churchyard. Subscriptions were opened in the *Malmesbury* and the *Medina* for the widow and two children he had left, '... meeting his death in endeavouring to safe the life of a fellow creature.' Blandford, the boatman, it is recorded, had meanwhile been picked up by a sailing vessel from Cowes.

In September, Capt James Page, master of the *George IV*, was fined £3 for 'running against and damaging the boat of Mr Hiscroft, the *Good Intent* (44 tons) of Cowes,' a seemingly unimportant event compared with what was to follow the next month. For in October he was sent to prison for three months for having 'refused to deliver up the certificate of registry of the *George IV* to the Collector of Customs at Southampton, by which he incurred the penalty of £100, under 6 Geo. 4 cap. 110, S.27'.

The stubbornness of Capt Page is not explained but it is known that some masters, perhaps when faced with dismissal or loss of their commands, would refuse to part with this essential document on which the master's signature was required before the vessel could proceed to sea. The vacant command of the *George IV* again went to Capt David Corke of Cowes, whose association with the Southampton steam packets was to continue until his death in 1866.

The winter service of 1829-30 was maintained by sailing passage vessels, '... fitted up with superior accommodation'. The *Mermaid* sailed from Southampton every morning at 7.0 o'clock and returned from Cowes at 4.0 o'clock with the mail; while the *Thetis* and the *Ant* (31 tons) alternately sailed from Southampton at 9.0 am and at 2.30 pm. And we are assured, 'Every attention is paid to the delivery of goods and parcels.'

Steam vessels employed on the island passage were by now considered, presumably, a profitable undertaking and on 23 June 1830 yet another steam packet was launched for the Southampton to Cowes passage. This was the *Duke of Buccleugh*, built by Joseph White of Cowes for Alexander Fletcher and

John Young, ironfounders of Millbrook, Southampton. But before being placed in service, she was purchased by William Fitzhugh, 'Out of the profits of the other vessels.'

Carvel-built of wood, the 38-ton *Duke* was single-masted and sloop-rigged, with a bowsprit, 'man bust' head—possibly a likeness of His Grace—and a square stern adorned with sham galleries. Her dimensions were 72ft 4in x 12ft 10in x 8ft, and her single engine was rated at 15 hp.[15] Early reports had suggested that she was to be employed on the Lymington-Yarmouth-Cowes–Ryde-Portsmouth service but, instead, she was placed on the Southampton to Cowes passage in opposition to the 'Matchless Little Steam Packet', the *Emerald*, a Hythe steamer whose exploits are described in Chapter 6.

Steamer fares throughout 1831 and 1832 remained the same as those of 1828. In July 1831 tow boats, to transport horses, cattle and carriages, were advertised for the first time on the Southampton to Cowes passage. These were towed astern of the steamers and slipped off near a conveniently level shore and rowed onto the beach. The fore-end of these barges had a bow ramp which could be lowered to allow cattle, horses or carriages to be driven on or off.

In June 1832 the *Medina* had occasion to stop and rescue a Hythe ferryman, named Elcock, whose boat had capsized in a squall, and there were several accidents off the Southampton breakwater—the Royal Pier not yet having been built. These accidents were the results of rivalry among the boatmen who rowed passengers to and from the steam packets as they lay off the Town Quay. In one instance, when a boat got under one of the paddle wheels of the *Medina*, the boat was crushed and two of the three occupants injured. Soon afterwards the *George IV* and the *Buccleugh* were involved in similar accidents but, as was usual, no blame was attached to the masters of the steamers. Instead, the boatmen were cautioned against running their boats alongside the packets before they had stopped their engines.

The first winter service from Southampton to the Isle of Wight started on 17 November 1832, when the *Duke of Buccleugh* began to make one round trip daily from Southampton to Cowes, Ryde and Portsmouth.

Traffic to the island was presumably still on the increase because, on 20 June 1833, yet another steamer for the Southampton to Cowes passage was launched for William Fitzhugh. Built by Alexander Cunningham at the Baltic Wharf, Chapel, Southampton, she was named the *Princess Victoria*: 'At half past twelve, everything being in readiness, the fastenings were loosened and she glided into the water, amidst the acclamations of a vast assemblage of persons. Miss Emily Fitzhugh, daughter of one of the proprietors, christened her with a bottle of sherry.' Described as 'a beautiful little steamer, adorned with a splendid figurehead' and 'fitted up in the most superior and elegant style', the *Princess Victoria* of 31 tons and 86 tons burthen, was single-masted and sloop-rigged. She had a 'woman bust' head (presumably a likeness of the Princess), a plain, square stern, and one engine of 24 hp. Her dimensions were: 74ft 2in x 15ft 9in x 9ft 7in and her engine-room length was $25\frac{1}{2}$ft.

Her first excursion was to the Royal Yacht Squadron Regatta at Portsmouth, held from 19 to 24 August 1833, which she attended with the *Buccleugh*. The latter vessel, during the following month, made an abortive attempt to cross the Channel to Cherbourg with Mr, Mrs and Miss Fitzhugh on board. She left Southampton one Thursday afternoon but encountered bad weather and was obliged to abandon the attempt and put back into Swanage the following Sunday.

The same month, September 1833, saw the development of a first-class row concerning Capt J. H. Knight Jnr after the secretary of a prominent yacht club inserted the following announcement in local papers:

> In consequence of the repeated complaints of the incivility and insulting conduct of J. H. Knight Jnr., Master of one of the

Southampton to Cowes steam packets, to several members of the Yacht Club and their friends, and more particularly on the night of the 30th August, when from the inefficiency of the steam vessel, she failed in making her passage to Cowes, and remained off Calshot during the night, contrary to the earnest entreaties of the passengers to be relanded at Southampton, the Yacht Club have ordered application to be made to a steam boat company in London to put on two efficient vessels, to which they have promised their individual influence and support.

The unfortunate Capt Knight immediately reported to his principal employer, William Fitzhugh, who referred him to another proprietor, William Hearn, who requested an explanation 'to answer such strong and unexpected charges.' The Captain's subsequent statement to justify his conduct and vindicate his character was also published in a local newspaper:

On Friday evening, August 30th, about half past 5 o' clock, we left Southampton Pier for Cowes, in the *Victoria* steam packet (a new vessel and one I was not accustomed to), the wind blowing a fine sailing breeze from the south-west, with rain at intervals; we had some difficulty in getting clear of the Pier Head on account of the *Lord Beresford* [cross-Channel] steam packet laying at the north side, which prevented us from going ahead. Consequently, we were obliged to get a warp on our starboard quarter and back the engine, to bring our bow round sufficiently to clear the *Lord Beresford* and my whole attention was engaged to prevent damage being done to either vessel. At this time, I was in the act of clearing, and a lady who appeared alarmed wished to be put on shore, thinking there was danger. I told her that she was quite safe, that no boat was at hand and that the plank was hauled in. She appeared satisfied. I thought no more of it. All went well down river until we reached the Spit Buoy to the southward of Calshot Castle, when it came on to blow very heavy from the south-west with rain and a heavy sea. I immediately made up my mind not to risk the vessel or passengers but to return back and either bring up between Fawley Beacon and Cadlands, or go to Southampton. The lady beforementioned became greatly alarmed and I begged her to be assured there was no danger, that we had altered our course and were going back

50

into smooth water, that I would oblige her either by bringing up in the river or go on to Southampton. She could not decide on either. I then brought up in the former position in order to examine the engine, it being quite new and had never been in a seaway before. We found the packing of the bonnet of the foot valve of the air pump had given way; it was repaired in a few minutes and I then gave orders to weigh anchor when the lady desired NOT to weigh anchor until daylight. I assured her we would not and wished her to go below, fearing she might take cold in such bad weather. She did so and immediately sent a gentleman, who made me pledge myself most solemnly NOT to weigh until daylight. I desired him to assure the lady I would attend to her wishes. At half past five o'clock on Saturday morning, we got under way, the wind being at north-west, blowing heavy, and made our passage to Cowes, everyone appearing satisfied. As to the inefficiency of the vessel, I need only state that during the gale on Friday evening August 30th, the *Lord Beresford*, 100 hp (sic), brought up near us and did not weigh until the morning.

Capt Knight's second explanation followed:

On Sunday, 1st September, it blew a strong gale from the northward, being direct into Cowes Harbour and a strong tide running out caused a heavy sea. The *George IV* did not call at Cowes on account of the bad weather. I left Southampton for Cowes with the *Earl of Malmesbury* and in Cowes Harbour had great difficulty in clearing two vessels, the *Phoenix* and the *Fox*. At that moment, when I was most anxious for the safety of the vessel, someone—I did not see who—asked me if I would tow his yacht out of Cowes. My answer was 'Wait a bit! I can't talk to you now.' We were then drifting with the tide across the hawser of the *Phoenix*. We did but just clear her, indeed, our stern boat struck her bowsprit. The gentleman, I am sorry to say, took offence at the words, which I was in hopes he might have overlooked, taking the weather and difficulty I was in at the moment into consideration. Signed: J. H. Knight Jnr, Master of the *Earl of Malmesbury*.

These explanations appear to have satisfied all parties because the announcements ceased and the threatened London steam boats failed to materialise. Furthermore, Capt Knight continued his service afloat and was later to become 'Superintendent of the Isle of Wight Steam Navigation Company' (sic). The Yacht Club secretary, Richard Stephens (Secretary of The Royal Yacht Squadron 1825-34), who was also Tidal Surveyor of Customs at Cowes, was promoted Collector of Customs at St Ives, Cornwall, in February of the following year, it being then remarked that his service in the Customs totalled thirty years.

A serious accident occurred on board the *Buccleugh* one day in August 1834 when, while on passage to Cowes, one of her stokers, Thomas French, caught his foot under the beam of the engine, crushing the bones. He was put into a cutter which happened to be nearby and taken back to Southampton for medical attention. And as was usual in these days, a subscription list was opened for the injured man by one of the passengers, a Mr Hawkins of Cowes.

The summer service of 1835, which started in May, opened with a severe gale sweeping along the south coast and causing considerable damage to craft in Cowes harbour. The *Zoe* and the *Fox* parted their moorings; the *Hero* and the *Fidelity*, pilot-boats, were damaged; and the steamer *George IV*, not to be outdone, rammed the pilot-boat *Jane*, carrying away her bowsprit and bulwarks, before finally colliding with the Lymington steamer *Glasgow* and bringing down the latter's foremast. This contrasted with the peaceful scene reported later that summer: 'Cowes is crowded and several steam boats from the neighbourhood arrived and remained in the Roadstead, literally crammed with passengers, while the bands on board struck up some lively airs'.

In September 1835, during a yacht race off Cowes, James Taylor, master of the mail packet *Thetis*, was washed overboard and would have drowned had not Capt Edward Stephens in the *Sons of Commerce* effected a gallant rescue. Two years previously, Capt Taylor had himself rescued three occupants of a Portsmouth wherry, who had been obliged to seek refuge up the mast when their boat sank in 14ft of water.

Page 53 (above) The cross-Channel packet *Ariadne* of 1824 outward bound in the Solent, flying the French courtesy flag at her foremast; (below) the paddle steamer *Camilla* of 1824, shown with a carriage stowed on her foredeck

Page 54 (*above, left*) George Ward of Cowes (1751-1829), the 'Island King' and pioneer steamship owner; (*above, right*) William Fitzhugh (1757-1842), a principal owner of Southampton steamers; (*below, left*) The Rev W. A. Fitzhugh (1793-1881), another principal owner from 1842 to 1861; (*below, right*) Capt David Corke Snr (1797-1866), master of the *George IV* in 1829 and later superintendent of the Southampton steamers

Records concerning early mail services to the Isle of Wight are few but it is known that, in March 1801, an unsuccessful attempt was made in Portsmouth to acquire the island mail contract and have the mail sent through Portsmouth. It was not, however, until October 1805 that Stephen Moore obtained a contract to convey mails between that port and Ryde for the sum of £20 per year. The Southampton to Cowes contract was granted to Perkins and Harris in June 1816, who shared the payment of £70 per annum. By March 1818, Harris had been disqualified and Perkins, unable to provide the two boats necessary to operate the service, went into partnership with Capt J. H. Knight, the contract being signed in March 1818. This was renewed in 1820 when the *Prince of Cobourg* went into service. The proprietors of the *George IV* attempted to secure this contract but were not successful, the islanders presumably not wishing to support the opposition. It would appear, however, that the steamers lost the contract to sailing packets, during the winter months at least, for it was reported in December 1836 that gale-force winds had prevented the sailing vessel from making the passage and a steamer had had to be put into service, the resultant delay being the worst for twelve years. More complaints followed in January 1838, leading to a new contract in March requiring two trips daily between Southampton and Cowes. The steamer mail contract was finally implemented in June 1838, the award going to the 'Cowes Line', or Isle of Wight Royal Mail Steam Packet Co, presumably at the instigation of Capt J. H. Knight who had been connected with previous contracts. The mailbag at this time was said to be a small satchel, containing at times less than six letters. Postage rates for letters were 2d from Southampton to Cowes, Portsmouth to Ryde, and Cowes to Newport; but letters from Cowes to Portsmouth cost 7d because they were sent through Southampton.

Changes followed in September 1843, when the departure time of the Southampton mail steamer was altered to 5.30 am in summer and 6.0 am in winter 'in order to give the inhabitants of Ventnor and Shanklin longer time to answer letters'. And in the spring of 1846, a special steamer left Cowes at 7.30 am to connect with the newly-introduced daily Southampton to London mail train. The Southampton to Cowes mail contract was finally acquired by the present Southampton company on its formation in 1861. Four years later, in 1865, the mail steamer was leaving Cowes for Southampton at 9.0 pm on weekdays, and Southampton at 2.0 am with the island mail, which was delivered that same morning. The contract was for £750 per annum, or £14 5s 0¾d per week, whereas the expenses were estimated to amount to £22 11s, made up as follows:

Two tons of coal per day .... £14 0s p.w.
Captain and engineer .... £4 4s p.w.
One fireman (20s); two seamen (36s); one boy (10s) £3 6s p.w.
Steward or mail-keeper .... £1 1s p.w.

The last mention of the *Thetis* in the local press was in January 1851 when, during a severe gale one night, several boats were destroyed at Southampton Town Quay, '... one of them being the only means of getting his living by poor old Taylor, who carried the mails in the *Thetis* or his boat for many years....'

In October 1836 the *George IV* made a special crossing to Le Havre and the following month the sailing passage vessel *Fox* (Capt Stephens) had her cabin broken into and some clothing and provisions stolen. Apprehension of the culprits was forecast, however, because '... one of the party left a shoe behind which will probably lead to their detection....'

A slight reduction in fares took place in 1837, and these now became:

Single:	Southampton to Cowes	2s 6d and 1s 6d
	Day return	4s 0d and 2s 6d
	Southampton to Portsmouth	3s 6d and 2s 6d
	Day return	5s 6d and 4s 6d
	Cowes to Portsmouth	2s 6d and 1s 6d
	Cowes to Ryde	2s 0d and 1s 6d

A four-wheel carriage with two horses cost £1 13s between Southampton and Cowes; and between Southampton and Ryde, £2. A four-wheel carriage without horses between the former places cost £1 5s and between the latter places, £1 10s. Between Southampton and Cowes, a two-wheel carriage and one horse cost £1 5s, and between Southampton and Ryde £1 10s. (See Note 6 for sailing packet charges.)

In September 1837 came news of the death of Samuel Price, engineer of the *Medina*, who had been celebrating with a friend, William Blow, in the Prince of Cobourg Inn, Southampton. He fell down some stairs and died from the injuries he received. At the subsequent inquest, held at the same inn, evidence was given as to his sobriety at the time of the accident and the verdict brought in on the victim, who had left a widow and nine children, was accidental death.

Two months later another fatality occurred when Richard James, the 37-year old steward of the *Princess Victoria*, collapsed and died following a heart attack while rowing some passengers out to the *Medina* which lay moored off the Royal Pier. The verdict, sad but quaint, was 'Visitation of God'.

In January 1838 the death was announced of Capt J. H. Knight Snr whose obituary included the comment: 'The introduction of steam navigation on the Southampton station was made at his suggestion and under his superintendence.' He was succeeded as superintendent by his son, J. H. Knight Jnr, who also inherited his father's large mansion, situated between the estates of the Ward family and Lady Osborne, which had been provided by George Ward.[16] The early steamer masters were apparently well remunerated, since the Knights were not only able to maintain such a large house but the son could also afford to purchase, in 1832, a 7/64th share, valued at £314 17s, in the *Duke of Buccleugh*. In addition to their normal shipboard responsibilities, the masters of these early steam vessels were also required to handle the ship's finances, and this involved collecting the passage money, out of which they paid crew and staff wages and the working expenses of the steamer, including the cost of repairs and coaling ship.

In April 1839, when the river Medina was reportedly frozen 'to the ferry steps', the proprietors of the *George IV* announced that a new steamer was to be built to be ready to meet '. . . . the vast increase of passengers' expected upon the opening of the London & Southampton Railway. And, it was added, 'She is to be commanded by Capt David Corke, what he justly merits, for a more attentive, civil and obliging fellow never commanded a vessel.'

The new steamer was named the *Gem* as she was launched from Thomas White's yard at Cowes on 5 September 1839, and on 8 October she was towed to Millbrook to have her engines fitted, presumably by Summers & Co. Carvel-built of wood, the 47-ton *Gem* was two-masted and schooner-rigged. She had a fixed bowsprit, a 'woman bust' head, and a square stern ornamented with mock galleries. Her dimensions were: 99.7ft x 14.9ft x 8.2ft and she had two engines totalling 40 hp.[17] (Pictures, p35.)

Under the command of Capt David Corke, the *Gem* went into service in the spring of 1840 as the 'fastest and largest' of the Southampton to Cowes steamers—and not before time. There was now considerable dissatisfaction with the service, despite the owners' claim that the vessels had been refitted 'on a scale of great comfort and elegance.' There was complaint that, throughout one week, neither of the two steamers on station had made the passage to Cowes in less than two hours, and that neither had attempted to make the passage to Portsmouth— 'There being no communication between Cowes and Portsmouth for seven days!' It was also pointed out that the smallest parcel sent from Southampton to Cowes cost 10d; that all passengers landing at Cowes and requiring carriages were obliged to take them from the Fountain Inn; and, last but not least, that the steamer sailing times did not fit in with the train arrival and departure times already being forecast.

Capt Corke and the *Gem* were presumably expected to remedy these several defects in communications with the island, but in the meantime public attention was being directed elsewhere. There had been much talk of an opposition company which was about to be established and, inevitably, there had also been rumours of the imminent introduction of iron steam ships on the island passage.

CHAPTER TWO

SOUTHAMPTON AND COWES
STEAMERS: 1840-65

THE OPPOSITION company was announced in January 1840 when the South Western & Isle of Wight Steam Navigation Co issued a prospectus seeking a capital of £12,000 in £20 shares with which to build three iron steamers of 40 hp each at an estimated cost of £10,800. The first vessel was promised for May and '. . . the opening of the London & Southampton Railway' when it would sail for Cowes, Ryde and Portsmouth at 9.30 each morning upon the arrival of the train, '. . . there being no packet at present which accommodates itself to persons travelling by train'. Whereupon the older established companies altered the sailing and arrival times of their steamers to suit those of the expected trains and lowered their fares by sixpence.

The threatened opposition, however, never materialised. The first and only steamer built for the company, and designed to rival the seven already in service, was launched from the Northam yard of Summers, Groves & Day, on 14 October 1840. Named *The Pride of the Waters*, she was described as 'A magnificent iron steamer', and it was said, 'From her length, power and light draught of water, she must become a favourite with the passengers'. Built to the design of a draughtsman named Heighington who departed from the accepted rule of this time, she had an 'unusually sharp bow, by which she will cleave the waves with greater ease and rapidity . . . the whole vessel in the water is a most graceful model.'

The launching of this, the first iron-built Island steamer, was recorded at the time and is the earliest detailed account of such an event:

> At the time of High Water, a crowd of visitors arrived and preparations were made under the direction of Mr John Vaux, shipbuilder of Northam, for the launch, a task of no small importance, considering the great length of the vessel, 122 feet (sic). The cradle having been adjusted, at half-past twelve o'clock, the wedges which supported the metallic fabric were struck away, and she seemed like a newly created being, to have a tremour in her frame, as for the first time she glided into her native element. At the moment of quitting 'terra firma', Miss Haque, sister of Mrs Summers, dashed a bottle of champagne at the retreating voyager and appropriately named her *The Pride of the Waters*. The rippled surface of the Itchen sparkled under a brilliant sun as she received into her bosom the handsome stranger, and the assembled multitude made the hanging woods around echo with their cheers. We had the opportunity of going aboard. She has a splendid saloon and handsome cabin forward with separate cabins for the Captain and the Steward. She is divided by iron bulkheads into three compartments, so that if she were to have her plates—not timbers—stove through in one division, the others would preserve her buoyant. She measures 167 tons (sic).[1]

The *Pride* was next towed by the Hythe steamer *Forester* to Millbrook to receive her engines. Of 49.5 tons, she was single-masted and sloop-rigged, with a square stern ornamented with sham galleries. Her dimensions were 114.9ft x 16.4ft x 8.1ft and her two engines had a combined rating of 44 hp.

Her launching, however, was both the highlight of the South Western & Isle of Wight Steam Navigation Co's activities and its swansong, because the company thereafter faded into obscurity and was not heard of again. The *Pride* was then bought outright by William Fitzhugh for the Southampton Steam Navigation Co upon the recommendation of Capt David Corke, and was renamed the *Ruby*.

In December 1840, Capt J. H. Knight Jr, superintendent of the 'Cowes Line' or the Isle of Wight Royal Mail Steam Packet Co, died at the age of forty-two and was succeeded by Capt David Corke, of the 'Southampton Line'; '... being so well known as anxious to please and advance with the times that we shall not much longer have to complain of the rate at which our steamers do the passage, their taking two hours to carry the mails between Southampton and Cowes.' This was an appointment of interest because, presumably, the two fleets were now under a single superintendency. David Corke's brother, Capt James Corke of the *George IV*, was promoted to the *Gem* while David was appointed master of the *Ruby*, which made her first trip to Cowes in April 1841, achieving what David Corke claimed to be 'the quickest passage in his experience'. The *Ruby* was engaged on excursion work and, in September 1843, she became the largest steamer to berth at Yarmouth Pier. During Cowes Week of 1844, she accompanied the yachts of the Royal Yacht Squadron.

Meanwhile, the London & Southampton Railway line had opened in May 1840, and within a few weeks the local populace were astounded to learn that a Chaplin engine with one carriage had steamed from Southampton to Nine Elms, London, in 2hr 5 min.

In May 1840, also, the *Medina* was again in the news following a rescue effected while she was on passage to Cowes. She had closed a capsized sailing boat, a Hythe wherry, off the river Hamble and picked up six workmen, the only survivors of a party of twelve men who had been working on the construction of Southampton Dock, and the boatman, 32-year old James Welch, who was taking them on an excursion to Calshot Castle. They had put into Hamble on the outward journey and spent several hours drinking heavily in the Victory Inn (which is still in business) before getting under sail again in a freshening wind. Had it not been for the *Medina*'s timely appearance when their boat capsized in a squall, the whole party would probably have drowned.

Comment concerning this tragedy was, nevertheless, blunt: 'They were all the worse for drink and Welch was in a beastly state of intoxication', yet at the funeral of the seven victims, hundreds of people lined the route or attended the burial at Peartree churchyard in the parish of Jesus Chapel, St Mary Extra, Peartree Green, Itchen. Reports of this accident included a complete list of the crew of the *Medina*: Captain Samuel Summers, engineer Joseph White, stoker George Nicholson, steward George Kleet, and seamen David Drayton and Robert Read.

The following month, the *George IV* ran aground on the Vine Causeway, West Cowes, but was got off safely without having incurred any serious damage.

The year 1840 closed with a report that an island steamer had 'tendered' the Atlantic steamer *British Queen* (picture, p71), bringing sixty passengers and the mail from Motherbank to Southampton; and the news that the *Duke of Buccleugh* was being lengthened: '. . . 9 feet above and 6 feet below the water-line, an extension of her grace which will not be unacceptable to her many admirers'. The *Buccleugh* at this time was maintaining the passage together with the *Medina*, the *Malmesbury*, the *Princess Victoria* and the *Gem*, but there was general criticism of their performance on passage, which seems hardly fair in view of their small size, lack of power and the kind of weather to be encountered in the Solent. On one occasion, one of these steamers bound from Cowes to Portsmouth ran into a severe gale and took two hours to make the passage, and then was unable to approach the landing at Gosport with any degree of safety. The passengers had, therefore, to be landed

by wherries of the hardy boatmen, who in each instance, pulled for their own and their passengers' lives. The waves rolled in with such tremendous impetuosity and threatened to dash the boats in pieces on the shore. Numbers of sturdy arms were extended to the drenched passengers as they neared the pales (sic) and they were dragged up as the boats swept past.[2]

In May 1842, in anticipation of the opening of the dock at Southampton and a forecast that fourteen large mail steamers were to use the port, a light-vessel was stationed off Calshot Spit to facilitate navigation in the approaches to Southampton Water, and has remained to the present day. The tonnage dues which helped maintain the light in 1842 were: vessels on overseas trade, in and out, $\frac{1}{2}$d per ton; and vessels on coasting trade, in and out, $\frac{1}{4}$d per ton. The Southampton dock, which finally opened on 1 July 1842, was nearly blown sky-high barely nine months later when the brig *Tartar*, loaded with explosives, caught fire. Luckily, the fire was brought under control in time.

The death was reported in April 1843 of Capt David Corke's son-in-law, Capt William Burridge, the son of Capt William Burridge Snr, master of the *George IV*, of Feathers Hill (since renamed Market Hill), Cowes. Captain Burridge Jnr was master of the coasting schooner *Matilda* of Southampton and was killed when struck on the head by a 'shoot' while loading coal at Newport, Monmouthshire. Only two years previously he had married Capt Corke's daughter, Sarah. He is buried in St Mary's churchyard, Cowes and the memorial stone marking his grave reads: 'Beneath are deposited the mortal remains of Wm. Burridge, who was called into eternity by an accident whilst faithfully discharging his duties as Master of the *Matilda* on the 12th day of April, 1843, aged 28.'

The death of another son-in-law of Captain Corke was reported seven months later, in November 1843. This was Capt William Mitchell, master of the schooner *Nimble* of Cowes, which disappeared with all hands while on passage to Llanelly where she was to load a cargo of coal. She had put into Hayle, Cornwall, for shelter and sailed out again on the morning of

Friday, 27 October, in company with another schooner but that evening, 'the *Nimble* bore up and has not been heard of since.' Mitchell was only thirty years of age. 'So in little more than six months, two of Mrs Corke's daughters have lost their husbands and returned again to their father's roof.'

In March 1844 Capt Corke and his family moved from Cowes to Southampton, taking with them a handsome silver cup presented to Corke by the people of Cowes as a token of their esteem and regard: 'It is very chaste and elegant and of the value of £10. To admit of its being participated in by many persons of limited means, the subscription was limited to 2s each person.'

Shortly after his arrival at Southampton, Capt Corke was selected as one of the three newly-appointed Sub-Commissioners of pilotage for Trinity House. The other two were Samuel Price Edwards, collector of customs at Southampton, and Capt John Love, Trinity agent at Yarmouth and late master of the Earl of Malmesbury's yacht *Medina*. These appointments dated from 1 March 1844 and were made in anticipation of the development of the port of Southampton which, in 1843 '. . . had an aggregate tonnage of 19,042 tons and 7,226 hp.'; and because, it was said, 'If a Cowes pilot is engaged, his recommendations, of course, are sure to be in favour of Cowes'.

The Sub-Commissioners' first action was to examine their Southampton pilots, increase their number from fourteen to eighteen and to station six of them at Calshot with powers to supersede any other pilot. It appears that 'other pilots' were not held in high esteem, . . .

> never bringing a large vessel up Southampton Water without running her aground somewhere or other. This does not arise from ignorance but with a view to damage the port. They know that no danger can take place, let the vessel ground where she will, and as a loss of time is likely to occur, which in the case of steamships is highly vexatious and harassing, they hope by such courses to get the vessels removed to another port.[3]

It was explained that the Isle of Wight pilots were called

'Cowes pilots' because their boats were registered at that port. And of these boats, in 1843, only two from Cowes and two from Portsmouth were capable of making extended cruises to 'Land's End and beyond Scilly' in order to place pilots on board. Local pilots, one imagines, were understandably jealous of the Southampton pilots whose number was to increase, by 1853, to 23 pilots and 5 boats, although at the same time there were 53 Cowes pilots with 19 boats and 43 Portsmouth pilots with 13 boats. In 1853 pilots' average annual earnings were: Southampton £58, Cowes £53, and Portsmouth £57. The present separate inward and outward branches of the Isle of Wight pilotage service were not to be established until 54 years later, in 1907.

Capt Corke's principal duties as superintendent of the island steamers were further increased during Queen Victoria's frequent visits to the Isle of Wight, her liking for the island having developed when, as Princess, she had spent holidays with her mother at Norris Castle. Once Osborne House was built, the royal family invariably travelled by train to Gosport and embarked in royal yachts for the crossing to East Cowes. They landed at the Trinity House Depot, where Sir John Pelly, the Deputy-Governor of Trinity House, had erected a wharf and special landing-stage for the use of the Queen, so that she could 'land and disembark without intrusion.' This landing stage, a special inset pontoon, together with a neat lawn and small pathway, were carefully maintained until the depot and wharf were rebuilt in 1965.

The royal family's staff, baggage, stores, horses and carriages, however, were usually sent from Portsmouth and Southampton to Cowes by Southampton steamers, and during the late 1840s some of their passages were recorded:[4]

Ruby and *Malmesbury*: Master of the Horse and department. 25 horses, 4 carriages, 4 baggage vans and respective jockeys, grooms, attendants and domestics.

Queen and *Malmesbury*: brought over 23 horses, some of the

royal carriages and part of the household.
Ruby and *Queen*: departure of Court to Buckingham Palace.
A division of police and remaining royal carriages.

On one occasion there was consternation when a van forming part of a Gosport-bound train and containing the dresses of the Princess Royal, broke down at Fareham. Capt Corke was instructed to have the van sent by tow-boat immediately it arrived at Southampton, even if it arrived late at night and a special steamer had to be laid on.

The Captain's other interests included that of ship-owning, which was noted in 1844 when he was named as principal owner of the schooner *Comet* (Capt Jewell) which, bound from Botley to Penzance, Cornwall, with a cargo of flour, foundered off Fowey with the loss of all hands. The owners later opened a subscription for the master's widow and two small children.

Another island-steamer master distinguished himself during the 1840s. This was Capt John Stephens of Feathers Hill, Cowes, who, in 1843, invented a useful life-preserver called the 'Stephen's Life Ball'. The ball consisted of a hollow metal sphere, cased with cork and quilted with canvas. Attached to it were grummets to serve as handles, and a bight or loop, large enough to slip over a person's head and shoulders. The whole, attached to a long line, stowed neatly in a bucket and was kept handy on deck ready for instant use. It was adopted by many British foreign-going and coasting vessels, the Italian and Portuguese navies and by Lord Adolphus Fitzclarence in the royal yacht *Victoria and Albert*. The Society of Arts gave the ball its blessing and the Philanthropic Society of Le Havre ordered thirty. Capt Stephen's invention might well have earned him world-wide fame had its general acceptance not been forestalled by an adverse report from the superintendent of the Royal Navy Depot, Woolwich, who considered: '. . . the form and shape being non-stable, renders it, therefore, useless.'

Worse still, on one of the few occasions when the inventor had occasion to use his ball, the intended recipient turned his back on it! This was in January 1844, when the *Medina* (Capt Stephens) was on passage from Portsmouth to Southampton. A passenger named Moses Goodman jumped over the side off Calshot with the intention of drowning himself and when a life ball was thrown towards him he chose to ignore it. He was even less appreciative of the efforts of two of the *Medina*'s crew who, launching the stern boat, managed to drag him to safety and return him to the steamer. He was later handed over to the police at Southampton who discovered that he had written a suicide note before leaving Portsmouth. Not long afterwards Goodman died in Southampton's workhouse but there was no inquest as body-snatchers had made off with the corpse before the surgeon could conduct his examination. The culprits, to show that they were not entirely dishonest, returned the sheets which had been taken with a note attached: 'The ghost of Moses Goodman— Bah!'

In March 1844 the island-steamer fleet comprised only six vessels—the *Medina*, the *Malmesbury*, the *Buccleugh*, the *Gem* and the *Ruby*. The *Princess Victoria* had been sold to the Royal West India Mail Steam Packet Co (later to become the Royal Mail Line) for use as a tender to convey passengers, luggage and workmen to and from the company's vessels in the Roads and a large floating workship moored in Southampton Water. And so, after nearly eleven years of service on the Southampton to Cowes passage, the *Princess Victoria* passed into the workaday life of a tender, coming to public notice on one occasion only, in August 1847, when her 23-year old engineer, Samuel Green, was drowned. He was stepping from the after sponson of the mail steamer *Avon* onto the paddle box of the *Victoria* when he slipped and fell into the water: '. . . No more to rise again.'

The *Princess Victoria* was replaced by the *Pearl*, the second iron steam vessel constructed for the island passage, built by Summers, Groves & Day in two months. William Fitzhugh owned fifty-eight of the sixty-four shares. She was launched at Northam on 2 May 1844 and it was reported that:

> Her deck space displays the space of a vessel double her tonnage and her saloon accommodation will be replete with every comfort and convenience. Her appearance on the stocks was the admiration of many scientific men who honoured the launch, after which the friends and owners and builders were regaled with an elegant 'dejeune'.

The *Pearl*, of 32.7 tons, was single-masted and sloop-rigged, with a square stern ornamented with sham quarter galleries, and a 'woman bust' head. Her dimensions were: 89.8ft x 13.3ft x 7.9ft and her single engine was rated at 26 hp. Under the command of Capt David Corke Jnr, she went into service for the Isle of Wight Royal Mail Steam Packet Co in the summer of 1844.

Shortly after her launching, the inhabitants of East Cowes asked for a steamer service but, at first, their request was refused. And it was not until they advertised in local papers, threatening '... to hire two of the swiftest steam boats on the Thames that would perform the Southampton to Cowes passage in three-quarters of an hour ...' that an East Cowes service was introduced—and, despite occasional interruptions, has continued to the present day.

In May 1845 some members of the crew of the *Pearl* hired a four-wheel chaise in Cowes to view the route of the proposed $4\frac{1}{2}$-mile railway line from Cowes to Newport. The party included the mate, engineer, steward and stoker—

> ... but as the party had been accustomed to place their lives in the hands of the engine-driver when on board, they considered it equally safe for him to drive them on shore. On their return, upon entering Cowes, the engine-driver having the steam well up, increased the speed to a racing pace. Slash went the whip and off went the horse, and when coming to the sharp corner at the bottom of the hill opposite the Duke of York Inn, out went the crew. The Mate had his shoulder put out and was bruised on the

forehead, the rest escaped unhurt but deploring the damage they had sustained by the mud to their clothes.

The railway, the first to be built on the island, eventually opened on 16 June 1862 and survived until 1968.

The year 1845 came to a close with the news that Thomas Sharp, a member of the Royal Yacht Squadron, had erected a 'brilliant gas light' in front of the clubhouse to assist vessels entering Cowes harbour at night. This, presumably, replaced the light erected in December 1838 by the Earl of Yarborough.

Throughout 1846, tow-boat charges were advertised which were to remain unaltered for the next fourteen years. These were: four-wheel carriage drawn by one horse 14s; two-wheel carriage drawn by one horse, 10s; horses 5s each; beasts 4s; calves 1s; sheep, per score, 6s; and lambs, per score, 5s. Fares in the summer of 1846 were also slightly reduced, '. . . and taken advantage of by the holiday folks.'

Occasionally, the daily routine on board the steamers was interrupted, as in October 1846, when the *Pearl* was again involved in an accident which might have had fatal results. She was steaming up Southampton Water, under the command of Capt D. Corke Jnr, when a Customs boat hailed, asking for a tow up-river to the preventative cutter moored in the Iitchen. Capt Corke agreed but while a line was being passed to the boat, the inexperienced boatmen manoeuvred their boat under one of the paddles which cut the boat in two, spilling the occupants into the water. Luckily for them, the *Pearl*'s stern boat was got away instantly and picked the men up within seconds, which was just as well since it subsequently transpired that two of the four men could not swim at all. For their rescue, the seamen in the *Pearl* were given a guinea each by the son of Sir Arthur Paget, who happened to be on board at the time.

The island steamer fleet was further increased in May 1848 by the launching at the Northam yard of Summers, Day & Baldock of yet another iron steamer, the *Queen*. Again William

70

Page 71 (*above*) The cross-Channel steamer *Atalanta* of 1836; (*below*) the paddle steamer *British Queen* of 1838, the first steamer on the Southampton-New York passenger service and 'tendered' by the Island steamers

Page 72 One of the first screw steamers on the South Coast, the *Princess Royal*, off Brighton's Chain Pier, c 1841

Fitzhugh held most of the shares, fifty-four out of sixty-four. The *Queen*, of 56.2 tons, was single-masted and cutter-rigged, with a plain unadorned bow and plain square stern. Driven by two side-lever engines totalling 40 hp, she was 117.1ft in length, with a beam of 14ft and a depth of $7\frac{1}{2}$ft. She was described as 'A clipper, to run to Cowes in 40 minutes, as quicker transit on this station is a great desiridatum, more especially now that passengers are accustomed to the rapid travelling by railway. Her saloon is most richly fitted up and the accommodation in every respect is profuse.' Despite her claim to speed, however, the best the *Queen* could do was '. . . under 50 minutes to Cowes.'

Her entry into service in the summer of 1848, under the command of Capt D. Corke Jnr, marked the demise of the old *Medina* whose name, by the end of the year, was withdrawn from the sailing schedules and, presumably, the passage. Perhaps she went on to towage duties, for she is not mentioned locally again until 1852 when she was transferred to Liverpool. In 1873, she was again transferred, this time, to Ardrossan, and was finally lost on a voyage from Belfast to Garston in 1880. She was the longest-lived of all the island steamers.

The crowded decks of these small steamers, during the summer months especially, presented opportunities which the 'light-fingered gentry' were quick to grasp, judging by contemporary reports. In May 1848, Mrs Hayes of Southampton was in the *Pearl* on passage to Lymington when a pickpocket was caught red-handed taking a handkerchief from her pocket containing more than ten sovereigns. He was taken before Capt J. Stephens, who handed him over to the Newport superintendent of police who happened to be on board and he was later brought before the magistrates at Lymington. Here he was 'summarily sentenced to three months' imprisonment and to be privately whipped'. Another pickpocket was caught in September 1849 on board the *Malmesbury*. His name was Nisbett and he was reported by a Mrs Welch of Southampton, who saw him pick the pocket of

73

E

another passenger as they sat on 'the seat across the bowsprit'.

An incident in lighter vein occurred when a passenger making for Portsmouth did not realise that packets from the Fountain Quay also sailed to Southampton. He boarded the first steamer to come alongside, the *Gem* and, after stowing his luggage, proceeded to promenade the decks, at peace with the world and his own arrangements, until the vessel sailed. It was not until the steamer was nearing Calshot that he realised anything was amiss and, dashing up to the captain, he asked where the steamer was going. 'To Southampton,' he was told. 'What!' exclaimed the passenger, 'I thought I was on board the packet for Portsmouth. I want to go to Brighton—Southampton is the last place I wish to go!' To which the captain replied that he thought, in this instance, the last must be first and the first last!

A similar mistake was made in August 1851 when a passenger boarded the cross-Channel steamer *Transit* at Southampton bound for the Channel Islands under the impression that she was going to Cowes. He did not realise his predicament until the steamer was off Calshot when he enquired casually of a fellow passenger the expected passage time and received the assurance, 'Not less than fourteen hours!'

Sombre news was recorded in May 1849 when the *Queen* (Capt D. Corke Jnr) was chartered to convey the body of General Sir Edward Paget from Trinity Wharf, East Cowes, to Southampton, en route to Chelsea Hospital. His widow, who died in March 1855, was described as '. . . the last survivor of the former occupants of Cowes Castle.'

A local newspaper of this time, June 1849, explained the origin of an interesting port practice which, slightly modified, is still in use today. Now, when tenders take their leave of departing mail and passenger vessels in the Roads, three prolonged blasts are sounded on the tender's siren or whistle as she draws away, and repeated by the larger vessel. Then, after a slight pause, the tender gives one short blast which is also echoed by the larger vessel as passengers and visitors cheer and wave good-bye.

This custom originated in the 1840s when the larger mail steamers could not complete their loading of cargo, coal and mails alongside in the dock owing to their comparatively deep draught. In consequence, they moored in Southampton Water or Cowes Roads for their last three or four days in port, and on sailing days the last cargo, mails and passengers were taken out by the island steamers which were generally crowded with visitors, friends and officials:

> They give three hearty cheers to the persons on board the mail steamer, just as the latter is getting under way, the crew of which immediately mount the rigging and reply by three vociferous huzzas. This draws forth a rejoinder of one more cheer from the Isle of Wight steamer. Then commence the final adieus, wavings of handkerchiefs, and wafting of kisses between passengers and friends as the former are gliding down Southampton Water. Sometimes these scenes are very affecting—mothers parting in this way from their children and wives from their husbands.[5]

The death of Capt Samuel Summers was announced in August 1849. He had commanded the *Thames* in 1821 and was '... one of the oldest commanders in the Isle of Wight steam packets and commanded the *Ruby* ever since she was built'. He had been taken ill one Sunday afternoon at Cowes, but rather than remain and receive medical attention had chosen to wait until his arrival at Southampton the following morning. He was then sent to his home, at 16 College Street,

> ... where he went to his bedroom, looked at his tongue in the glass and exclaimed very solemnly, 'I'm a dead man!' He went to bed and medical assistance was immediately procured but it was too late. He died about four o'clock the same day. Capt Summers was much respected by his employers and the public.[6]

It is possible that he was a victim of cholera, which was prevalent at this time in Southampton.

It was the *Queen*'s turn to feature in the news in February

1850 while on passage from Portsmouth. For upon arrival there the crew and passengers reported having heard a 'fearful explosion' from the direction of Norris Castle as the *Queen* paddled past. It later transpired that the stables at the Castle were being used to stow gear and stores from yachts, including the *Ganymede* and the *Kate*, and that the young son of Robert Bell, the Castle owner for eleven years and proprietor of a popular magazine *Bell's Messenger*, had heard a hissing noise coming from the stable loft immediately prior to the explosion. He was on his way to obtain a key in order to investigate when the stables blew up, killing two workmen instantly.

Local steamer news was rather more cheerful in June 1850, when it was reported that forty-five Polish refugees, emigrating to the United States, had been given a free passage in the *Buccleugh* from Southampton to Mother Bank, where they boarded the packet *American Eagle*, bound from London to New York. But this was a lull before the storm which threatened to break out a little later following an announcement to the effect that a war of opposition was about to begin on the Southampton to Isle of Wight station. A new company, it was said, was to place two new large steamers on passage to the island. They were to be 'clippers', performing the passage in less than one hour, '. . . against the two hours at present being allowed' to convey the swarms of visitors expected to come over to the island during the Great Exhibition of 1851. An early launching of the rival's first steamer, *The Times*, was also forecast.

However, the months went by without further news of the vessel and it was not until May 1852 that the mystery was partly explained. *The Times* had indeed been built—by John and Robert White of Cowes—but for more than a year she had lain, uncompleted and engineless, in the river Medina. Presumably, her owners had exhausted their finances, for she was eventually acquired by the Isle of Wight Royal Mail Co—William Fitzhugh owning fifty-eight of the sixty-four shares. She was then engined

76

by Summers, Day & Baldock and renamed the *Medina*. She was wooden-hulled, of 55.34 tons, single-masted and sloop-rigged, with a 'female bust' head and a square stern ornamented with mock galleries. Her two engines totalled 56 nhp and her principal dimensions were: 120.8ft x 14.9ft x 8.6ft.[7]

On one occasion, during the summer of 1852, it was claimed that her average passage, from the Royal Pier to Cowes, was 46 to 47 minutes: '. . . She has, however, with the tide in her favour, made the passage in 42 minutes.' From this, it would appear that the *Medina* was the fastest steamer in the Solent. Subsequently, she was for many years queen of the local excursion work.

On the evening of the 27 March 1851 the *Duke of Buccleugh* was in collision with the 15-ton yacht *Sea Dog*, owned by J. Barfoot of Lymington. The steamer was abeam of Calshot, bound for Southampton, when the yacht, having the owner and three other men on board, suddenly tacked and ran across the bows of the steamer. Capt William Calpine immediately put his helm hard over and stopped the engines, but to no avail. The two vessels collided and within seconds the yacht went down. A boat from the *Buccleugh* was got away quickly, picked up the three men, and was searching for the owner who had been below deck at the time of collision when Capt Calpine plunged over the side with a life-line. Swimming in the direction he thought he had heard a cry, he found the missing man and both were hauled back to the steamer and safety. On arrival at Southampton, the yacht-owner took full responsibility for the accident, entirely acquitting Capt Calpine of any blame. It was further stated at this time that 'This is the first accident occurring to or by one of the entire line.'[8]

The *Pearl* was also involved in a slight accident in May of the same year when making her way up Southampton Water in the dark. She was run into by a small coasting sailing vessel which afterwards made off, having refused to give her name. The *Pearl* suffered damage to the amount of £5 and the only

77

suspect vessel that could be traced but not positively identified was the coaster *Rising Sun*, which returned to Southampton the following day with a damaged bow.

The following month, Capt J. Stephens effected a notable rescue outside Portsmouth harbour while in charge of the *Malmesbury*. The gig of HMS *Prince Regent*, containing the captain and five of his crew, was making for Southsea beach in a heavy sea when the boat was swamped close to the 'white buoy', the occupants being pitched into the water. The accident was seen by the crew of the *Malmesbury*, laying at Victoria Pier, and Capt Stephens steamed off to the rescue and managed to save five of the occupants—a seaman, William Hawkins of Landport, unfortunately being drowned.

In August 1851, following implementation of the Act of Parliament relative to steam navigation, the lot of the passenger in local steam vessels was, at least in theory, considerably improved. This Act, among other requirements, forebade overloading with passengers under penalty of a fine of up to £20 and 5s for each person over the stated number, while passengers who forced their way into a full vessel were liable to a special £2 fine of their own.

The year 1852 opened on a dismal note with 200 men on strike at the Northam yard of Summers & Company, and the appearance of a letter in the local press, written by an aggrieved passenger, complaining about the catering prices in Southampton steamers: 'It is well known they carry on a lucrative trade in refreshments but if they continue to make such an enormous overcharge as they did in the trip to Lymington last Saturday— 6d for a glass of brandy—they may rely upon the public not to tolerate it!'

A less personal complaint was made in September 1852 by a 'John White' of Cowes, who indignantly referred to the 'disrespect shown to the memory of the late Duke of Wellington ...' in the *Gem*, 'No flag at half-mast! No flag at all! I felt disgusted at being on board a vessel where such a manifest insult was offered to the honour of our great Duke!' Which prompted 'Vectendis' (?) of Cowes, and presumably a 'Stirer', to reply:

The Cowes and Southampton steamers have got into very 'Liberal' hands and I am sure you will agree when I tell you our respected townsman, Captain Burridge, lost his situation through voting for Colonel Harcourt. I hope an opposition company will be started and Captain Burridge given a situation. The Portsmouth & Ryde Company got put to rights by an opposition and I hope it will not be long before the 'Liberals' of Southampton will receive a similar lesson!

All of which proved too much for Joseph Clarke, manager of the *Gem*, who felt obliged to join in, pointing out that Capt Burridge had no county vote and in consequence did not vote for Col Harcourt and, therefore, did not lose his situation for this reason, as declared by the Captain himself. Whereupon, the correspondence ceased. An opposition company on the Southampton to Cowes passage was not to materialise for another nine years.

The *Buccleugh* and the *Queen* were each involved in a fatal accident in February 1853, when James Clarkson, a Post Office porter, was drowned while taking mails on board the *Queen* at the Royal Pier during the early hours. He slipped off the gangplank and was drowned, his body being recovered some time later by means of 'creepers', used by Charles Marteil, a bricklayer, and taken to the Cobourg Inn and thence to the workhouse.

At the subsequent inquest it was explained that the two steamers were lying alongside each other at the Royal Pier, the *Buccleugh* lying outboard. Henry Blake, fireman in the latter vessel, gave evidence as also did the mate of the *Queen*, Henry Summers, who admitted that as he had turned in at 11.0 pm there was no one on deck to receive the mails. When pressed, he insisted that this was the steward's responsibility, adding that he had been a steward himself some years previously, which infers that stewards in the island steamers at this time were seamen rather than culinary experts. Notwithstanding the fact that no watch had been kept on board the vessels, no blame for the accident was apportioned to any party and a verdict of 'Accidental death' was brought in.

In 1854 there was criticism of the island steamer fore cabin fares, which were now: Southampton to Portsmouth 2s 6d, and Southampton to Cowes 1s 6d. 'These are more than the labouring classes can afford! 1s 6d and 1s would be ample charges!' It was no doubt merely coincidental that, at about the same time, the office of the island steamers at 10 Bugle Street, next door to the Duke of Wellington Inn, caught fire. The fire was got under control before much damage was done and the inn is still in business today.

In March 1855 Capt William Calpine was in command of the *Buccleugh* on passage to Cowes during a gale, when a woman passenger was taken ill off the Brambles buoy. Having done all he could for her comfort, the captain then made for Cowes '. . . as fast as the power of steam and speed of the vessel would permit'. On reaching the Fountain Pier, medical assistance, in the persons of the surgeons Cass and Hoffmeister, was procured, and under an awning rigged over the poop of the steamer, the woman was delivered of a son, unfortunately still-born. The mother was later taken to the Fountain Tap to recuperate.

In June 1856 news of the coming withdrawal from service of the 'Fast and favourite', 'Oldest and dearest of friends', the *Earl of Malmesbury*, was received glumly by her admirers, despite the promise of a new steamer in her stead: 'In future, we must put up with being whisked from Cowes to Southampton in one hour. Our old friend used to give us one and a half hours, indeed, sometimes two hours steam for the same money that we are now to be charged for it's being done in half the time.' The *Malmesbury* was sold and transferred to Plymouth the same year, being acquired by the Earl of Mount Edgcumbe who had an interest in Cremyll Ferry. Her final end is obscure, because after the owner's death in 1861 all trace of the vessel was lost, a fact confirmed in 1885.

Her place on station was taken by the new iron steamer, *Emerald*, which was launched on 22 July 1857 from the Northam yard of Day, Summers & Co, and christened by Miss Elizabeth Lamb, the daughter of Andrew Lamb, engineer superintendent of the Peninsular & Oriental Co in Southampton since 1840, who was later (1861) to become chairman of the present Southampton company. The *Emerald*, as was reported significantly at the time, was built 'Under the joint superintendence of Capt D. Corke Snr and Joseph Clarke', the respective managers of the separate companies. Described as an 'elegant and clipper-looking paddle steamer', she was of 43.5 tons register, single-masted and smack-rigged, with a 'straight' stem and an unadorned elliptic stern. She was driven by two oscillating engines totalling 32 nhp and her dimensions were: 105ft x 14.1ft x 8.1ft. (Picture, p35.) The *Emerald* went into service for the Isle of Wight Steam Packet Co under the command of the senior master, Capt James Corke, heralded by the optimistic forecast that, 'From her appearance, she will become a favourite of the public and prove fast and commodious.'

Meanwhile, in September 1856, Capt W. Calpine in the *Pearl* had effected another gallant rescue while on passage from Cowes to Portsmouth. A four-year-old child playing on deck had managed to open a gangway door and fell through it into the water. The Captain immediately gave orders to stop the vessel and, fully clothed, dived over the side, and within a few minutes had returned with the child to the ship. '. . . After giving himself one or two good shakes [the Captain] mounted the paddle box and took the *Pearl* to her destination.' This was the fourth life saved by Capt Calpine, and one for which he received an award of £24 5s, a not inconsiderable sum in those days, together with a gold watch in a hunting case, 'suitably inscribed and supplied by Mr Dudley of Newport at cost price'. In March 1857 Capt

Calpine received the gold medal of the Royal Humane Society.

The end of the *Duke of Buccleugh*, or 'Little Duke' or 'Old Duke', as she was sometimes called, was forecast in January 1857, and one of her many fans suggested that her successor, understood to be an iron steamer, should be named 'The Iron Duke'. But from other quarters came comment that she could not be withdrawn from service quickly enough because '. . . her passage times, of from one-and-a-half, to one-and-three-quarters of an hour, and sometimes two hours, were within a quarter-of-an-hour of the old sailing-packet time.' (On one occasion in 1856, she took $3\frac{1}{2}$ hrs from Southampton to Cowes.) The *Buccleugh* was eventually taken out of service, sold and transferred to Penzance in January 1859, and broken up eight years later. Her replacement on the island station, the *Sapphire*, was not launched until July 1860.

On 8 June 1858, the *Pearl* and the *Emerald* were involved in an accident which nearly had fatal results. The *Pearl* had broken down the previous day while on passage to Cowes and had been obliged to anchor overnight off Calshot. The following morning the *Emerald* was sent down with six men to assist with repairs but as the men, together with the master, Capt Henry Summers, were stepping into their boat to row across to the *Pearl*, their boat capsized, spilling the occupants into the water. George Clark, mate of the *Pearl*, set about lowering a boat but the captain, William Short, promptly jumped over the side, passed lifebuoys to the men struggling in the water, and himself rescued two non-swimmers. All the men were saved and Capt Short was later appointed manager of the present Southampton company.

The *Ruby* also nearly came to grief in December 1858 when approaching Portsmouth from Ryde in dense fog. Off Haslar she was informed by a fisherman that the *Ruby* was steering straight for Southsea beach, whereupon, the Captain altered course to port and promptly ran ashore high and dry between the hospital and the fort. And as the tide was then falling, she did not get afloat again until the next day.

In February 1860 the two Southampton companies were apparently in a healthy financial position. The mail company, owning the *Ruby*, the *Medina*, the *Pearl* and the *Queen*, paid a 30 per cent dividend; while the steam packet company, owning the *Gem* and the *Emerald*, had put aside £5,000 for the acquisition of another steamer, the *Sapphire*, which was then on the drawing-board. But before this vessel came down the launching ways, an opposition company was formed to challenge the established monopoly of the old companies on the grounds that the old vessels, being slow and inefficient, were providing an unacceptable and inadequate service.

The new company had the impressive title of Southampton, Isle of Wight & Portsmouth Improved Steam Boat Co. Formed in March 1860 with a capital of £15,000 in £10 shares, the company's bankers were the National Provincial Bank; the engineer, Charles Kernan of the Vulcan Iron Works, Millbrook; the solicitor, Charles Bridge of Aldermoor; and the secretary, Alfred Barton. Among the shareholders, it was claimed, were William George Ward, the Marquis of Bath, Earl Wilton, the Marquis of Conyngham, and other members of the Royal Yacht Squadron. The new company claimed that their vessels were to be larger, faster and more powerful than those of their rivals, and were to be built on the modern 'American principle'. And instead of the usual open decks and small, badly-lit cabins situated below deck level as in the older vessels, the new company's vessels were to have cabins on deck and fitted with an ample number of windows. In addition, it was proposed that the time-delaying and sometimes dangerous use of tow boats would cease, and that these would be replaced by a 'floating bridge'—a large beamy vessel with an open deck for the transport of carriages, cattle and horses. It was also proposed to place floating pontoons at the landing places in Southampton and Cowes to facilitate the landing and embarkation of passengers.

Presumably undeterred by the threat of these major improvements, the Isle of Wight Steam Packet Co launched yet another of their conventional steamers on 5 July 1860 from the Northam yard of Day, Summers & Company—the iron steamer, *Sapphire* of 51.74 tons register. She was single-masted and smack-rigged, with a 'straight' stem and a square stern ornamented with quarter badges. Her dimensions were: 120.3ft x 14.5ft x 7.5ft and her two oscillating engines developed 40 nhp and 200 ihp. She was launched by Miss Macormac, daughter of the superintendent of Day, Summers' shipbuilding department. The only reference to the *Sapphire*'s deck layout: 'Her skylights are arranged to afford seats', implies that the saloons were below deck level. Later, on a trial passage from Southampton to Portsmouth and home again, she averaged 12.4 knots, '... without setting sail either way', which suggests that even at this time the use of sail in the island steamers was not altogether unusual.[9]

The new and rival company's first steamer, the iron-hulled *Lord of the Isles*, was designed by James Ash and built at the Thames Iron Works. Of 91.49 tons register, she was single-masted and smack-rigged, with a bowsprit, a 'man bust' head—representing a Highland laird in costume—and a rounded stern. Her dimensions were: 135.5ft x 18ft x 7ft, and her two oscillating engines, built by J. Stewart, developed a total of 60hp. (Picture, p36.) Boilers 20lb per sq. inch. Vacuum 26. Cyl. diam. 33in. Stroke 3ft. Paddle wheels at 45 r.p.m. Fuel consumption 8½cwt per hour. 'Engines with double eccentrics and the link motion the same as for locomotives for starting and stopping.' Each engine has double ported slides. The registered owners were: Robert Pinnock of Cowes; William Rawlings of Winchester; and James Alfred Mew of Newport.

The *Lord* was the first local steamer to have saloon cabins on deck, or deckhouse saloons, the deck level of the saloons being recessed slightly below that of the main deck. The after saloon measured 28ft 3in in length and had attached a ladies' small cabin, both extending the full width of the hull. The First class saloon was carpeted and seats were upholstered in velvet. The Second class saloon deck was covered with 'Floor cloth' and the cushions were of 'American cloth'. A promenade deck fitted with seats and handrails was provided on top which, incidentally, must have restricted the vision of the helmsman who steered from the stern. Doors were set in each side and at the after end of the saloon, while the plate-glass windows could be opened. The forward saloon was set inboard slightly, thus allowing a narrow walk for passengers along the deck, and was rounded at the forward end. Both saloons were heated by hot-water pipes, presumably an innovation at the time.

The *Lord of the Isles* made her first passage on 6 May 1861 under the command of Capt James Piers and with a party of directors, their friends and the brass band of the Volunteer Rifle Corps on board. She steamed to Cowes and Ryde, then, over-taking the Ryde steamer *Prince of Wales*, went through Spithead and circled the 110-gun 1st Rate HMS *Trafalgar*, and the 41-gun 2nd Rate HMS *Edgar*. Later, she made 14.18 knots over the measured mile in Stokes Bay. The *Lord* went into service the same month and, on 21 May made her first excursion, which was to Bournemouth, calling at Cowes out and home.

The new company's second iron steamer, the *Lady of the Lake*, was launched at the Thames Iron Works in August 1861. She was designed by James Ash and was similar to the *Lord* but with a 'bust head, depicting a Highland lady in costume'. Of 104 tons register, her dimensions were: 147.6ft x 17.9ft x 7.6ft and her two oscillating engines, built by J. Stewart, developed a total of 60 hp. (Picture, p36.) Her registered owners were the same as for the *Lord of The Isles*. The *Lady*'s two deckhouse saloons, slightly different from those of the *Lord*, were both set inboard. The forward saloon was also almost oval in shape and again, the level of both saloons appears to have been slightly recessed below

that of the main deck. It is possible that a promenade was provided on top of the after saloon, because luggage was sometimes
stowed there. The paddle-box louvres of the *Lady* also differed
from those of the *Lord*. Both ships, however, had light blue hulls
and were generally referred to as the 'Blue Boats'.

The *Lady of the Lake* arrived at Southampton on 19 September 1861 and the following day, under the command of Capt
George Cooper, was said to have made the passage from
Southampton to Cowes in $37\frac{1}{2}$ minutes. On 24 September she
made an excursion around the Isle of Wight in five hours, and
two days later made a special trip to Portsmouth with the directors and their guests on board. Overtaking the *Lord* and the
Sapphire (said to be the 'crack boat' of the old company) en
route, the *Lady* steamed into Portsmouth where the party on
board was shown over HMS *Emerald,* and the 9,000-ton armoured
ship HMS *Warrior,* before returning to Southampton. The *Lady*
went into service on the Southampton to Cowes passage on 1
October 1861 and on one occasion, in 1864, is known to have
steamed from Southampton Docks to Cowes and back in two
hours. Her behaviour in bad weather was the subject of criticism,
as was the nautical ability of Captain Cooper. Upon leaving Ryde
Pier, instead of letting go forward and going astern on a back-
spring, thus lifting the bow clear, he persisted in going ahead and
forcing her out, bow first, "impaling his paddle box on the bowsprit
of the *Princess Royal,* removing some of her gilding in the process,
scraped across the bow of the *Prince Consort,* wrenching away her
bowsprit, figurehead and part of her bulwarks, all of which fell
overboard to join the figurehead of the *Lady* which he had knocked
off last week by an equally clever feat of seamanship"! In October
1863, the *Lady* (Captain Henry Summers) had the misfortune to
run down and sink a fishing boat off the Hamble River, drowning
one of the occupants. The Captain was subsequently charged with
manslaughter and although there was much adverse comment
about an inefficient lookout being kept and considerable delay

86

before the vessel was stopped and a boat lowered, he was acquitted.

The formidable challenge presented by the arrival of these two new, fast and large steamers on the island passage had not been unanticipated by the two older companies, who now decided upon an amalgamation of fleets and resources to better oppose the rival newcomers. A committee of management was formed by the two companies on 9 April 1861 and they ceased to exist on 7 August 1861 when the shareholders elected a new board of directors under the chairmanship of Andrew Lamb, a resident of Southampton and engineer superintendent of the P&O Steamship Co from 1840 onwards. It was this board which, on 10 September 1861, registered the superbly named South-ampton, Isle of Wight, & South of England Royal Mail Steam Packet Co Ltd, which acquired the mail company's *Ruby*, *Pearl*, *Queen* and *Medina* and the Isle of Wight Steam Packet Co's *Gem*, *Emerald* and *Sapphire*.[10] The *Emerald* under the command of Captain John Muston, was nearly sunk one morning in December 1861 off the Sturbridge Buoy when she was struck by a huge cannon ball during a practise firing of Armstrong guns. The ball smashed into the *Emerald*'s starboard quarter, denting the side and tearing off scroll work, capsized the binacle, made the helmsman duck and 'took the rosey hue from the passengers' faces'.

The following month, October 1861, the rival Improved Steam Boat Co launched their third iron steamer, the 'floating bridge' *American*, built at the Vulcan Iron Works, Millbrook. Of 173.27 tons, she was mastless and had a rounded stern. Driven by an 80 hp engine, her dimensions were: 130ft x 25.5ft x 8.25ft, though her draft at launching was only 2ft 3in forward and 2ft 6in aft. To keep the main deck clear and utilise as much space as possible, it was extended along most of its length to the outer edge of the paddle boxes on each side, and on the overhang, long, narrow saloons were erected for the passengers' accommodation. The *American* was provided with both bow and stern rudders—she was presumably a 'double-ender'—and had paddle wheels, the patent of which was held by Muntz, one of the registered owners. The others were Rawlins and Pinnock. Pinnock, incidentally, was chairman of the Improved Steam Boat Co and on occasion boasted of his small shareholding in the rival company's steamer, the *Gem*, which entitled him to free travel in that vessel.

The enterprise underlying the development of such a revolutionary type of craft as the *American* for the island passage at this time was undoubtedly commendable but, unfortunately, she did not prove successful. Indeed, it is doubtful if she was ever in service. She was advertised as about to commence on the Southampton to Cowes passage from 28 December 1862 to the 8th February 1863; then the advertisements in local newspapers ceased and a report on 1 February referred to the vessel having rammed the pontoon at West Cowes, which may have occurred on a trial trip. Years later, in 1889, it was stated in the *Hants Independent* that: 'The *American* never ran.'

The Improved Steam Boat Co, nevertheless, got off to a flying start by acquiring a 21-year lease of the Fountain Quay, Cowes, from the owner, William George Ward, who was presumably tired of haggling with the older companies and their usual two or three year leases. But the first intimation the old companies had of this was when one of their vessels steamed into Cowes and, mooring alongside the *Lord*, which was lying at the quay, attempted to discharge her passengers across the deck of the latter steamer. To their surprise, they found the way ashore barred by the *Lord's* crew, demanding a toll of twopence a head. 'But we don't pay tolls!' argued the old companies' employees, 'We've got the lease!' 'Not since 12 o'clock today!' came the reply, 'Come on now, twopence a head!' And to add insult to injury, the old companies were obliged to vacate their office on the Fountain Quay and move into the Vectis Brewery nearby.

At Southampton, the Improved company also made changes. Rather than pay tolls on the number of passengers passing

Page 89 (*above*) The steam packet *South Western*, the first iron steamer on the Channel Islands service, fighting a gale in the Great Roads, Jersey, in September 1845; (*below*) a two-funnelled Channel Islands steamer of c 1874; contemporary reproductions identify her variously as the *Courier* or the *Dispatch*

Page 90 (above) The cross-Channel mail packet *Wonder* in the great storm of 1846; (below) the silver salver presented to her master, Capt J. Goodridge Jnr, in recognition of his 'nautical ability so consistently displayed throughout the fearful storm of Wednesday, 21 October 1846'

through the Royal Pier, it acquired a pier and pontoon for a rental of £150 per year from the Itchen Floating Bridge Co, situated on the Southampton shore of the river Itchen. And when the pier commisioners sought legal redress, the company successfully defended its action.

The *Lord of the Isles* and the *Lady of the Lake*, each making only four round trips daily between Southampton and Cowes, could not hope to better the service provided by the old companies' vessels to both East and West Cowes, Ryde and Portsmouth. Nevertheless, the competition led to a reduction of fares which was no doubt much appreciated by the travelling public. These were now, between Southampton and Cowes: single 1s 6d and 1s; and return 2s and 1s 6d.

The competition also led to races between the rival steamers, as was commented at the time: 'The old boats with one exception have been running for years with boilers and machinery weakened by age and are now working up to highest pitch— puffing and blowing to compete with the *Lord of the Isles*. The old boats take an hour, an hour and a quarter or even an hour and a half, on passage.' The 'one exception' was the *Sapphire*, and even she was hard pressed to beat the *Lord*. Indeed, races between these two vessels became a daily affair and a frequent cause of apprehension on the part of smaller vessels which could not get out of their way. Another report appearing at this time states that the *Queen* took fifty minutes on passage and the *Medina* and the *Sapphire* forty-five.

As the competition grew fiercer, so tempers mounted and the culmination was a hectic free-for-all in an opposition war similar to that which had occurred on the Portsmouth to Ryde passage some years previously. The rivals raced each other for berths, hampered each other's movements, cut each other's mooring ropes and generally did everything to harass one another. And to further inflame tempers, when racing into Cowes, the winning steamer sported a gamecock at the masthead. This led to fights,

F

legal battles and appearances before the local magistrates. Certainly, our forebears took their competition seriously.

One irate Sotonian complained of the chaos caused by the uncontrolled rivalry of the opposing steamers at the Royal Pier:

> A half-hour or twenty minutes before the opposition steam boat starts, the call boy, an urchin of 12 or 14, is sent to ring the bell. And this he does with all the zeal and gusto which a knowledge of the annoyance he can inflict with impunity, is calculated to afford him. At the second stroke of the bell. up jumps the opposition boy and begins his bell, and one or two of the steamers add, from time to time, an accompaniment of prolonged screams from their steam whistles. The effect of this noise is that two or three passengers who are quietly walking along the Quay, fancy themselves late and set off running down the Pier. Near the end, they are attacked by half-a-dozen rival touters, shouting, yelling and abusing one another, and by the time the breathless and confused passengers have got on board, they find that they have some half an hour to wait in the midst of all this din. The bell ringing lasts for about five minutes and then ceases for a minute or two whilst the ringers rest. Then on it goes again from both steamers and so the annoyance keeps up till the boats start. . . .[11]

Unfortunately for the Improved company, and despite its commendable innovations, enterprise and early popularity, it was unable to weather the financial storm it had steamed into so deliberately. Within twelve months mounting losses led to bankruptcy proceedings, with liabilities of some £15,000, the principal creditor being the Thames Iron Works. By June 1862, the Improved company was sharing a timetable with its rivals, and four months later, in October, came a winding-up order. In May 1865 the company, together with most of its assets, was acquired by the present Southampton company. Henry Pinnock, chairman of the Improved company was taken on to the board and was vice-chairman at the time of his death in 1889. Alfred Barton, secretary to the Improved company, was appointed Cowes manager to the present company. The New company's original secretary, Charles Bridges, committed suicide in November 1861, following 'heavy percuniary losses'. The *Lord* and the *Lady* were taken over but not the *American*. She was sold in 1868 to a Mr B. H. Hartley of London for conversion to a pontoon and in 1870 was re-sold abroad.

Past differences were presumably soon forgotten following the take-over and the acquisition of the new company by the old proved an immediate success. The experience of the old combined with the initiative and enterprise displayed by the new made for a vigorous efficiency which has since prevailed for more than a hundred years.

A singular honour was accorded the *Sapphire* in April 1864 when she was placed at the disposal of the Italian statesman, Giuseppe Garibaldi, during his sojourn in Southampton, and no doubt he took passage in her when he visited Lord Alfred Tennyson at Farringford. The same month, two other Southampton steamers ran into trouble at the ceremonial opening of Cowes Green, presented to the town by George Robert Stephenson, son of Robert Stephenson, of railway fame. Both ships were dressed overall near Cowes when, in the first instance, a seaman named Early, of Itchen, fell from the bowsprit of the *Lady of the Lake* (Capt Henry Summers) and was injured by one of the paddle wheels; in the second instance, the *Ruby* was in collision with J. Broadwood's yacht, *Galatea*. The impact knocked Capt Stephens off the paddle box onto the deck, breaking several of his ribs.

The first steamer built for the Southampton, Isle of Wight, & South of England Royal Mail Steam Packet Co was the wooden-hulled *Vectis*, built by Joseph White of Cowes and launched at 1.0 pm on 14 June 1866 by Miss Elizabeth Lamb, daughter of the chairman. The *Vectis*, of 122 tons (140.7ft x 18.2ft x 8.2ft), was single-masted and smack-rigged, with a bowsprit and square stern.[12] Her 'female bust' head was 'A likeness of the young lady who launched her, represented as wearing a turban hat and a white yachting jacket, trimmed with gold.' The poop was higher than the upper deck, '. . . so that her after-cabin is rendered much loftier and more commodious. It is exceedingly elegant and tastefully got up and her fore-cabin is capacious and unusuaily commodious, owing to the arrangement and construction of the skylights which give light to the saloons.'

The *Vectis* went into service in August 1866 under the command of Capt John Muston, and claimed a passage time from Southampton to Cowes of forty-seven minutes. Later, she was used mainly on excursion work, replacing the *Medina*, now employed on the more mundane passage.

It was not until 1889 that the last of the older steamers, having generally spent their latter days as cargo vessels following conversion, were finally sold out of service: the *Pearl* in 1867 after twenty-three years on the Southampton station (broken up five years later); the *Emerald* in 1871—fourteen years; the *Ruby* in 1872—thirty-one years; the *Sapphire* in 1873—thirteen years; the *Queen* in 1876—twenty-eight years; the *Medina* in 1882—thirty years; the *Gem* in 1883—forty-three years (being broken up six years later); the *Lady of the Lake* in 1887—twenty-six years; and the *Lord of the Isles* in 1889—twenty-eight years. It is of interest to note that the wooden-hulled *Gem* outlived all the iron steamers, while the *Medina* was second only to the iron-built *Ruby*.

The wooden-hulled *Vectis*, however, built in 1866 and converted for cargo work in 1887, was not disposed of until 1910 (being broken up the following year), and was in service for forty-four years. She was the prototype of many Southampton paddle steamers which were subsequently employed on this station for almost a hundred years. The last paddle steamer of this company was the *Princess Elizabeth*, built by Day, Summers & Co at Northam in 1927, and finally sold out of service in 1959.

The present company, the Southampton, Isle of Wight, & South of England Royal Mail Steam Packet Co, known latterly

94

also as 'Red Funnel Steamers', celebrated its centenary in 1961 and today continues to maintain the passage which began in 1820, when the old *Prince of Cobourg* began to paddle furiously between Southampton and Cowes.

CHAPTER THREE

LOCAL CROSS-CHANNEL AND COASTING STEAMERS

All darkling dangers of the Channel crossing gone—
You, who would not the waves be tossing on,
Haste, in the *Ariadne*, now embark with me,
You'll be at Jersey safe, before it's dark at sea.

—Part of 'Address to the *Ariadne*',
Southampton Herald, 1824

THROUGHOUT THE nineteenth century, Southampton's cross-Channel traffic in passengers, mail and cargo was chiefly to and from the Channel Islands[1] and Le Havre.[2] And in 1820, while the paddle steamer *Prince of Cobourg* operated between Southampton and Cowes, local cross-Channel services were still being maintained by sailing vessels. Those from Southampton included the 107-ton schooner packet *Britannia* (Capt Ben Winder), managed by Weeks & March, Southampton packet agents, which had been built at Northam in 1819; and the 70-ton cutter, *Prince of Cobourg* (Capt James Page), built in 1816 and boasting 'Three separate cabins, 24 large beds, a large skylight, and a w.c. separate from the cabins'. One of these sailed for Le Havre every Tuesday and Friday, returning the following Tuesday and Friday. In addition, Weeks & March's cutter *Elizabeth* sailed to Caen once a fortnight.

The 110-ton packet *Chesterfield* (Capt Starr Woods, master and owner) also sailed for Le Havre every Friday, returning on the following Monday, providing 'a large stateroom with 25 single beds and two private cabins for ladies with six beds in each'. His cutter, the *Venus*, sailed for Caen every Wednesday. Sailing packets on passage between Southampton and the Channel Islands about this time included the *Hero*, the *Speedy*, the *Aeolous* and the *Diligent*.

Within a matter of years, however, these packets were all to be replaced by steam vessels, one of the first to operate locally being the steam yacht *Royal Tourist* (Capt William Bain) which, in April 1822, sailed from Brighton to Le Havre every other day. Her fares were £2 12s 6d in the cabin and £1 11s 6d (no refreshments) on deck. The following month, the steam yacht *Swift* (Capt H. MacGregor) of 80 hp, sailed from Brighton for Dieppe on Wednesday and Saturday, returning on Thursday and Sunday, but charged a more modest £1 15s cabin and £1 5s 'steerage'.

The first cross-Channel steamer to enter Southampton, however, was the French steamer *Triton*, which arrived with some passengers from Le Havre on 7 June 1823 and which for the remainder of the summer season sailed for Le Havre every Thursday and returned every Monday, calling at Portsmouth, out and home. Fares were two guineas cabin, and one guinea on deck, 'Children and servants, half price.' The *Triton* also operated this same service in June 1824.

The first local steamer to cross the Channel was the island steamer *Medina*, which was also the first steamer to enter Guernsey and Jersey, making this historic voyage in June 1823, although the honour has frequently been attributed to the steam yacht *Royal Charlotte* (Capt R. C. Godfrey), which traded between Jersey and Southampton from November 1821 to October 1823. Unfortunately, details of her registration cannot be traced and only brief references are to be found in contemporary news-

97

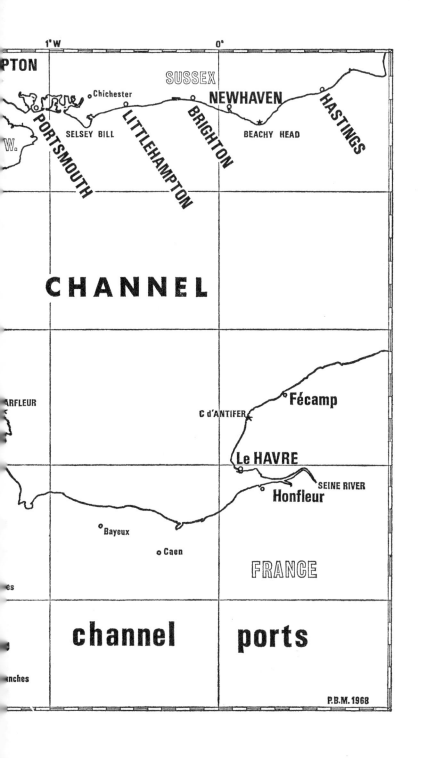

PTON

1°W

0°

SUSSEX

NEWHAVEN

HASTINGS

Chichester

BRIGHTON

SELSEY BILL

PORTSMOUTH

LITTLEHAMPTON

BEACHY HEAD

W.

CHANNEL

ARFLEUR

Fécamp

C d'ANTIFER

Le HAVRE

SEINE RIVER

Honfleur

Bayeux

Caen

FRANCE

es

channel

ports

inches

P.B.M. 1968

papers. One records the purchase by several Jersey merchants of the 'steam yacht *Royal Charlotte*' to convey passengers and cargo from Jersey to Southampton, the passengers at 15s each and cargo at '7s per foot' while another newspaper the following week reports the first arrival of the 'steam yacht *Royal Charlotte* with a number of passengers and a cargo of cows from Jersey.' And although her arrivals at and her sailings from Southampton are regularly recorded from that date until October 1823, no further reference was made to her as a steam vessel. Likewise, contemporary accounts of her loss, although detailed, make no mention of steam, engines, paddles etc. In the early hours of the morning of 31 October 1823, she was driven onto a lee shore at Cape le Hogue during a gale and became a total loss, the crew and passengers, however, being saved.

On the other hand, the *Medina*'s arrival in the Channel Islands evoked a report which clearly states she was the first steam vessel into Guernsey, and similarly implies that she was also the first into Jersey. She sailed from Southampton on Sunday, 9 June 1823, having on board, Col Fitzgerald of the 72nd Regiment, and anchored off Cowes until Monday morning when she proceeded to Guernsey

> ... *being the first steam vessel that ever visited the place*, the novelty attracted a vast number of the inhabitants, and as soon as the Col. and his family were landed, the commander (Mr Knight) politely invited those who were desirous of viewing the machinery, to come on board. Many respectable individuals accepted the invitation, and expressed their astonishment at the mechanism, and admiration at the accommodation on board her. On the next day (Weds. 11th.), the *Medina* started for Jersey, and so had his urbanity won the good will of the islanders, that 130 accompanied Mr K. (sic) in the trip. *The same curiosity was excited there as at Guernsey*, and Mr K. issued a general invitation. In the evening, he left for Guernsey, cheered by the numbers assembled in boats to witness his departure. . . .

The *Medina* took 4hr 5min from Guernsey to Jersey and

15½ hours on her return passage from Guernsey to Southampton. Another account states that thousands of spectators had thronged the Jersey shore to witness her arrival, among whom was a distant horseman, who seeing smoke issuing from the *Medina*'s funnel, galloped off to fetch help for the 'packet on fire'!

The *Medina*'s voyage to the Channel Islands and the *Triton*'s season on the Le Havre to Southampton passage in 1823 heralded the establishment of local cross-Channel steam navigation, which took place the following year.

Southampton shipowners, lead by William Chamberlayne, MP, answered the challenge of the French steamer *Triton* by ordering a steam packet of their own—the *Camilla*—for the Le Havre service, to be ready for the spring of 1824. And hearing that some Jersey merchants were having a steamer (the *Lord Beresford*) built for the Channel Islands to Portsmouth service, they ordered another steamer, the *Ariadne*, to operate on the Southampton to the Channel Islands passage '. . . to keep the advantages they had so long reaped by the trade to and from these islands'.

The first of these steamers to enter service was the *Ariadne*, a 130-ton wooden-hulled vessel built by William Evans of Rotherhithe. Three-masted and schooner-rigged, she had a 'woman bust' head, and a square stern with quarter galleries. Her dimensions were: 115ft x 17ft 4in x 8ft 9in, and her two engines totalled 74hp.[3] The *Ariadne* arrived at Southampton on 6 June 1824 and sailed for Guernsey and Jersey the following day under the command of Capt John Bazin, taking thirteen hours on passage. Thereafter, she sailed every Tuesday for the Channel Islands and, in September 1824, once made a passage from Southampton to Brighton.

As the *Ariadne* began her passage work, her rival, the Jersey-owned *Lord Beresford*, named after the then Governor of Jersey, had just undergone trials in Swansea, where she had been built by William Scott & Co '. . . attaining a speed of 10 or 12 miles per hour without producing any unpleasant sensation'. Carvel-built of wood, the *Lord Beresford*, of 81 tons, was two-masted and schooner-rigged, with a square stern and quarter galleries. Her dimensions were: 100ft x 18ft 2in x 11ft 9in and her two engines developed 70hp.[4] She went into service between Portsmouth and the Channel Islands in June 1824, a week or so after the *Ariadne*, and in October of that year was the first steam vessel to enter St Malo while on excursion from Jersey under the command of Capt Robert Masterman. He was principal owner of the *Lord Beresford*. He died the following year. In 1825 and later, she sailed from Southampton to the Channel Islands, calling at Portsmouth, out and home.

The *Camilla*, built for the Le Havre service, did not arrive at Southampton until 23 June 1824, much later than had been anticipated. Her passage meanwhile had been maintained temporarily throughout May 1824 by the Isle of Wight steamer *Medina*, which sailed from Southampton to Le Havre at 6.0 am on Tuesdays, returning on Fridays—'Crossing by daylight'. She took up to fifteen hours on passage. Built by William Evans of Rotherhithe, the *Camilla* was wooden-hulled and carvel-built. Three-masted and schooner-rigged, she had a 'woman bust' head, an unadorned square stern, and two engines totalling 60 hp. Her tonnage was 102 and her dimensions: 107ft 10in x 17ft 10in x 10ft.[5]

The arrival of the *Camilla* was celebrated by the presentation of a silver cup to Capt J. G. Doran, who had supervised her building and she went into service on 25 June, under the command of 'Master, T. Brown, under the inspection of an Officer in the Royal Navy' (presumably, Capt Robert Forder, RN, one of the shareholders), and sailed on Tuesdays and Fridays for Le Havre, where she met the steam packet *Duchesse de Berri*, on passage between Le Havre and Rouen. The *Camilla*'s fares were: best cabin, £2 2s; children under twelve and servants, half price;

carriages £4 4s each, and dogs 5s. Her passage time averaged $12\frac{1}{2}$ hours and her arrivals at and departures from the Town Quay, together with those of the *Ariadne*, brought large crowds of spectators to the waterfront. On the Channel Island passage, both the *Ariadne* and the *Lord Beresford* called at Cowes if required and passengers from the latter vessel could board, if desired, the Cowes steamers to Southampton at the expense of the owners of the *Lord Beresford*.

The year 1824 closed with a report that the *Camilla* had been 'towed in crippled' by the *Lord Beresford*. Both the *Ariadne* and the *Camilla* were laid up in December, although the *Lord Beresford* maintained a winter service from Southampton until the end of January 1825—the steamer services being replaced by sailing vessels until April 1825.[6]

Fares to the Channel Islands by both steamers remained the same throughout 1825: main cabin 31s 6d, fore cabin 16s, fore deck 10s 6d and, between Guernsey and Jersey, 7s 6d and 5s.

In April 1825, another steamer appeared regularly in the Solent—the 218 ton *Brunswick*[7] (Capt James Mill) of the Plymouth & Portsmouth Steam Packet Co (1823-55). She was joined on the same passage in June 1826 by the 118-ton *Sir Francis Drake* (Capt Sadler) which, together with the *Brunswick,* made the Plymouth to the Channel Islands passage and, in 1828, called at Portsmouth homeward from the Channel Islands while the *Brunswick* sailed from Plymouth to Portsmouth and called at the Channel Islands outward. A service to Falmouth was also maintained by these two steamers, and in October 1829 the *Sir Francis Drake* was temporarily relieved by the *Sophia Jane*[8] which, in May 1831, was to be the first steam vessel to arrive in Australia.

The *Sir Francis Drake* continued to trade to the islands for almost thirty years, putting into Southampton occasionally and making frequent excursions around the Isle of Wight. In November 1836 she towed the first Itchen floating bridge from Plymouth to Southampton, and in July 1837, while on passage from Guernsey to Jersey, she was nearly lost by fire. She was off Gronez when smoke was seen issuing from the deck abaft the funnel and the master, Capt Nicholls, fearing the worst, steered into St Ouen's Bay in order to run her onto the beach. But by the time she had entered the bay, Pengelly, the carpenter, had broken open the deck with an axe and, pouring in copious quantities of water, had dowsed the flames. Whereupon, the vessel was put about to clear the land—only to strike a rock. Again she was lucky, for after the passengers had been landed safely by boat in St Ouen's Bay, Capt Nicholls managed to kedge his vessel off into deep water and take her into Jersey for repairs.

On her Portsmouth, Plymouth and Falmouth service in 1837, fares on board the *Sir Francis Drake* were: Portsmouth to Plymouth £1 5s, 15s and 10s; and to Falmouth £1 12s 6d, £1 and 14s.

From December 1825 to March 1826 inclusive, the three local steamers were laid up and their stations maintained by sailing vessels, including the *Elizabeth* (Capt Burton), the *Watersprite* (Capt Page), and the *Lady Wellington* (Capt Fuszard).

The *Ariadne* began her 1826 season on 4 April, taking forty passengers to the Channel Islands and, in July, her passage times and those of the *Lord Beresford* were said to 'average 14 hours'. And on one voyage in June, the *Camilla* took 100 passengers to Le Havre, while in September the *Beresford* put into St Malo. The year, however, was a quiet one for the steamers and it closed with the report: 'The *Beresford* in her last trip disarranged some of her works and was obliged to put into Lymington to repair.'

In April 1827 James Weeks of Southampton placed another steamer on the Le Havre station in opposition to the *Camilla*. This was the 180-ton (56 tons register) *St David*[9] (Capt Brice) which shared a timetable with the *Beresford* and, as if in retaliation, the *Ariadne* improved her Channel Island service by the introduction of monthly calls at St Malo. The *St David*, however, was not seen again locally after November 1827 for, after being put up for sale in October, she was taken out of service and replaced on the Le Havre station in March 1828 by the 180-ton (126 tons register) *George IV* from Bristol.[10]

These early years had not been without incident. In addition to the occasion in 1824 when the *Camilla* had broken down and been towed into Southampton by the *Beresford*, in January 1828 the *Speedy Packet* (Capt Bishop) was wrecked, luckily without loss of life, and in April of the same year Capt Priaulx of the sailing packet *Aeolus* was washed overboard and drowned.

Another stranger appeared in the Solent in August 1828, when the General Steam Navigation Co's steamer *Brocklebank* maintained a brief service between Portsmouth, Ryde and Brighton— the same month that the *Ariadne* acted as guardship at the Southampton Regatta and flew the 'Grand Standard of England'. The *George IV* also achieved a little notoriety the same month when two of her engine-room complement, William Wilcox and John Kinch, were each fined £100 for attempting to smuggle into Southampton '1½ gallons of Geneva spirit, concealed in an oil jar'. But this was a minor seizure compared to another in October 1829, when seven hundredweights of silk were found hidden on board.

During the summer of 1829, yet another strange sail appeared in the Solent—the 130-ton Bristol steamer *Bristol* (Capt Hermann)—which operated a service from Southampton to the Channel Islands with occasional calls at Sark and St Malo. She returned to Bristol at the end of the season and was broken up in 1859. Throughout the same season, the *Ariadne* sailed from Southampton every Tuesday evening for the Channel Islands, leaving the islands every Friday for Southampton, except once a month when she called at St Malo on the Thursday, leaving there on the following Saturday for the islands and Southampton. Her fares were: main cabin £1 11s 6d, fore cabin 18s, and fore deck 10s 6d. At the same time, the *Camilla* and the *George IV* sailed for Le Havre every Wednesday and Saturday, calling at Portsmouth, out and home, and leaving Le Havre on the following Saturday and Wednesday. Fares for this eleven-hour crossing were: £2 2s, servants and children under twelve £1 10s; carriages and horses, each £4 4s.

The *Ariadne* had a spell of bad luck during the latter months of 1829. While laying at moorings one night in Cowes harbour, a boatman, William Duncombe, rowed the steward out to the *Ariadne* and was drowned while returning to the shore. Then, in October, she ran down and sank a fishing-boat off Hurst Point, luckily without loss of life, though the owners were later obliged to pay half the cost of a replacement boat. Finally, in November, she was compromised yet again in the West Solent while giving a tow to a small boat—it capsized and one of the occupants was drowned.

In 1831, three much larger steamers began calling regularly at Cowes, the *Shannon*, the *Thames* and the *City of Londonderry*, all of 513 tons and with engines of 160hp. Every Sunday, one of them left London for Cowes, Plymouth, Falmouth and Dublin. Fares from Cowes were:

	1st cabin	2nd cabin	Deck
To London	£1 3s 6d	17s	5s
To Plymouth	£1 3s 6d	17s	5s
To Falmouth	£1 12s 6d	£1 3 6d	7s
To Dublin	£2 5s 6d	£1 13s 6d	10s

During the summer of 1831 the General Steam Navigation Co's steamer *Superb* (350 tons and 100 hp) maintained a service between Southampton, Plymouth and Bordeaux and, in addition, made several excursions around the Isle of Wight and from Southampton to Brighton. Her master was Capt William Major.

In the summer of 1831 the London, Guernsey & Jersey Steam Packet Co, formed with a capital of £11,520, traded between London and the Channel Islands with frequent calls off Brighton. Services were also operated to and from the Channel Islands from Southampton and Brighton. The company's 'new and beautiful' steamer, the 345-ton, 120 hp *Lord of The Isles*

Page 107 (above) Wreck of the Jersey mail steam-packet *Express* on the Grunes Houillieres, on the SW coast of Jersey in September 1859; *(below)* the Portsmouth-Ryde steamer *Chancellor* lying broken-backed off Ventnor Pier in July 1863

Page 108 (above, left) William Chamberlayne (1761-1829), principal owner of the *Camilla*, the *Ariadne* and the *George IV*; (above, right) George Player (d 1843), pioneer owner of Ryde steamers; (below, left) Charles St Barbe (1776-1848), principal owner of the *Glasgow*; (below, right) Capt John Bazin (1780-1836), master of the *Ariadne*

SOUTHAMPTON STEAM PACKETS.

THE

ARIADNE,

(CAPTAIN BAZIN,)

THE LARGEST STEAM PACKET ON THE STATION,

Leaves Southampton

FOR

GUERNSEY AND JERSEY

Every TUESDAY EVENING, at SIX o'Clock,

DURING THE SEASON,

And returns from THE ISLANDS every Friday.

☞ *The ARIADNE proceeds to St. MALO, and GRANVILLE twice a Month, after her arrival in JERSEY.*

THE

CAMILLA,

STEAM PACKET, (under the direction of an Officer of rank in the Navy, who is always on Board,)

LEAVES SOUTHAMPTON, FOR

HAVRE DE GRACE

Twice a Week during the Summer Months, and Once a Week in Spring and Autumn, calling at Portsmouth for Passengers both going and returning.

Passports for France may be obtained of Mr. W. J. Le FEUVRE, French Consul, Southampton, of whom further particulars may be had respecting the above Packets.

Joint timetable of the *Ariadne* and the *Camilla*

(Capt William Hide), had seventy-four sleeping berths and a dining saloon 22ft long and 15ft wide. She was claimed to be the fastest vessel on the Southampton to the Channel Islands passage, with an average crossing time of twelve hours. Competition on this route reduced her fares to 10s, 5s and 2s 6d. In November 1831, when forced by strong winds to put back into Southampton for more fuel, she ran down and sank the sailing vessel *Julie* from South America, which had been anchored in the West Solent overnight without showing lights. The steamer's owners, nonetheless, later had to find some £12,000 in damages and costs.

The steam vessels of H. P. Maples subsequently dominated the London to the Channel Islands passage until May 1864 when they were acquired by the newly-formed Channel Island Steam Ship Co, which continued to operate until May 1968, when regular services on this route terminated.

During 1832, competition on the Channel Islands passage continued and fares were again 10s, 5s, and 2s 6d, and races were the order of the day. A passenger in the *Lord Beresford* from Jersey to Guernsey describes a race with the 150-ton Weymouth mail steam packet *Flamer* (see Appendix 3): ...

> ... we were neck and neck and every quarter of an hour we found the *Lord B.* gradually drawing ahead and giving the crew of the *Flamer* an opportunity of looking into her cabin windows, and in 2 hours and 51 minutes we arrived in Guernsey Roads when the command was given to 'ease her'. At this time, the *Flamer* was nearly three-quarters of a mile astern and when she came alongside, the Commander politely acknowledged the victory of the *Lord B.* by touching his hat and saying, 'Goodridge, I wish you much joy!'[11]

Such rivalry might have been responsible for the collision which occurred in September 1832 between the *Lord Beresford* (Capt J. Goodridge) and the *Ariadne*, in which the *Ariadne* suffered a damaged lifeboat, cook-house, paddle box and bulwarks.

In May 1833, while laying at moorings in Southampton, the *Camilla* (Capt Le Sauteur), lost her bowsprit and suffered damage to her figurehead when she was rammed by the brig *Northumbria* (Capt Mills) which had a pilot on board named Edgar Rowecliff. Twelve years later this same pilot was 'Broken and rendered disqualified to act as a pilot any longer', despite an appeal heard by an Elder Brother of Trinity House in the course of an inquiry at the Dolphin Hotel, Southampton. In August 1833 the *Ariadne* was damaged in a severe gale while on passage from Guernsey to Southampton, one paddle box and part of the captain's cabin being carried away.

The following December, similar bad weather struck the *Flamer*, carrying away her bulwarks and a boat. Three of the crew were washed overboard but luckily were got back on board. One seaman was thrown through the skylight into the saloon and later died from his injuries. When the *Flamer* finally made port, five of her crew, were carried off the ship on stretchers.[12]

Three years later, a passenger was to describe a similar heavy-weather crossing from Guernsey to Weymouth, in February 1836, in the *Flamer*:

> When we left Guernsey the wind was favourable but in about two hours, a sudden calm came on which was speedily followed by a white squall, the forerunner of a tremendous gale. About 4 pm we shipped a heavy sea which knocked in the larboard paddle box and sent the ship's bulwarks on that side and one of the boats adrift. The Mate, Mr Roberts, had his collar bone put out. I do not know what we should have done without Captain Symonds who gave orders with great spirit. At eleven o'clock we shipped another heavy sea which filled the places forward, as well as the boats on the booms, in the bottom of which they had to make a hole to let the water out and we were thus left quite unprovided with boats. The Captain found we could not reach Weymouth and took us to the Isle of Wight. We were very near landing at Lymington but finally reached this place (Weymouth) at two o'clock this day. Had we been a few hours longer, we would have been out of coals.[13]

111

In May 1834 yet another steam vessel arrived at Southampton, this time to operate on the Le Havre service, despite the protestations of one of the proprietors of the *Camilla*, W. J. Feuvre, who claimed that her profits over ten years averaged less than $10\frac{1}{2}$ per cent which, minus a 'deterioration' of 5 per cent and insurance of $3\frac{1}{2}$ per cent, left a meagre '2 per cent profit'.

The new steamer was the 104-ton Glasgow-built *Apollo* which boasted 'an elegant dining-saloon, measuring 40ft long and 20ft wide; ladies' and gentlemens' cabins and upwards of 50 beds'. Built in 1832 for the Glasgow, Largo, Millport and Ayr passage, the *Apollo* was carvel-built of wood, single-masted and sloop-rigged. With a 'man bust' head, quarter galleries and one 100 hp engine, her dimensions were 131ft 2in x 16ft $1\frac{1}{2}$in x 9ft 1in and she went into service under the command of Capt James Weeks, late of the *George IV*.

Once the Apollo was in service on the Le Havre station in opposition to the *Camilla*, fares on both ships dropped from £1 10s main cabin and £1 fore cabin to 10s and 5s; and then to 5s and 2s 6d as the rivals fought each other for patronage. The *Camilla* claimed she 'neither forced nor raced her engines; was a safe sea-boat and having considerable advantage over a vessel *built for river navigation and having only one engine*' but this did nothing to lessen the humiliation of her defeat in service by the *Apollo*, whose 10-hour passages sometimes bettered the *Camilla*'s by as much as one and a half hours. Moreover, the *Apollo* was apt to rub it in on occasions by arriving at Southampton ahead of her rival with flags flying and a band playing on deck. Nor, apparently, was her master averse to some harassment of the *Camilla*, one of whose passengers once complained that

... the *Apollo* ran close alongside the *Camilla*'s stern, paddle box to paddle box, and so near that any person might have jumped on board, both vessels going at the rate of, at least, 8 miles per hour and the *Camilla* under canvas and close-hauled. The *Apollo* was either attempting to injure the paddle box or frighten the passengers, and if the latter, he surely succeeded.

112

Meanwhile, in May 1834, the 80-ton steamer *George Canning*, built by J. Lang for the Glasgow-Belfast service, which sailed between Jersey and St Malo (1833-36), made news when her engineer struck for an increase in wages. Unfortunately for him, the agents of the *Lord Beresford* were on board and transferred the waiting passengers to one of their own vessels, so breaking the strike.

More competition appeared in April 1835 as the *Ariadne* (Capt J. Bazin) and the *Lord Beresford* (Capt J. Goodridge) maintained the passage to the Channel Islands, and the *Camilla* (Capt Fuszard) and the *Apollo* (Capt J. Weeks) sailed to Le Havre. The first was the *Isle of Guernsey*, belonging to the London, Guernsey and Jersey Steam Ship Co, which frequently made the Channel Islands passage from Southampton; the second was the 500-ton London steamer *Liverpool* (Capt Hepburn), which was also placed on the latter service. She had a quarterdeck 68ft long and 26ft wide, and a state cabin measuring 27ft by 17ft with a height of 7ft 6in. She accommodated thirty-five passengers in cabins, some of which were two-berth and partitioned by means of collapsible bulkheads or screens. And a further innovation at this time, she had wash 'basons' with running water. Built in 1830 for the Glasgow Steam Navigation Co, the *Liverpool* was 136ft in length, with a beam of 22ft and a depth of 14ft 8in and was fitted with a 180 hp engine.

The *Liverpool*'s arrival at Southampton prompted some blunt comment in local papers: 'Strange sail . . . we do not want her here. Let Southampton people support their own . . .', followed a little later by a much stronger, 'Why do not the proprietors of the *Ariadne* coelesce and drive the lubber back again to her own filthy puddle at London?' She, nevertheless, stayed and fares to the Channel Islands which had been £1 6s, 16s, and 10s 6d now dropped to a ruinous 5s and 2s 6d, leading to a tremendous increase in passenger traffic and, no doubt, some embarrassing social upheavals as all and sundry, taking advantage of the phenomenally low fares, piled into the hitherto exclusive, almost sacro-sanct, state cabin.[14] This financial suicide was only terminated several weeks later when the owners of the *Ariadne* and the *Lord Beresford* managed to 'buy off' the *Liverpool* for £300, where-upon she was sold to the London & Dublin Steam Packet Co for 12,000 guineas and placed on the Falmouth to Lisbon service, Capt J. Goodridge Jnr going in her. Channel Island fares were then promptly upped to 25s, 16s, and 10s 6d.

This disastrous competition, however, was nothing in com-parison to what was about to follow. Indeed, the end was already in sight for the small, independent shipowner because the rail-way 'octopus', backed by seemingly unlimited capital, was spreading its tentacles across the countryside and reaching south-wards for ultimate steamship ownership, particularly in the Solent area. Sotonians and other locals, well aware of this threat, united and prepared to fight back.

In September 1835 they formed the South of England Steam Packet Co with a capital of £200,000 '. . . to secure the purchase of vessels plying between Southampton, the Isle of Wight, the Channel Islands and France, in view of the development of Southampton and the coming of railway steam packets'. The board of 'influential and practical men' included Capt Robert Forder, RN, Capt Ward, RN, Capt J. Bazin, Capt J. H. Knight, W. J. Le Feuvre, N. M. Priaulx, Joseph Clarke, John Rubie and W. C. Westlake.[15]

At about the same time, another steamship company, which was to play an important part in the development of local steam navigation, was formed in London to trade between London and 'other important British ports' to the Channel Islands, France, Portugal, Spain and the Mediterranean. This was the British & Foreign Steam Navigation Co which, soon after its formation, placed the 'new and powerful' *Lord Byron* on the Southampton to the Channel Islands station, sailing from Southampton on Tuesdays and Fridays. She was replaced in January 1836 by the 'new river-built' *Lady de Saumarez* (Capt J. Goodridge Snr) having twelve berths in the gentlemen's cabin, twelve in the ladies' cabin, and eighteen in the fore cabin, thus claiming more beds than those in the rival *Ariadne* and *Lord Beresford*. Of 500 tons burthen (157 tons register) the *Lady de Saumarez* was two-masted and schooner-rigged, with a 'female bust' head, sham galleries and two engines totalling 90 hp.

The South of England Co replied to this challenge by ordering two new cross-Channel steamers, but before the first was launched, Capt Bazin, who had been superintending the building of the *Atalanta,* died, and command of the *Ariadne* passed to his son-in-law, George Babot, whose own son of the same name later commanded vessels of the London & South Western Railway. The South of England Co's first steamer, the *Monarch,* launched in May 1836, at Northam, for the Le Havre service, was, at 174 register tons, the largest steam vessel built in Southampton up to that time. Built in only four months by Rubie & Blaker at Itchen, she was two-masted, schooner-rigged and carvel-built of wood. She had a 'woman bust' head, mock galleries and two engines totalling 120 hp. Her accommodation included 150 sleeping-berths, considerably more than her rivals could offer.

Despite the speed with which she was built, or perhaps because of it, she did not enter service until 4 April 1837, some difficulties having presumably been encountered.

The South of England Co's second steamer, the *Atalanta,* built for the Channel Islands station by Thomas White at West Cowes, was launched on 2 June 1836 by Mrs Compton, wife of the local Member of Parliament, the ceremony being watched by a large crowd of spectators, including 200 who had travelled from Southampton in the *Camilla* for this purpose. Of 380 tons burthen (162 tons register) the *Atalanta* was two-masted, and schooner-rigged, with a 'woman bust' head, mock galleries and two engines totalling 120 hp. Her dimensions were: 140ft x 22.4ft x 12ft 7in, and she was said to be, '. . . splendidly fitted up

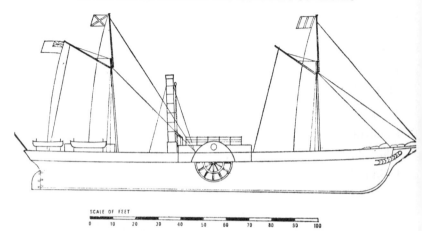

SCALE OF FEET
0   10   20   30   40   50   60   70   80   90   100

Conjectural drawing of the cross-Channel steamer *Atalanta*

with the cabins and saloons lined with mahogany, rose and satin woods—no suite of apartments in a home residence can excel her!' (Picture p71.) The *Atalanta* took up station on 30 August 1836 under the command of Capt George Babot and, the *Lord Beresford* having been placed temporarily on the Le Havre station, soundly thrashed her only rival, the *Lady de Saumarez*, making her first passage in 11hr 20min and beating the latter vessel by 1hr 43min. The following month she made the crossing from the Channel Islands to Southampton in 9hr 40min.

The *Atalanta* was met at Jersey by the *Ariadne,* which took passengers on to Granville. Whereupon, the British & Foreign transferred the steamer *Watersprite* from Weymouth to Southampton to oppose the vessels of the South of England Co. The inevitable drop in fares followed and passengers were, no doubt, delighted to find that these were now: to the Channel Islands, 10s, 6s and 4s—later, 5s and 3s; and to Le Havre, also 5s and 3s.

Several shipwrecks occurred locally in October 1836. The Jersey sailing packet *Gulnare* lost her rudder off St Helier and

was wrecked onshore—Capt Laurains, the thirty-five passengers
and crew of five, being saved—and the wreck was later sold for
£8. The *Atalanta* was stranded on the beach at Grange Chine,
about five miles west of Blackgang, at the back of the Isle of
Wight but was got off safely without loss of life or damage. But
the second vessel to run aground was not so lucky. This, the
worst shipwreck on this coast for twenty years, occurred when
the West Indiaman *Clarendon,* of 500 tons burthen, laden with
sugar and rum from the West Indies, with a crew of seventeen
and ten passengers—including four women—was driven onto a
lee shore during a severe gale in the early hours of 11 October
1836. She broke up within five minutes and only the mate and
two seamen were saved. This tragic loss, following upon similar
casualties, prompted the Elder Brethren of Trinity House to re-
place the lighthouse on the high land behind St Catherine's Point
with the present structure sited near the water's edge. This naviga-
tional safeguard, however, might well have been resented locally
because many people living along the coastline, sometimes on the
borderline of starvation, were often dependent upon cargoes,
stores and provisions being washed up on shore from wrecks.
Incidentally, the loss of the *Clarendon* was marked by the erec-
tion, close to the point where she foundered, of the Clarendon
Hotel, which still stands today.

By March 1837 cross-Channel fares to the islands had increased to 25s, 15s and 10s. Frequent visitors to Southampton at
this time were the British & Foreign steamers *Calpe* (157 tons
and 120 hp), commanded by Capt Thomas King, which had
been on service between London, Cadiz and Gibraltar, and the
City of Glasgow (218 tons and 120 hp) under the command of
Capt G. Barnett Snr, which maintained the London to Southampton passage. Both these steamers, together with the *Lord
Byron,* the *Watersprite* and the *Lady de Saumarez,* underwent
a change of ownership in August 1837 when the vessels of the
British & Foreign Co were acquired by the newly-formed Com-

mercial Steam Navigation Co, the demise of the old company resulting from its failure to obtain the Peninsular mail contract which went to the Peninsular Steam Navigation Co, later to become the Peninsular & Oriental Co.

Thereafter a veritable fleet of the new company's vessels steamed into Southampton. Among them were the *Transit* (267 tons and 120 hp) under Capt P. Wrightson, the *Chieftain* (600 tons and 200 hp) under Capt L. Wrightson, which had been employed on the London-Gibraltar service, and later the *Grand Turk* (243 tons and 150 hp), 'oak-built with four cabins and 100 berths', which had been on the London-Boulogne service. Other latecomers included the *Cornubia* (94 tons) built by J. Scott & Sons at Greenock in 1832, the *William IV* (151 tons register) originally owned by the St George Steam Packet Co, the *Kent* (135 tons register),[16] the *Robert Burns* (185 tons and 80 hp) and the *Edinborough Castle* (104 tons and 80 hp).[17]

Other 'strange sail' which regularly frequented the Solent in 1837 included the General Steam Navigation Co's steamer *Eclipse*, built in 1829, which sailed from London every Sunday, bound for Portsmouth, the Isle of Wight, Torquay and Dartmouth, calling off Deal, Dover, Hastings, Brighton and Ryde; and, in the following year, the four larger steamers of the St George's Steam Packet Co, the *Jupiter*, the *Juno*, the *Vulture* and the *Hercules*—'each of 600 tons and 240 hp'—and in service between Portsmouth, Plymouth, Falmouth and Cork.

The Commercial Co, however, suffered a blow in the early hours of 3 September 1837 when the *Apollo* (Capt Minter), bound from Yarmouth to London, was sunk off Northfleet, on the Thames, following a collision with the Scottish steamer *Monarch* (Capt William Bain), bound for Leith. The *Apollo*, unfortunately, sank quickly, taking with her the stewardess and two small children, although most of the crew and other passengers managed to scramble on board the *Monarch*, which had suffered less damage. It appears that the navigation lights of the *Apollo* had been burning so dimly that she had been mistaken for a vessel at anchor. Despite this fact and the admission that at the time of the collision the mate had been turned in below, and a boy had been at the helm, and despite Capt Minter's shameful testimony that he had been the first person to abandon his stricken vessel and climb on board the *Monarch*, the verdict at the inquest held on the stewardess, Mary Ann Jones, was that the *Monarch* and Capt Bain were to blame for the collision. British seamen, however, derided this verdict, quoting the occupations of the inquest jury—one grocer, two shoemakers, six licensed victuallers, one china dealer, one straw-bonnet maker, one draper, one clerk in a steam-packet office, one eating-house keeper, one broker, and finally, one half-pay Army officer. The verdict, nevertheless, stood and Capt Minter survived his humiliation to become harbour master at Granton, Scotland, in June 1838.

Attempts were later made to salvage the *Apollo* but the *Waterwitch*, connected to the *Apollo* by chains to effect a tidal lift, sank alongside the vessel she was trying to raise. It was not until August 1843 that the *Apollo* was finally raised by Capt Stone of the Port of London Authority and beached on nearby Black Shelf.

In February 1838 the Commercial Co announced a dividend of 6 per cent and placed the *City of Glasgow* on the Le Havre station in opposition to the South of England Co's *Monarch*; and opposed the latter company's *Atalanta* on the Channel Island service with the *Lady de Saumarez*. They also caused their rivals considerable annoyance by extending the *Lady*'s service with calls at St Malo, whereas the South of England passengers were obliged to disembark at Jersey and transfer themselves and their luggage to the *Camilla*, operating between Jersey, St Malo and Granville. In consequence, fares dropped from 21s and 14s, to 10s and 4s.

The Commercial Co also placed the *Kent* and the *Cornubia* on passage between Poole, Southampton, Portsmouth and London. This service proved successful, although the *Kent* was wrecked on the Shingles, West Solent, during a dense fog in February 1842 while on passage from Torquay to Southampton. No lives were lost and the following morning the *Edinborough Castle* (Capt Goodridge) was soon alongside 'with men and bars for the purpose of getting at the machinery'.

In September 1838 the Commercial Co's *Calpe* was placed on the Weymouth to Cherbourg service with calls at Southampton. Single fares between Weymouth and Southampton and Southampton and Cherbourg were 21s. At this time there was still room for sail, and the cutter *Lady of the Lake* (Capt Thomas Moses) was sailing between Plymouth and Portsmouth.

The Commercial Co stepped up competition on cross-Channel routes in 1839. The *Grand Turk*, and for a time the *Calpe*, were placed on the Le Havre station in opposition to the *Monarch*, the *Turk* sailing from Southampton every Tuesday and Friday, the *Monarch* every Monday and Thursday, and fares which had been £1 5s and £1, children under ten half price, soon dropped to 7s and 4s.[18]

The Commercial Co also placed the *Transit* (Capt J. Goodridge, Jnr) on the Channel Islands station to assist the *Lady de Saumarez* (Capt J. Goodridge, Snr) in opposing the *Atalanta*. The latter vessel sailed every Tuesday and Friday for Guernsey and Jersey, while the two Commercial steamers sailed every Monday, Thursday and Saturday—the Monday boat continuing on to St Malo and returning every Wednesday, in opposition to the *Camilla*, operating at this time between Jersey and the French ports. As a result, fares from Southampton to the Islands dropped from 21s and 14s to 5s and 2s 6d.

Nevertheless, the *Atalanta* repeatedly outpaced her rivals and they, smarting under the continual defeats, made the most of the old *Ariadne*'s lack of speed in their advertisements: '. . . on one occasion, the *Ariadne* was 10 hours from Jersey to St Malo, against the *Lady de Saumarez*'s 5 hours', but this can have done little to lessen their chagrin.

Passions aroused by this rivalry were said to have caused a collision in May 1839, which occurred when the *Transit* (Capt J. Goodridge, Jnr) and the *Monarch* (Capt Fuszard) were on an excursion from Southampton to Portsmouth to witness the launching of the 110-gun 1st Rate, HMS *Queen*. The 'scrape' cost the *Transit* her figurehead and bowsprit and for some time she was in a disabled condition. It was rumoured that the *Monarch* had refused to take off any of her rival's passengers but this proved false as, in fact, the *Monarch* had taken off sixty immediately following the collision. In September 1838 the *Transit* was placed temporarily on the Channel Islands to London station in place of the *Lord of the Isles*.

Another steamer service was operated during the summer of 1839 when the 57-ton *Rose*[19] (Capt F. Stavers) of the Weymouth & Southampton Steam Packet Co sailed between Poole and Portsmouth. Built at Blackwall in 1832, the *Rose*, two-masted and schooner-rigged, with standing bowsprit, square stern and sham galleries, was 108ft in length and driven by two 40 hp Boulton & Watt engines. But the greatest local event of 1839 was the arrival in the Solent of the British & North American Steam Co's steamer *British Queen*, the first passenger steamer to maintain a service between Southampton and New York. But as the dock at Southampton was not completed until 1842, she was necessarily 'tendered' at Motherbank or in Cowes Roads. Her trans-Atlantic fares were: saloon 40 guineas, lower saloon 35 guineas, fore saloon 25 guineas.[20]

In September 1839 great interest was aroused when the City of Dublin Steam Packet Co's steamer the *Royal Adelaide*[21] ran down the schooner *Gil Blas*, laden with gold dust and ivory, at the back of the Isle of Wight. Despite the value of her cargo, the schooner was quickly abandoned and for some hours was lost to

121

sight. When she was finally found afloat and salvageable, the missing deckboy was discovered fast asleep in his bunk.

In October 1839 Elizabeth Cooper, stewardess in the *Lady de Saumarez*, was fined the sum of £5 13s for smuggling into Southampton 10lb of tobacco and a gallon of brandy—a modest penalty compared with the previously usual '£100 fine or six months commital'. The year closed with the rescue by the crew of the *Grand Turk* of the *Ariadne*'s steward who had fallen overboard near the Royal Pier, evidence that the fellowship of the sea could still transcend the bitter inter-company rivalries.

The war of opposition between the South of England and the Commercial companies continued throughout 1840. The *Brunswick* and the *Ariadne* maintained the Southampton to Plymouth passage; while the *City of Glasgow* was placed, first, on the Southampton to London route and, later in the year, on the Southampton, Dartmouth and Torquay station. During the summer months the *Lord Beresford* sailed between Southampton and Brighton. No doubt the opening of the London & Southampton Railway in May 1840 brought about a considerable increase in passenger and cargo traffic locally and along the south coast generally.

A tragic accident occurred in August 1840, when the London Steam Navigation Co's steamer *Dart*, on an excursion from Brighton to Cowes, ran down and sank a small fishing-boat off the 'white buoy' near Cowes. Although a boat was quickly lowered from the steamer, a youth named Linnington, of East Cowes, was drowned. Accusations were made that a negligent lookout had been kept on board the steamer and the mate, Henry Adams, was held to blame. He was exonerated at the inquest, held at Newport, but the verdict did not apparently satisfy the dead boy's relatives and friends because soon afterwards 'Joseph Hamorton and others of East Cowes' were charged before the local magistrates with an assault on the mate, the proceedings being terminated at the last moment by mutual consent.

The appearance in Southampton, in September 1840, of 'two mysterious and heavily-armed, iron steam vessels' aroused considerable local speculation until it was learnt that these were the Honourable East India Co's *Proserpine* (Capt Hough) and *Phlegethon*[22] (Capt Cleveland), bound for China. Other large steamers calling regularly at Southampton throughout 1840 included the City of Dublin Steam Packet Co's *Royal William*, *Royal Adelaide*, *Duke of Cambridge*, *Devonshire* and *City of Limerick*.

The year closed with news, in November, of a successful salvage operation effected by Capt Robert Forder of the *Monarch*. He rescued the master and crew of the collier *Hopeful* (Capt Leslie), bound from Sunderland to Odessa with 400 tons of coal, which was lying disabled in mid-Channel. Encountering bad weather, she had been driven back on her course for two days and nights, and had lost most of her canvas and bulwarks, together with the mate and a seaman who had been washed overboard and drowned. Only the master, two men and a few boys were left to fight for their ship and were at the end of their tether when Capt Forder got them on board the *Monarch*. Then, putting some of his own crew in the *Hopeful*, he towed his prize into Southampton.

In March 1841 it was the turn of Capt J. Goodridge Jnr to effect a similar rescue and salvage operation, while in command of the *Transit* and on passage to the Channel Islands. He sighted a French sailing vessel wrecked on the Casquets, a dangerous group of rocks off Guernsey, and soon afterwards picked up the exhausted survivors, drifting nearby in a small boat. Then, despite a heavy swell and the fog which was closing in, he anchored close to the wreck—the *Jeanne Annette*—and put some of his crew on board to cut away the masts and rigging, and get the vessel upright. He then towed her off the rocks and into Guernsey. As the *Jeanne Annette*, bound from Rouen to Bordeaux, had been laden with a cargo of brandy of an estimated value of

123

£3,000, Capt Goodridge's salvage award was no doubt a substantial one.

The same month, March 1841, the South of England company announced a dividend of only 2 per cent on the paid-up capital, and there was apparently little chance of improvement because the *Monarch* on the Le Havre station was opposed by the *Grand Turk* and the *Calpe*; and the *Atalanta* on the Channel Islands station, with the *Camilla* in service between Jersey, St Malo and Granville, were opposed by the *Transit* and the *Lady de Saumarez*, the latter vessel sailing direct from Southampton to St Malo. The *City of Glasgow* was on passage between Southampton, Plymouth and Devonport, and the *Edinborough Castle* sailed between Southampton and Weymouth. Then in June 1841 the 500-ton, 140 hp French steamer *Hambourg* (Capt Vasse, Capt James Weeks) also came on to the Le Havre station, with the result that, by July, fares to Le Havre were down to 5s and 2s 6d, and finally, to 2s 6d and 1s 6d in the *Hambourg*.

In September 1841 the *Lord Beresford* (Capt Goodfellow) sailed into Southampton for the Falmouth & Southampton Steam Packet Co, maintaining a service as under:

		Chief cabin	Fore cabin	Deck
Falmouth to	Mevagissey	5s	3s	—
„	Plymouth	10s	7s 6d	5s
„	Torquay	£1	15s	7s 6d
„	Southampton	£1 10s	£1	12s 6d
Plymouth to	Mevagissey	7s 6d	5s	—
„	Southampton	£1 5s	15s	10s
Torquay to	Southampton	£1	15s	7s 6d

The service was temporarily suspended in November 1841, when the *Lord Beresford*, Plymouth-bound, ran foul of the steamer *Royal Tar*, carrying away her own bowsprit and funnel and suffering other damage. The new service never made money, and in May 1843 the *Lord Beresford* was sold to Joseph Price of Neath Abbey for service out of Swansea.

Another strange sail had appeared in the Solent in July 1841

124

Page 125 (above) The cross-Channel steamer *Southampton* of 1860 in her later days with only one funnel; (below) unidentified paddle-steamer leaving Ryde Pier in June 1840, with cabin-class passengers enjoying the luxury of an awning

Page 126 A steam packet with tow boat approaching Ryde Pier, top-hatted master at the helm. From an engraving by George Brannon, August 1828

and was to remain on the south coast for at least four years. This was the 101-ton screw steamer *Princess Royal* (Capt Light), owned by the Brighton & Shoreham Steamship Co (picture, p72). Her 'Smith's patent' two-bladed screw propellor, 5ft in diameter and driven by a 45 hp engine, made her one of the earliest screw steamers to see service on the south coast, though Wimshurst's screw steamer, the *Archimedes* (237 tons and 70 hp) had visited Portsmouth in May 1839. The *Princess Royal* sailed between Southampton and Brighton during 1842 and was later, in March 1845, purchased by Capt Fuszard of Southampton and placed in service between Southampton and Cherbourg.

In January 1842 it was reported that the *Camilla* of Southampton had foundered off Coquet Island on the east coast, following a collision with the brig *Commodore Napier* (Capt W. J. Clark), bound for Southampton with a cargo of coal. The *Camilla* sank almost immediately, taking with her the master, Capt Pearse, seamen John and William Harris, and a boy named MacDonald. Only the mate, James Rumney, was saved. This was not, however, the steamer *Camilla*, as has been erroneously recorded, but a sailing vessel of the same name owned by Capt Fuszard of Southampton, and the steamer *Camilla* (Capt Priaulx), replacing the *Atalanta,* was on the Jersey, St Malo and Granville station in June 1842. The following year she sailed from Plymouth every Tuesday for Guernsey and Jersey, leaving Jersey for St Malo every Wednesday. Her eventual fate was to be acquired by the New South Western Steam Packet Co in 1847 and to be broken up in 1853.

April 1842 proved a milestone in local steam navigation because in that month the Commercial Steam Navigation Co was acquired by the railway, or individuals with predominantly railway interests. Two separate companies were then formed: the New Commercial Steam Navigation Co with London as its principal port (and from which later derived the Southern Railway Marine Service), and the South Western Steam Packet

127

H

Co, with Southampton as its principal port. Which drew the comment, locally, 'Mr Chaplin and other directors of the South Western Railway are on the board of the new company. No doubt, the South of England Company will be next!',[23] clearly indicating that railway domination of local cross-Channel steamer services had commenced.

The South of England Co's first competition came the following month when the 'new' *Duchess of Kent* came temporarily on to the Channel Island passage, making 12-hour crossings; and the *Prince of Wales* similarly allotted to the Le Havre station, making 9-hour crossings. The *Prince of Wales* (700 tons and 260 hp) had 76 sleeping-berths and was said to be similar to the Liverpool-Glasgow steamer *Princess Royal*. In addition, the *Princess Victoria* (Capt J. Goodridge Jnr), built at Blackwall in 1835, went on service between Southampton and Bordeaux, but her crew of forty made her uneconomic and she was taken out of service in September 1842, although the *Calpe* maintained the same station the following year.

Pressure on the South of England Co further increased in July 1843, when the South Western Co placed their new iron steamer—the first on service to the Channel Islands—the *South Western* (Capt J. Goodridge Snr), on the Channel Islands station. Built by Ditchburn & Mare, London, she was of 132 tons register, two-masted and schooner-rigged, with a 'shield' head and sham galleries. Dimensions were: 145.4ft x 18.7ft x 9.8ft and she was driven by 80 hp Seaward engines. (Picture, p89.) Shortly after her arrival in Southampton, she made a special excursion, sailing from the Royal Pier at 11.45 am with 170 guests and a 'full band of music', passing Calshot at 12.15 and entering Portsmouth harbour at 1.0 pm. She steamed round the *Victory* and the *St Vincent*—the band playing 'Rule Britannia'—and then crossed over to Ryde. After circling the *Great Liverpool*, which was anchored in quarantine off Motherbank, and giving her three hearty cheers, she then altered course westwards through the

Solent and proceeded to the Needles. A dinner was provided for the guests and the later toasts were carefully recorded: 'The Queen'; 'Prince Albert and the Royal Family'; 'The Navy and Army'; 'Prosperity to the South Western Steam Packet Company'; 'J. W. Drew, Esq. the chairman and directors of the company'; 'The South Hants Infirmary'; 'Prosperity to the town of Southampton, its railways and docks'; and 'Captain James Goodridge Snr'. The festivities were terminated only by the *South Western's* sudden arrival back alongside the Royal Pier.

Once in service, the *South Western* was said to have averaged 12 knots on passage, and in July 1843 she beat the *Atalanta* into Guernsey by 2¾ hours. The following month, whilst accompanying the royal yacht *Victoria and Albert* in Southampton Water, she was obliged to ease speed to avoid overtaking her 'senior'.

Despite the increase in competition on the cross-Channel routes, however, the fares of the South of England Co and of the South Western Co remained the same during 1843: 21s and 14s to Le Havre; 25s and 18s to the Channel Islands; and 35s and 25s to St Malo.

Still, maintaining the pressure, the South Western Co added another new iron steamer to their fleet in October 1844. This was the famous steam packet *Wonder*, said to be 'a twin to the *South Western* and a beautiful model, she looks like a bird cleaving the air'. Built by Ditchburn & Mare, London, 137 tons register, she was two-masted and schooner-rigged, with 'billet' head, sham galleries and raised poop deck. Her dimensions were: 158ft x 20.6ft x 10.1ft and her three Seaward & Capel atmospheric engines totalled 140hp. She made the 190-mile voyage from the Nore to Southampton in 11½ hours and was later credited with a speed of 14 knots. In December 1845 she once made the 9½-mile passage from Cowes to Southampton in thirty-nine minutes, beating the 317-ton HM yacht tender *Fairy*—screw driven and powered by Penn oscillating engines—which claimed a speed over the measured mile of 13.4 knots. Indeed, the *Wonder's* reputation for speed was such that Queen Victoria is said to have wished to buy her for use as a royal yacht. She had the further distinction of having a public-house named after her—the Wonder Inn—near the corner of Northam and York Roads, close to Northam Bridge, Southampton. Although this was demolished in 1958, several stained-glass windows depicting the steam packet have survived to the present day. One of these windows is now on display in the Maritime Museum, Southampton. One other tangible link with the *Wonder* may also be seen locally. Among the trophies of the Master Mariners' Club, Southampton, is a silver speaking-trumpet or megaphone, about four times the size of an old ear-trumpet. Richly chased throughout its entire length and ornamented with pictures of the *Wonder*, it bears the following inscription:

> Presented to Captain James Goodridge Jnr of the Mail Packet *Wonder* on the 1st day of January 1847 in token of the high admiration in which his character for nautical ability so eminently displayed throughout the fearful storm of Wednesday 21st October 1846, and his uniform devotion to the interest and comfort of the public is held by the inhabitants of Jersey.[24]

The 'fearful storm' referred to in the inscription had overtaken the *Wonder* while on passage to Guernsey and Jersey. (Picture, p90.) She had left Southampton at 7.0 pm on Tuesday, 20 October and ran into the storm at eleven o'clock that night. It continued until the vessel's arrival at Jersey at half-past four on Wednesday afternoon. During this voyage—Capt Goodridge later described the crossing as the worst he had ever experienced—tremendous seas swept the decks, carried away part of the bulwarks and did other damage. '. . . But by his presence of mind alone and his seamanlike management of his vessel, she was brought safely to Guernsey at about one o'clock on Wednesday afternoon and then proceeded to Jersey.'[25]

The presentation of these testimonials to Capt Goodridge took place on the poop of the *Wonder*, in Victoria harbour, Jersey, in

130

the presence of local dignitaries and the assembled ship's company. The sum of £5 was distributed among the crew, and the first and second mates and the principal engineer were promised silver medals, though records do not show if these were ever awarded. One such medal survived and is now in the possession of P. R. Southall, Esq., of Southampton. Measuring about 2⅝in in diameter, it has the Channel Islands Arms on the front, surrounded by laurel leaves; and on the back is inscribed: 'Commemorative of William Turtle's able conduct as Second Officer of the *Wonder* Mail Packet in the Storm of 21st October, 1846.' After the ceremonies, Capt Goodridge entertained his guests in the state cabin where his health and that of Mr Matthews, who had arranged the presentation, '. . . were pledged in bumpers with all the honours'.

The arrival of the *Wonder* on the Channel Islands station in October 1844 sealed the fate of the South of England Steam Navigation Co, because the following month the South Western Steam Packet Co defeated their long-time rivals and 'amalgamated' with the South of England Co. And for the next two months the two companies' vessels were listed together on advertised sailing timetables under the heading 'South Western Steam Packet Co', although, strangely, from January 1845 to October 1846, the timetables of the South of England Co appeared in local newspapers under their own title.

As if by way of celebration, in January 1845 Capt J. Goodridge Jnr in the *Transit* put on a spectacular show for a large number of sightseers at Southampton dock who were awaiting her arrival from the Channel Islands. She steamed furiously through the entrance and then, without slackening speed or wavering from her course, continued straight across the dock and ploughed bow-first into the dock wall with a resounding crash. Her bowsprit, figurehead and cutwater were severely damaged and the crew and passengers not a little bruised and shaken. It was disclosed later that her chief engineer had been taken ill and left behind at Jersey—unknown to the captain—and that his relief 'didn't know how to "Stop" or "Back her"!'

In March 1845 the short-lived but long-named Poole, Isle of Purbeck, Isle of Wight & Portsmouth Steam Packet Co placed the 150-ton, 70 hp *Waterwitch* (Capt Richard Stanworth) on station between Poole and Portsmouth, calling at Brownsea, South Haven, Yarmouth and Cowes. Another 'strange sail' passing through the Solent at about this time was the steamer *Zephyr* (Capt Beer) from London to Torquay, calling at Portsmouth, Cowes, Weymouth and Topsham.

From April 1845 mail for the Channel Islands was being sent through Southampton instead of through Weymouth, and sail was still represented on the former station by the cutter *Star* (Capt James Ozonne).

The following year, 1846, saw the final defeat of the South of England Co when, in July, another important change of local steamship ownership took place 'destroying two well-established and paying companies'. A new company was formed with capital supplied by the London & South Western Railway Co, some of whose directors sat on the new board. This was the New South Western Steam Packet Co which purchased, first for £29,500, the South of England Co's vessels *Atalanta, Ariadne, Camilla* and *Monarch*; and, secondly, for £58,500, the South Western Steam Packet Co's vessels *Wonder, South Western, Grand Turk, Lady de Saumarez, Transit, Calpe* and *Robert Burns*. The three older and less powerful steamers, *Transit, Calpe* and *Robert Burns*, were soon disposed of and three other steamers were based temporarily at Portsmouth, much to the disgust of Sotonians, who had just given the company five acres of land in South-ampton!

The New South Western Co's first steamer, the *Express*, was built in six weeks by Ditchburn & Mare on the lines of the *Wonder*. Of 170 tons register and iron-hulled, she had a 'shield' head, no galleries and two Maudslay engines totalling 180 hp.

132

Her dimensions were: 159ft x 21.4ft x 10.4ft, and it was reported that 'her 19ft diameter paddle-wheels with a dip of floats of 5ft, at 42 rpm, give her a speed of 12 to 13 knots'. She was the first local cross-Channel steamer to have two funnels.

The first voyage of the *Express*, from Blackwall to the Nore under the command of Capt Paul, took 2hr 7min. Her internal decorations were said to be: '. . . worthy of her speed, being of bird's eye maple and Spanish mahogany. Her ceiling is white and gold and the coup d'oeil has an elegant and durable character'. She was placed on the Le Havre station in July 1847 and in the same month brought the body of the Irish patriot, Daniel O'Connor, from Le Havre to Southampton. She made her first call at Jersey on 28 May 1848, and in March of the following year she brought Louis Philippe, King of France, from Le Havre to Newhaven. An inscribed brass plate to commemorate this voyage was placed on the berth in which the king slept.[26]

During the summer and autumn months of 1847, the *Grand Turk* steamed between Southampton and Plymouth and Penzance, her fares being, respectively, 25s, 18s 6d, and 10s 6d; and £1, 15s and 7s 6d.

The New South Western Co's second iron steamer, the *Courrier*, built for the Channel Islands station, arrived in Southampton in November 1847, and was described as 'the handsomest and most speedy vessel that ever sailed out of Southampton'.

Of 147 tons register and built by Ditchburn & Mare, she was two-masted and schooner-rigged, with a 'shield' head, quarter galleries and two funnels. Her dimensions were: 167ft x 22.5ft x 10.8ft and her Maudslay engines totalled 200 hp. She made her maiden voyage to the Channel Islands on 12 November 1847, one of her passengers being Henry Maudslay, son of the founder of the marine-engine firm of that name, and in the same month she claimed a passage time of 7hr 10min from Southampton to Guernsey. But like all these comparatively small steam vessels she was, presumably, quite lively in a seaway, as instanced on

133

one occasion when an elderly passenger was hurled out of his seat as the vessel rolled heavily and injured his head so severely that he later died. The *Courrier* once claimed a speed of 17 knots.

The *Lady de Saumarez* (Capt P. Wrightson) came to the fore in March 1848, when she brought 'many badly treated English' —presumably refugees from the republic which had just replaced the Orleans monarchy—from Le Havre to Southampton. The Peninsular & Oriental steamer *Iberia* had also put to sea for the same purpose but her services were ultimately not required. The following month, it was the turn of the *Monarch* (Capt Priaulx) to steal the limelight when she towed a Chinese junk from St Helier, Jersey to London where she was placed on exhibition. This was the 750-ton *Keying* (160ft x 33ft x 16ft), built in Hong Kong and sailed to Europe via the Cape of Good Hope, Boston and New York. This was one of the last notable duties of the *Monarch*, because in February 1849 she was sold, for £900, plus £180 for her machinery, '. . . to a gentleman connected with emigration to New Zealand'. Her engines were then removed and she was converted to a 356-ton brig. Her end came in 1869, when she was stranded and wrecked in Hobson's Bay, Victoria, Australia.

The New South Western Co's third iron steamer, the *Dispatch* (Capt John Babot), made her first voyage to the Channel Islands on 2 May 1848 and claimed a passage time of $1\frac{1}{2}$ hours between Jersey and Guernsey. On trials she was said to have attained a speed of '18 statute miles per hour at 40 rpm' and a speed of 15 knots over the measured mile. Of 149 tons register and built by Ditchburn & Mare, she was two-masted and schooner-rigged, with a 'shield' head and quarter galleries. Her dimensions were: 166.7ft x 22.1ft x 11.6ft, her Maudslay engines were described as 'two common, vertical, direct-acting engines' developing a total of 200 hp.[27]

From May to September 1848 inclusive, the three Channel Islands steamers were based at Poole, despite the fact that the first mail and passenger train began operating between London and Southampton in May. Throughout 1847 and 1848, fares from Nine Elms to Paris were: single: 1st class 48s, 2nd class 36s; and to Le Havre or to the Channel Islands, 21s and 14s.

In August 1848 the vessels of the New South Western Steam Packet Co were leased by the London & South Western Railway Co for a period of fourteen years, railway companies at this time being prohibited by Act of Parliament from owning steamships.

The close of the year saw the retirement of Capt George Babot of the *Ariadne,* the *Atalanta* and the *Dispatch* and other vessels, and in recognition of his twenty years' accident-free service in cross-Channel steamers, he was presented with a suitably inscribed silver salver.

The *Grand Turk* left the Solent in February 1849, under charter to Newbolt, Hall & Brothers for the Alexandria and Beirout mail service. She did not return until April 1851, to operate the Southampton-Guernsey-Morlaix service under the command of Capt John Goodridge.

By the summer of 1849 the New South Western Co vessels had left the Royal Pier and were berthing in Southampton dock, but this transfer had not been effected without a struggle. The pier commissioners and traders in the Holyrood area had already lost a considerable amount of business following the opening of the dock in 1842, when the larger P & O vessels and the West India mail steamers had moved there. To protect their interests, the pier commissioners had sought to evoke a clause in the Act of Parliament governing the use of the pier which required all steamers landing and embarking passengers and their luggage to do so at the pier, and Capt George Babot of the *Atalanta* and Capt Richard White[28] of the *Monarch* had each been fined £4 in July 1845 for failing to do so. For some time afterwards, the South of England and the South Western companies had made alternate use of the dock and pier for four-monthly spells but, in January 1848, the New South Western Co, still averse to having to use the pier, refused to pay for the damage allegedly caused to it by their vessels. The commissioners then had recourse to law but lost their case, 'the Act containing this clause being imperfectly drawn'. Some form of compromise, however, was reached soon afterwards and until 1864 cross-Channel passengers embarked at the Royal Pier and were landed at the docks. Cargo was, of course, loaded and discharged in the docks.

In August 1849 the financial resources of the New South Western Co were obviously under some strain since it was reported that its offices had been moved from Southampton High Street to the railway terminus or station, '... for economy's sake and [now] occupy what was once the gentlemen's waiting room'. The following month, railway ownership of steam vessels was openly acknowledged in the heading to the sailing timetables in local newspapers, which read: 'The London & South Western Railway Steam Packet Company's Swift and Powerful Ships, *Courrier, Dispatch*...'. Two weeks later, the words 'Steam Packet' were omitted, but the tempo quickened soon afterwards because up to 500 passengers per train were arriving at Southampton from London, the modest return fare being 8s first class and 7s second class. Some of the excursionists also went on to Cowes and on one fine day the *Lady de Saumarez*, the *Atalanta* and the *Express* between them landed 1,850 people in Cowes where they remained five hours and practically denuded the town of supplies. Nothing like it had ever been seen before.

In September 1850 two steamers were lost off Jersey. The first was the *La Polka* (Capt Priaulx) which, in place of the *Superb* undergoing repair, had left Jersey for St Malo with thirty-five passengers on board. But when about six miles off the Minquiers Rock she sprang a leak and while being run in towards the shore in order to beach her, struck a rock and sank, her crew and passengers being forced to abandon ship and seek the rugged safety of nearby Matrielle Rock. Here they were marooned through the night, their only provisions being some biscuits,

136

bread and water supplied by three fishermen who had chosen to live on this small, barren and isolated rock. They were taken off the following morning by the *South Western* (Capt J. Goodridge) on passage from Weymouth to St Malo. The second wreck occurred barely a week afterwards when Capt Priaulx, commanding the *Superb* on passage from St Malo to Jersey, was prevailed upon by his passengers to close the wreck of the *La Polka* so they might have a look at its remains. In doing so, the *Superb* struck the same rock and sank with the loss of eleven lives.

In November 1850, two new screw steamers went into service between London and the Channel Islands, the *Caesarea* and the *Sarnia*. Both were of 265 tons burthen (133.5ft x 20ft x 13ft), three-masted and schooner-rigged and with engines of 40 hp. Each vessel had 'cabins on deck' and sixty sleeping-berths. Sotonians at this time, however, were annoyed because the LB & SCR, engaged in a price war with the L & SWR, was trying to win greater patronage by reducing fares between London and Portsmouth to '4s return'. A Southampton newspaper commented, 'How paltry is this conduct and how unjust to us, to whom no such advantage is offered!'

In September 1851, the *Atalanta* was lengthened eighteen feet at White's yard, Cowes, the old bow being upended and used as a workmen's shelter in the same yard. J. Clement, Esq., of Gravesend has a contemporary scale model of *Atalanta* with two funnels. It has never been vandalised but expert examination shows that deck fittings have been moved slightly and that the model had only one funnel originally. It is surmised that this was a builder's model (White's), and was probably altered when the parent ship was lengthened in 1851.

The year 1851 closed with a report of a victim of the changeover from sail to steam. This was Capt Thomas Bedbrook, formerly master of the cutter *Speedy Packet,* on the Southampton to Jersey station. 'He was a good navigator but his habits were those which belong to the drinker and the dissipated. For some

137

time past he had been ship's keeper on board the *Ariadne* in the dock. . . .' One morning his body was found in the water resting on one of the paddle floats, and it was assumed that he had fallen off the gangplank and drowned.

In August 1852 the P & O steamer *Jupiter* became the largest steam vessel to make a local excursion when she took 502 passengers from Southampton to Portland for a day's outing, while the *Express* made a more modest trip to Brighton. But these were quiet months for the local cross-Channel steamers. They were not named on sailing timetables and, in the absence of contemporary newspaper reports or comments, are assumed to have been steaming about on their lawful occasions with monotonous regularity. Only rarely do they catch the limelight, as in June 1853, when the body of a man, secured to a boat by means of a rope tied about the waist and his pockets filled with stones, was found washed up on the beach at Brighton. The body was later identified as that of George Young, for many years steward in the *Atalanta*. Meanwhile, the old *Brunswick* was still diligently steaming between Portsmouth and Plymouth, her fares being 17s 6d main cabin, 12s 6d fore cabin, and 7s 6d on deck.

Throughout the summer of 1853, railway steamers left Southampton for Le Havre and the Channel Islands every Monday, Wednesday and Friday—the Jersey, St Malo and Granville services now being maintained by the vessels of the Jersey Steam Packet Co, whose fleet included the *Rose*, the *Venus*, the *Comete* and the *Dumfries*. Single through rail and boat fares were: London to Paris, 24s and 17s; London to Le Havre, 22s 6d and 16s; London to the Channel Islands: mail boat 30s and 20s, cargo boat 21s, 12s 6d and 10s.

In March 1855 the New South Western Steam Packet Co launched the iron paddle-steamer *Alliance*, named after the Anglo-French Crimean War alliance. Built by Ditchburn & Mare and of 168 tons register, she was two-masted and schooner-rigged, with a 'shield' head, sham galleries and two funnels. Her dimensions were: 175.5ft x 23.7ft x 14.6ft and her engines, by Seaward & Capel, developed a total of 225 hp. Her cost was said to be £19,460. She had accommodation for 150 passengers and was credited with a speed of 13¾ knots on trials. She went into service on the Le Havre station on 11 July 1855 under the command of Capt Walter Smith, with expectations of making the passage in nine hours—'About three hours faster than the company's old packets'. At about this time, from 1 January to 30 June 1855, passenger traffic was mainly to and from the Channel Islands; arrivals totalling 5,671 as against 2,471 from Le Havre.

On 5 April 1856 the New South Western Steam Packet Co's iron steamer *Havre*, designed by James Ash and built by Ditchburn & Mare, was launched by 'Mrs Ash and Miss Johnstone'. Of 200 tons register (184.7ft x 24ft x 14.5ft) she was two-masted and schooner-rigged with a 'shield' head and two engines totalling 225 hp. She went into service on the Le Havre station during the summer of 1856.

On 21 November 1856 the *Atalanta* (Capt John Lewis), relief boat for Jersey, was run into by the P & O steamer *Sultan* at the mouth of the river Itchen and lost her port-quarter boat and bulwarks, extending from the forward sponson to the taffrail, but luckily without injury to passengers or crew.

A much more serious collision occurred in 1858 when on 28 April, the *Havre* (Capt Walter Smith), bound from Le Havre to Southampton, collided with the *Wonder* (Capt E. B. Clements, relief master), outward bound, both vessels making about twelve knots at the moment of impact. The *Havre*'s bowsprit completely demolished the *Wonder*'s port lifeboat and carried away most of the bulwarks on the port side. Luckily, damage to both vessels was above the waterline and each survived what might have proved a major disaster.[29] At the subsequent Board of Trade inquiry, although the *Wonder* was held to blame for the collision, the master was exonerated, but the second mate, Robert Woodcock, was censured for having failed to call the captain on deck when collision had seemed imminent. There was also some adverse comment on Woodcock being an uncertificated officer.

Rail and steamer fares in January 1860 could hardly be considered exorbitant: single, Southampton to Le Havre, 21s and 15s; and London to Paris, 28s and 20s.

The last vessel to be dealt with in this chapter is the iron-hulled paddle steamer *Southampton*, built and engined by Palmer Brothers and launched in April 1860 for the New South Western Steam Packet Co. Of 299 tons register (215.5ft x 25.4ft x 12.7ft) she was two-masted and schooner-rigged, with a 'shield' head and two oscillating engines totalling 200 hp.[30] (Picture, p125.)

The arrival of the *Southampton* heralded the end of the formative years of local cross-Channel steamship services which had commenced in 1823 when the Isle of Wight steamer *Medina* made her historic voyage to the Channel Islands. In 1862 the New South Western Steam Packet Co was formally acquired by the London & South Western Railway Co—an Act of Parliament allowing railway companies to own steam vessels having been passed that year. Subsequently, the railway company maintained local cross-Channel services until 1965, when the mail and passenger vessels were withdrawn from service at Southampton, thereby causing almost as much local resentment as had been the case more than 123 years previously on the arrival of 'railway-owned' steamers.

THE WEYMOUTH TO CHANNEL ISLANDS MAIL PACKET SERVICE
The Government mail-packet service on this station was established in 1794 when two 60-ton cutters, the *Royal Charlotte* and the *Rover*, were placed on station. A third cutter, the *Earl of Chesterfield*, was captured by a French privateer in 1811, many of the passengers and crew being killed. Two other cutters, the *Francis Freeling* and the *Hinchinbrook*, were wrecked in 1826.

Nevertheless, during the French War communication between England and the Channel Islands was maintained principally by

140

the cutters *Diligence* and *Brilliant*, sailing from Southampton. The *Brilliant* was captured in 1814 by an American privateer, the *Prince de Neufchatel*, but the prize-master, mistaking Alderney for part of France, sailed blithely into the harbour, no doubt much to the delight of the helmsman and others on board who had discreetly refrained from correcting him.

Mail-carrying steam packets were placed on the Weymouth station by the Post Office in July 1827, the first official mail delivery being made by the *Watersprite* to St Helier on 7 July. In January 1837, these vessels came under Admiralty direction, but the service proved uneconomic and in April 1845 the Weymouth mail-packet service ceased operating. The mail contract, 'worth £6,000 per year', was then granted to the New South Western Steam Packet Co at £2,000 per year, increased to £4,000 in 1848 when the attractions of Southampton's new dock and the recently-opened railway line to London prompted the Government's decision to transfer the service from Weymouth. The South Western company did, however, operate an auxiliary mail service through Weymouth to the Channel Islands in 1850 and the fares were then 15s and 10s single; steward's fee 1s 6d and 9d; horses £2 5s each; carriages £2 5s each, and dogs 4s.

The New South Western Co re-established the Weymouth service in 1857 when an opposition company, the Weymouth & Channel Island Steam Packet Co, was formed and put into service the *Aquila* and the *Cygnus*, iron paddle steamers built for the North of Europe Steam Navigation Co. (For details see Appendix 3.) A third steamer, the *Brighton*, built for the Marples & Morris Newhaven to Dieppe service, was placed in service in 1858. In January 1887 the *Brighton* was wrecked off Guernsey and two years later the Weymouth and Channel Island Steam Packet Co ceased to exist. Subsequently, the steamship service from Weymouth to the Channel Islands was maintained by vessels of the Great Western Railway and the London & South Western Railway.

141

CHAPTER FOUR

PORTSMOUTH AND RYDE STEAMERS

PORTSMOUTH DERIVED its name from the Roman title of Great Port or Chief Porta. Although it has one of the greatest natural harbours in the country, it is not mentioned in the Domesday Book and for centuries was little more than an outpost of the harbour of Southampton. Its number of vessels were greatly exceeded by those of Hamble, Lymington and the Isle of Wight.

The importance of Portsmouth began with its development as a naval port in the 1480s, when Henry VII caused the heavy fortfications to be built. The Close Rolls of 1205, however, state that King John had then ordered the harbour to be improved when he addressed the Sheriff of Southampton, 'We command you, that without delay, by view of lawful men, to cause our docks at Portsmouth to be enclosed with a good and strong wall.'

The first dry-dock in the world was built here in 1495-96. The Square Tower, a prominent landmark, was built in 1494 by Henry VII and the Round Tower, on the eastern shore, was begun in the reign of Edward III. From the Round Tower, a huge chain was laid across the seabed at the harbour entrance to the Gosport shore and hoisted when required effectively to 'close' the port. Large links of iron chain discovered near the

Page 143 The crack iron steamer *Her Majesty*, closing **Ryde** Pier, c 1850, under the stern of the R.Y.S. *Titania*. The mail flag at her foremast depicts a galloping horse and rider

Page 144 (above) A cartoon showing seasick passengers lining the rail of the Lymington steamer *Solent* on her maiden voyage in 1841; (below) the oldest known photograph of an Island steamer, showing the master, top-hatted, on the starboard paddle box, helmsman at the wheel aft and furled foresail

Round Tower in 1856 are reputed to have been used for this purpose. Little remains today of Southsea Castle, which was built by Henry VIII in 1539, blown up in 1759, repaired in 1814, and strengthened in 1850.

In 1800, Portsmouth's naval dockyard covered 82 acres, while Southsea Common still consisted of open fields dotted here and there with a few houses. In 1816, Southsea was a fashionable watering place.

The outer wet-dock of the London & South Western Railway opened in 1841, the Great Steam Frigate Dock of the Royal Navy in 1848, and the inner dock in 1851. The first pier, Victoria Pier, opened in 1835, and the first floating bridge, operating between Portsmouth and Gosport and designed by James Meadows Rendell, went into service in 1840. The spire of St Jude's Church of 1815 is the principal seamark and is still used today by vessels entering the harbour from seawards and through the Swatchway.

Ryde, the other town with which this chapter is mainly concerned, was known in Norman days as La Riche or La Rye. Originally part of the parish of Newchurch, it was burned by the French during the reign of Richard II.

Owing to deep mudbanks which extend a considerable distance from the shore, Ryde could be approached at low water only with the greatest of difficulty:

It was customary except during the short interval of High Water for the passengers to be crammed into a common luggage-cart and then drawn by a horse over the sands and through the waves till it reached a depth sufficient for a boat to float alongside it, in which they are transferred and conveyed off to the packet. As may be inferred, this united cart and boat process of reaching the vessel or shore could not be inviting at the best of times; but it was really terrific to weak and timid persons during the concurrence of a fresh gale, driving rain, and the tide perhaps at its lowest ebb, to say nothing of the horrors of landing in a dark and squally night.[1]

145

The lot of the traveller, however, was greatly eased in 1814 when the Ryde Pier Co, formed in 1812, erected the 1,240ft 'Long Pier'. In March 1818, 750ft of the structure was carried away during a storm, but repairs were soon effected. It was extended in 1824 and 1833, and a new head was built in 1842. The old pier was finally replaced in July 1880 and the present one was acquired by the Southern Railway Co in 1924.

THE PORTSMOUTH AND RYDE STEAMERS

The Portsmouth and Ryde steamers which eventually replaced the Union sailing packets came into service some years after George Ward and William Fitzhugh had placed the *Cobourg* on the Cowes passage in 1820, though a steam vessel had operated between Portsmouth and Ryde as early as 1817. This was the *Britannia*, which went into service on Monday, 19 May 1817, sailing from Portsmouth every morning at 8.30 and again at 3.0 pm, returning from Ryde at 10.0 am and at 5.30 pm. A coach met the steam boat at Ryde to take passengers on to Newport. The *Britannia*, of 15 hp and 70 tons burthen, was built in 1817 by Titterton at Stockwith, near Gainsborough, Lincolnshire, with engines by Butterley & Co.

The *Britannia*, however, had been designed for the London-Southend service and not surprisingly was withdrawn from the Portsmouth-Ryde service within four weeks, '. . . it being ascertained that boats of this description are not calculated for situations liable to heavy seas, accompanied by adverse winds and strong tides'.[2] Thereafter, local enthusiasm for steam vessels appears to have waned considerably, for it was not until 1825 that another steamer was placed on this passage.

This was the steam packet *Union* which, for the two previous years, had been employed on the Ramsgate to Calais passage. It was recorded:

> She possesses the rare quality of great swiftness with a com-
> paratively small power in consequence of the small resistance she

offers to the water. Her engines (of which she has two) have been examined by an engineer of great eminence in the Dock-yard, who pronounces them to be of the best construction and the most capital workmanship and in perfect repair.

On trials, the *Union* made the passage to Ryde in thirty-four minutes, '. . . without showing a sail to the wind' and commenced in service for the Portsmouth & Ryde Steam Packet Co on 5 April 1825 under the command of Capt James Groves (1780–1860). So reliable did she prove that in the following thirteen days she had made eighty trips, the shortest being of 28 min duration and the longest, with a strong headwind and tide against her, 40 min. The average passage time was 34 min and only one turn was missed because, we are assured, the engineer packed a piston too tightly. Built by William Evans of Rotherhithe in 1822, the *Union* (36 tons and 16 hp) was two-masted and schooner-rigged, with a standing bowsprit, 'woman bust' head, square stern and sham galleries. Her main dimensions were: 76ft x 12.2ft x 8ft.

In June 1825 the Portsmouth & Ryde company placed another steam packet, the *Arrow,* on the same service under the command of Capt James Beazley, owner of the smack *Eagle.* Built by Lang at Dumbarton in 1822 and owned by W. S. Forsyth, the *Arrow* had been stationed at Liverpool before her transfer to Portsmouth. A wooden-hulled vessel of 46 tons, she was two-masted and schooner-rigged with a standing bowsprit and square stern, but without figurehead or galleries. Her dimensions were: 92ft 8in x 11ft 11in x 7ft 7in and it was reported in 1826 that she 'goes about nine miles an hour'. Both the *Union* and the *Arrow* used tow boats for the carriage of horses and cattle, and offered their services for towing vessels in and out of Portsmouth harbour. And, during the summer of 1825, the *Arrow* ran excursions round the island.[3]

A third steamer, the 47-ton *Lord Yarborough,* whose figurehead depicted the nobleman of that name who was to become the first commodore of the Royal Yacht Squadron, was built for the Portsmouth & Ryde company by Daniel List of Fish-bourne, Isle of Wight and launched on 14 June 1826. Single-masted and schooner-rigged, she had a wooden hull, fixed bow-sprit, square stern and quarter badges. Her two engines totalled 30 hp and her dimensions were: 81ft 7in x 14ft 4in x 9ft 5in. The *Lord Yarborough's* entry into service in July 1826 almost spelt the end of the *Arrow* which was put up for sale that same month, but apparently there were no takers as throughout the summer of 1827 the *Union* and the *Arrow* maintained the Ryde passage, sailing daily from Portsmouth at 8.0 am, 10.0 am, 3.0 pm and 6.0 pm and from Ryde at 9.0 am, 12.0 pm, 5.0 pm and 7.0 pm. Fares were 1s 6d quarterdeck and 1s forecastle, single. Occasionally, one of them made excursions around the island or to Netley Abbey, 'and other interesting places'. The *Lord Yarborough* went further afield. Every Monday and Friday morning, she started from Cowes at 9.30, after the arrival of the Southampton boat, and sailed to Brighton, calling off Ryde, Portsmouth and Worthing, and returning from Brighton at 8.0 am on Tuesdays and Saturdays, to join the Southampton-bound packet at Cowes. On Wednesdays, the *Lord Yarborough* sailed from Portsmouth to Poole at 8.0 am, calling off Ryde, Cowes, Yarmouth and Lymington, and returned from Poole on Thursdays.

During the summer of 1827, the Southampton steamers *George IV* and *Earl of Malmesbury* had joined forces and were '... forming a line of communication with the Ryde steam packets'. The Ryde steamers, however, were the first to provide a winter service to the Isle of Wight, effected in November 1827 with a packet sailing from Portsmouth daily at 8.30 am and 2.30 pm and from Ryde at 9.30 am and 4.0 pm.

Another Portsmouth steamer of this time, which most probably made trips to Ryde was the 13-ton *Pelham*, presumably named after Charles Pelham, Lord Yarborough. Built as an open boat in 1826, she was converted to steam in 1828. Her owners were

148

Andrew Awe, William Lee and John Little, all of Portsmouth. The latter, Capt John Little, master of the Wootton Bridge boat, is later mentioned as having joined the 'Friends of the Temperance Society' and that by so doing, he '. . . had been enabled to save 5s per week, as he had been in the habit of drinking 10 to 12 glasses of spirits daily, and even then considered himself a temperate man'.

The small Ryde steamers, however, were subject to the vagaries of weather and the service was sometimes suspended or altered, as in April 1829 when one steamer was unable to land her passengers at Ryde because of the rough seas prevailing and was obliged to put them off at Nettlestone. The number of passengers carried through Portsmouth and Ryde nevertheless increased, and in March 1830 it was recorded that by far the greatest proportion of passengers to the island used this route. The following summer, these steamers were making four round trips daily to the island.

Another new steamer, the 38-ton *Earl Spencer,* was launched for the Portsmouth & Ryde company on 4 June 1833 at the yard of Benjamin Denham, Ryde, and christened by Miss Lind, daughter of Mrs Lind of Westmont, who later entertained fifty guests to dinner at her house whilst Capt Beazley played host at the Eagle Inn to Mr Denham and his friends. The *Earl Spencer* (77ft x 13ft 8in x 8ft) was single-masted and sloop-rigged, with a fixed bowsprit, 'crest' head, square stern and mock galleries. She went into service the following month but her first passage to Brighton was delayed for two days owing to severe weather conditions. The *Arrow* having since been disposed of, there were now three Ryde steamers on service but there is still mention of sailing wherries. One of them, the *Mary Ann* of Gosport, was swamped in December 1835 and the occupants, Mrs Matthews of Portsea and Mr G. H. Denick of Gosport, innkeepers, and the boatman, W. Parryman, were 'launched into eternity'.

In January 1836 an 'octagon' lamp was fitted on Ryde pierhead, an improvement which was no doubt much appreciated by Capts Groves and Beazley and others who, the following summer, were maintaining a busy service leaving Portsmouth for Ryde at 7.0 am, 8.0 am, 10.0 am, 12 noon, 2.0 pm, 3.0 pm, 4.0 pm and 6.0 pm on weekdays; and leaving Ryde at 7.0 am, 9.0 am, 11.0 am, 12 noon, 2.0 pm, 3.0 pm, 5.0 pm and 7.0 pm. On Sundays, the steamer left Portsmouth at 8.0 am, 10.0 am, 2.0 pm and 4.0 pm; and Ryde at 9.0 am, 12 noon, 3.0 pm and 5.0 pm. Fares were 1s 6d aft, and 1s forward single, and only 2s for the round passage 'if you do not disembark'. There were no tow boats on Sundays.

Despite the light on Ryde pierhead, a small brig was driven through the pier during a severe gale one night in February 1838, tearing a 50ft gap through the timbers and piles. The following morning only the brig's two topmasts could be seen projecting out of the water and her crew were presumed drowned. In May 1839 the pier was further improved by the installation of a bell, to be sounded fifteen minutes before the departure of each steamer to ensure the punctuality of passengers who, at this time, were complaining that the steamers often refused to go alongside the pier, so obliging them to embark and disembark by means of boat at extra expense. The pierhead was rebuilt and enlarged at a cost of £400 in 1842 by James Langdon of Ryde, and in the same year the New Victoria Pier at Portsmouth was opened. Two years later, in April 1844 the steamers were 'leaving Gosport New Pier five minutes before touching at Victoria Pier, Portsmouth, first thing on entering and leaving Portsmouth Harbour'.

Another Ryde steamer, the 46-ton *Prince Albert* (Capt James Jones) went into service in June 1847, making her first passage from the 1,249ft-long Albert Pier, Portsea, newly opened on the first of that month as a terminus for the South Coast Railway at a cost of £1,200. Built by George and James Inman at Lymington and launched in February 1847, the wooden-hulled *Prince Albert* (96ft x 12ft 4in x 8ft) was single-masted and cutter-rigged with a fixed bowsprit, 'man bust' head and a plain square stern. She was fitted with 'Captain Smith's Patent Paddle Box Boats'—the paddle boxes could be unshipped in an emergency, inverted and used as lifeboats—an innovation which, commendable though it was, could hardly fail to draw attention to the complete absence of boats on the other Ryde steamers. This was gleefully seized upon by the local Portsmouth newspaper, which further complained that the Paddle Box Boats were actually screwed down, head and stern. Disparaging remarks were also made about the state of the wooden hulls of the Ryde steamers, the lack of inspection and, indeed, their actual seaworthiness. All of which proved too much for Alfred Heather, secretary to the Portsmouth & Ryde Steam Packet Co, who replied indignantly that not only were all the Acts for the Regulation of Steam Navigation strictly complied with, but that he was cancelling all company advertisements and timetables in the newspaper that had suggested otherwise. He was as good as his words and the boycott lasted several months.

By Coronation Day on 28 June 1848, tempers had presumably cooled for, by way of celebration, fares each way between Portsmouth and Ryde were only 6d, though the reduction could have been prompted by the rumours then abroad that an opposition company was to operate a steam-packet service between Portsmouth and Ryde. The L & SWR line had just been extended to Portsmouth and the LB & SCR line had arrived the previous year, so that a considerable increase in passenger traffic to Ryde was now anticipated.

Coincidentally, or perhaps in anticipation of some sort of trouble, about this time J. H. Hearn, secretary to Ryde Pier Co, advertised the 'Office of Policeman to the Company' at a wage of 17s per week and a suit of clothes annually to persons between the ages of 21 and 35. And policemen were certainly required when the rumoured opposition materialised.

The new company was formed in December 1849 under the

151

title of The Portsea, Portsmouth, Gosport & Isle of Wight Steam Packet Co, with offices at 170 Queen Street, Portsmouth. It set out to oppose the old company and destroy its monopoly by reducing fares and improving the boat service to suit the arrival and departure of the Portsmouth trains. At a shareholders' meeting held at the Crown Hotel, Ryde, the company secretary, R. W. Ford, announced that two new 'superior' steamers had been ordered from J. White of Cowes, and that Capts Stallard and George Beazley Jnr, both of Ryde and late of the old company, had been engaged as commanders. Capt Stallard soon resigned and his place was taken by Henry Knapp, 'a steward in the old company', whereupon the old company promoted Capt Albert W. Stratton of Ryde to the vacant command, engaged Capt Cribb of Lymington, and altered their timetables to fit in with those of the Portsmouth trains. Thus battle commenced.

The new company's first steamer, the *Prince of Wales,* was launched from the yard of Joseph White, East Cowes, on 6 May 1850 and, after trials, went into service at the end of June. Wooden-hulled and of 57 tons register, she was single-masted and sloop-rigged and had a square stern. Her dimensions were: 107.6ft x 13.2ft x 8.3ft and her two engines by Day, Summers & Co totalled 40 hp. Her registered owners on behalf of the new company were John Friend Pratt of Portsea; William Butt of Ryde; and Samuel Pring of Newport, all merchants.

In July 1850 the *Prince of Wales* was joined on passage by her sister ship, the *Princess Royal* (Capt Henry Knapp) which came from the same yard and was identical in every way with the *Prince of Wales.* The *Princess Royal* made her maiden voyage during the second week of July, taking a party of directors and their friends from Ryde to Portsea, where an hour was spent celebrating in the Kepple's Head before sailing to Cowes to show the flag. She had crossed from Ryde to Portsea in 23min with paddles turning at 37rpm 'which will not doubt be increased to 45rpm when all is in order'.

152

The new company operated from Portsea pier, which the old company had discreetly vacated, and set about their war of opposition with gusto, introducing yearly tickets and weekly tickets at competitive prices, much to the delight of the travelling public who took the new company straight to their hearts. Soon afterwards, however, the old company also lowered their fares and, within several weeks, fares had dropped by 40 per cent, the new company claiming credit for having led the way.

In August 1850, presumably in an attempt to win back support and defeat their rivals, the old company launched the new iron-hulled steamer *Her Majesty*, the first iron steamer on this passage. Built by Robinson & Russell of Millwall, and of 66 tons register, she was three-masted and schooner-rigged, with a standing bowsprit, 'woman bust' head and square stern. Her dimensions were: 129.1ft x 14ft x 7.2ft and her engines developed 50 hp. (Picture, p143.) Her registered owners, on behalf of the old company, were James Player Lind and Edward Utterson, both of Ryde.

The new ship claimed a record $15\frac{1}{2}$ to $18\frac{1}{2}$ minutes passage between Portsmouth and Ryde and was known as the crack steamer of the old company. She must have soundly thrashed the new company's vessels, especially the little *Lindsey*. Nothing is known about the *Lindsey* except that she was not registered locally, was not new and remained on the Ryde station for only three months. She also caused the new company and its supporters considerable embarrassment when she broke down in mid-Channel while on excursion to Cherbourg and had to be towed home.

The opposing fleets now comprised the old company's *Union, Lord Yarborough, Earl Spencer, Prince Albert* and *Her Majesty,* and the new company's *Prince of Wales, Princess Royal* and *Lindsey.* Not only did they race but they fought each other by impeding their rivals' approach to berths and harassing their manoeuvres. The public took sides with equal enthusiasm and the new company was the subject of a particularly scurrilous pamphlet in August 1850.[4]

However, after twelve months of warfare it was said that the popularity of the new company was so great that, although their rivals were charging lower fares, they were enjoying greater patronage:

> ...this has exasperated the employees of the losing company to such a degree that they have been guilty of the most extraordinary proceedings, and which must end, if not put a stop to, in some terrible calamity. As soon as a steamer starts from either side, she is followed by a rival steamer, the Captain of which tries all in his power to drive the other steamer ashore to avoid a collision. The confusion with the passengers and the fighting and swearing of the crews are truly alarming. This has been going on almost daily for months. The touters at the different landing places take sides and desperate fights take place among them. There have been inumerable police cases arising out of these feuds and both the Magistrates and local press have been unable to put a stop to the War...[5]

The inevitable calamity occurred when the new *Prince of Wales* (Capt Knapp), bound for Portsmouth, and the old *Prince Albert* (Capt Groves), bound for Ryde, came into collision. The *Prince Albert* sustained considerable damage and her thoroughly frightened passengers were transferred with some difficulty to the *Prince of Wales* while the stricken vessel was towed in for repair. By this time, it was said, so much 'terror and timidity' had been aroused among the passengers that many preferred to travel by way of Southampton and Cowes.

Claims arising from the collision were brought before the local magistrates but the matter was finally settled by arbitration. The referees, William White, RN, and George Allen, RN, held Capt Groves of the *Prince Albert* to blame, although they also criticised Capt Knapp for not having taken avoiding action sooner. Nevertheless, the jubilation of the new company and its supporters knew no bounds, and when the *Prince of Wales* arrived at Ryde on her last trip of the day upon which the verdict was given in her favour, 250 supporters greeted her arrival and gave three hearty cheers for the captain and crew. Ryde town hall was also engaged for a 'public demonstration' and more than 200 rallied to the celebration dinner and ball that followed. Not long afterwards Capt Groves was dismissed by the old company and Capt Knapp suspended by J. P. Lind, chairman of the new, though both were subsequently reinstated.

Both companies by now, however, had just about had enough and in March 1851 negotiations were opened for an amalgamation. It was not before time because the passengers themselves had now become embroiled in the fighting, as one complained bitterly that same month. He had been waiting at Portsmouth in the *Princess Royal* when an old steamer came alongside to discharge her passengers across the *Princess Royal's* deck when '... without any provocation, the crew commenced fighting with the crew of the *Princess Royal*. One of the ruffians rushed at an innocent gentleman in the stern and nearly succeeded in throwing him overboard!'

Peace came eventually in May 1851 when a majority of shareholders voted in favour of amalgamation—50 for and 28 against. The two companies were thereupon dissolved and there came into being The Port of Portsmouth & Ryde United Steam Packet Co, with a fleet comprising the *Prince of Wales, Princess Royal, Her Majesty, Prince Albert* and *Union*; and six horse boats. The *Lord Yarborough* and the *Earl Spencer* had, presumably, already been taken out of service on this passage.

The service provided by the United company in 1852 was considered excellent. There were eleven daily sailings on weekdays from Ryde to Portsmouth and Portsea, nine of which continued on to Gosport, and five sailings on Sundays. In the reverse direction, there were eleven daily sailings from Portsmouth on weekdays and four on Sundays. First and last departures from Ryde were 7.30 am and 8.30 pm. The efficiency of the service was reflected in the company's balance-sheet and at the half-yearly meeting in October 1852 a 'dividend of 10s on each share of £7 10s' was declared. At the same time it was announced that another company was to place a steamer in service between Bembridge, Seaview and Portsmouth, but she did not appear until August of the following year and proved to be a small steamer, the *Dart,* which had previously been stationed at North Shields. She operated between Bembridge and Portsmouth, touching at Ryde and Seaview, but this service could not have been successful for, although two more steamers were promised for 1854, together with tow boats to discharge goods onto Brading Quay, the service ceased at the close of the summer season of 1853.

In July 1853 the *Prince of Wales* was again in the news when she ran aground shortly after leaving Portsea pier for, despite the fact she was carrying mails, passengers and a considerable quantity of luggage, she was ignored and left high and dry for two hours by the other Ryde steamers. It was not until a passing Southampton steamer stopped to help that the passengers, mails and luggage were eventually landed. Relations between the Ryde and Southampton steamers were said to be excellent for although the latter sailed between Southampton, Cowes, Ryde and Portsmouth, and had done so since 1825, they refused to carry passengers or goods between Portsmouth and Ryde and did not interfere in any way with that traffic.

In November 1853 a master of one of the United steamers was reported to have engaged in a fight with a flyman (flymen plied for hire in small, fast-sailing craft), for smoking in the fore cabin. 'Fighting with a passenger on his own ship!' exclaimed the report, though it later transpired that the captain had merely 'snatched the pipe out of the man's mouth!' A dig at the Southampton steamers, '... where the practice of allowing drinking and smoking in the fore cabin must prevent any respectable person from venturing below, accompanied as it is with ribaldry and obscenity most foul . . .' implied that Ryde steamers were above that sort of thing.

In November 1853 it was decided to increase Ryde steamer fares to ensure an adequate dividend and passengers, recalling the cheap fares and splendid service of the competitive days, were bitter—'The new packet company had destroyed the monopoly of the original possessors of the field and reduced fares, but now UNITED, they are putting them up!'

The entrance to Victoria pier was fitted with a new glass roof in January 1855 and berthing arrangements were improved at Ryde in March 1856, the pierhead being extended to a length of 280ft and a width of 120. This 'improvement' was not seen in quite the same light by passengers who were obliged to trek the full length of the pier and, indeed, representations had been made to the Ryde Pier Co in August 1852 requesting the introduction of some means of getting passengers from one end of the pier to the other—a facility for which, in the event, they had to wait another eight years, until 1864.[6]

In April 1855 there were again rumours of an opposition boat being placed on the Ryde station, to operate between Stokes Bay and Ryde, in anticipation of the railway line being taken to Stokes Bay and other lines being constructed on the island. In fact, the Stokes Bay Railway, an extension from Bishopstoke of the L & SWR's London-Southampton line, was not to be opened until 6 April 1863 but in February 1856, the Stokes Bay & Isle of Wight Ferry Co was formed, and in November 1857 royal assent was given to an Act of Parliament authorising the purchase of the Stokes Bay Railway and Pier, Isle of Wight Ferry, Ryde Pier; the improvement of the river Medina and the construction of works at West Cowes. But not all these grand schemes were implemented. The Ferry company remained independent of the Pier company until September 1860, when they issued their first joint report. And in 1863 it was said that the 'Isle of Wight Ferry Co is a united body with the Stokes Bay Railway and Pier Co'.

The Stokes Bay to Ryde service began on Easter Monday, 6 April 1863, when the 45-ton iron steamer *Gareloch*, '... a long narrow boat', began making five passages each day, averaging about fifteen minutes on each trip. With a length of 140ft and capacity for 300 passengers, the *Gareloch* was said to 'sit low in the water' and to steer badly though, contrary to the prevailing practice, she was steered from a position between the paddle boxes. She had one mast forward with a topmast and gaff and her funnel was pink. Within two weeks of entering service under the command of Capt George Beazley Jnr, the *Gareloch* was in collision with the *Her Majesty* (Capt Craske) off Nettlestone. The damage was not severe but at the subsequent inquiry, which attached no blame to either master, each was warned that 'certificate suspension' could follow any repetition of the incident.

Southampton steamers also maintained a service from Stokes Bay to the Isle of Wight but made the passage to Cowes direct. It would appear also that this service was of short duration because it was advertised only from 4 May to 3 June 1863. Sailing times were to accommodate train passengers at each terminal; leaving Cowes at 10.0 am, 1.15 pm and 5.15 pm; leaving Stokes Bay at 11.0 am, 2.5 pm and 6.5 pm. Single fares were 1s 9d and 1s 3d.

The second steamer destined for the Stokes Bay to Ryde service arrived at the beginning of May 1863 from the Clyde, '... having covered the 700 miles in 53 hours'. This was the iron-hulled *Chancellor*, a large two-funnelled steamer of 160.71 gross tons and 70.35 tons register which had been built and engined by Denny for the Loch Long & Loch Lomond Steam Boat Co to operate on the Arrochar and Glasgow passage. She had two diagonal engines totalling 80 hp, with haystack boilers, and her after cabin was 30ft long, 18ft wide, with 7ft headroom, and was capable of seating 60 persons. The seats and sides were covered in crimson velvet, the panels being ornamented with stained glass. A large mirror was fixed over an elegant fireplace.

The fore cabin was 24ft in length and 18ft wide. Principal dimensions were: 167.4ft x 17.1ft x 7.1ft. Great things were expected of her, and in addition to maintaining the Stokes Bay to Ryde passage she was to make excursions round the island, to Guernsey, Jersey, Poole and Le Havre.

The *Chancellor* made her first excursion on 29 June 1863, taking holidaymakers from Stokes Bay to Ventnor. The boat was so crowded that the passengers had to rough it on the ropes, paddle boxes and anywhere they could be seated. They were further disappointed at Ventnor because instead of going alongside the pier, then under construction,[7] the vessel anchored nearby and passengers were obliged to disembark and embark by means of boats.

The second and what was to prove the *Chancellor's* last trip to Ventnor was made on 1 July 1863. She arrived from Stokes Bay at 1.30 pm, about forty-five minutes behind the advertised time, and although the tide was ebbing, the company's manager who was on board—probably remembering the complaints about the use of boats on her previous visit—'. . . considered it quite safe' to land the passengers directly onto the pier. The steamer having been put alongside and the passengers landed, it was then decided to leave the vessel alongside despite the ebbing tide and to let her take the bottom, on the theory that the flooding tide would have her afloat again long before her departure time. Instead, on taking the bottom, she was holed forward and as the tide rose, her forward compartment—one of three—filled. The pumps proved inadequate, as did the baulks of timber which were lashed to her bows in attempts to get her afloat. She was eventually moved about six feet and then settled with her stern floating high in the water and projecting beyond the half-completed pier, exposed to wind and tide. The wind freshened during the night, so that she was slewed round and deposited broadside onto the beach where she broke her back, the two portions of the ship lying almost at right angles. It was after-

159

wards said she had seen her best days on the Clyde and '. . . although painted up very showily, she was quite rotten, the wonder being, how she clung together so long'. (Picture, p107.)

Undaunted, the proprietors of the *Chancellor* soon announced plans to place more steamers into service and to make excursions to Yarmouth and Alum Bay. At the latter place, they intended to build a jetty, erect a large hotel, and '. . . to take the railway from Newport' but little came of these grandiose schemes, and the pier at Alum Bay was not built until six years later, in 1869.

Ventnor harbour was used by the little steamer *Antagonist* from 9 May 1864 until the beginning of September of that year. Built in 1857 by Lungley of Deptford and engined by Stewart, she had previously been employed on the Thames.[8] The *Antagonist* maintained a daily service between Ventnor and Littlehampton, sailing from Ventnor at 7.0 am, and from Littlehampton at 3.0 pm, the passage time being about three hours. She also brought coal to Ventnor. She could hardly have been considered satisfactory because on one occasion, in July 1864, when she made an excursion from Ventnor to Littlehampton, calling at Sandown and Shanklin, with about seventy passengers, she missed the tide, encountered bad weather and did not arrive at Littlehampton until 4.0 pm. And as she sailed from there at 6.0 pm and took another six hours homewards to Ventnor, the lot of the seasick passengers, '. . . crammed to capacity in this steam tug', must have been anything but pleasant.

The mysteriously abrupt termination of her service on this passage in September 1864 was followed by an appeal in the local press, 'Lost, Stolen or Strayed. The Steamer *Antagonist* left Ventnor on Monday as usual and has not been seen since!' Her disappearance was explained several days later. After her last departure from Ventnor, her master had sighted a drifting and abandoned wreck, laden with cargo. Making all speed to Littlehampton to dispose of his passengers, he had then returned to the wreck and towed his 'prize' into Portsmouth. That he did not subsequently resume the Ventnor service suggests that his salvage award was a substantial one. The service, however, was later temporarily maintained by the *Ursa Major,* a wooden-hulled paddle steamer of 82 tons, built at North Shields in 1856 and owned by William Ray of Landport. Single-masted and sloop-rigged with a'rounded stern and 'bear's head' head, her main dimensions were: 90.3ft x 17.2ft x 9.4ft and her engines developed 45 hp.

Meanwhile, in October 1859, the United had added another steamer, the iron-hulled, two-masted *Prince Consort,* to their fleet. Of 103.77 gross tons (65.38 net) she had been built and engined by John Scott Russell at Millwall at a cost '. . . in excess of £5,000, on the lines of *Her Majesty*', and was launched on 6 October by Mrs R. W. Ford, '. . . who sprinkled champagne liberally over her bows'. She had a 'male bust' head—presumably a likeness of Prince Albert—two oscillating engines totalling 60 hp and her dimensions were: 154ft x 15.1ft x 6.7ft. One dark night in September 1861, the *Consort,* under the command of Capt Beazley, ran down and sank the yacht, *Amazon,* fortunately without loss of life. Capt Beazley had mistaken her anchor lights for those of Ryde Pier.

An opposition steamer commenced service on the Portsmouth to Ryde station in 1860. Named the *Victoria,* she was a small paddle steamer of only 37 tons gross, with a waterline length of 65ft, and was the first steam vessel especially designed for vehicular traffic to the island. Her square stern was fitted with a watertight door which, hinged at the bottom, could be lowered to serve as a ramp. Cattle, horses and carriages could then 'drive on and off'. The *Victoria* was the first vessel built by Wigham, Richardson & Co at Wallsend-on-Tyne, who launched her in July 1860, but there is little information as to her stay on the Ryde station, though there is reference to her as the company's 'steam horse boat'. This pioneering forerunner of today's car ferries was referred to at the time, somewhat scathingly, as 'rude and absurd looking, puffing and screeching about and very busy carrying horses, cattle, carriages, merchandise and luggage which if not available, she disappears and returns within a few hours with a cargo of shingle or bricks'.

Within three years of her arrival in the Solent, *Her Majesty* had the misfortune to be wrecked and sunk off Bembridge on 15 August 1863, while returning from an excursion. Approaching the 'Black Buoy off Coal Rocks', which should have been passed on the outside, the mate, William Tyhurst, ordered the helmsman to steer inside. Thinking that the order came from the captain, the helmsman obeyed and the few moments which elapsed before the captain realised what was happening proved fatal. She had struck at full speed on Coal Rocks, holing herself forward. Capt Tate, who had been for many years mate in the vessel and had relieved Capt Craske on his retirement only a month previously, managed to get her off and ran her ashore on a sandbank, '50 yards west of Lane End'. Within a few minutes, however, the engine-room had flooded and she slowly filled and sank, passengers and crew having meanwhile been taken off by boats nearby. A Board of Trade inquiry, held on 4 September 1863, found the mate entirely to blame for the accident in having altered course contrary to a previous order given by the master and his certificate was suspended for six months. This was not, however, the end of *Her Majesty*, for within two weeks she was raised by means of a tidal lift and towed into Portsmouth for repairs.

Another United steamer, the iron-hulled *Princess of Wales*, of 100.47 tons gross (79.15 net) took to the water on 28 July 1865. Built by Lewis & Stockwell at Blackwall and launched with steam up, she left Blackwall Pier at 12.30 pm and arrived at Woolwich twelve minutes later. She made 13.5 knots over the measured mile with her feathering paddle wheels turning at 46 rpm. Single-masted and sloop-rigged, with a round stern and no figurehead, the *Princess* was 140ft long, with a beam of 16ft and a moulded depth of 6ft 9in. Her two engines, by James Watt & Co, totalled 50 hp and she had a 'commodious promenade' above the large saloon aft which was lit by means of sliding windows. Next to this was a ladies' cabin. The entrance to these saloons was said to be '. . . not as in older boats by means of a winding flight of stairs but by a straight staircase and very short. The entrance is over four feet wide.'. . . Following her trials, it was estimated that she would average 'under 19 minutes' on passage between Southsea and Ryde piers, but records do not show if this speed was attained.

Not quite four years later, the United's iron steamer, the *Duke of Edinborough,* 92.54 tons gross and 60 tons net, was launched from the Blackwall yard of Wigram & Co—on 27 February 1869. Although described as 'A beautiful model and well adapted to these waters' she was to be the subject of much criticism. On her trial trip from Southsea to Ryde pier, she made the passage in eighteen minutes and would have improved on this, we are assured '. . . had not a train of barges, laden with shingle and cement for the Spithead Forts, crossed her path'. She was not christened until just prior to her departure from Ryde pier on a 'maiden voyage' cruise to Alum Bay with the company's directors and friends on board. Then Miss Batchelor, a granddaughter of the company chairman, Mr Yelf, 'threw a bottle of wine at the cocked hat of His Royal Highness, exclaiming "Prosperity to the *Duke of Edinborough*"! Flags were then unfurled and a band struck up some lively airs. Later, a luncheon was enjoyed on board, followed by music and dancing.' Two-masted and schooner-rigged, the *Duke* had a 'three-quarter man' head, a round stern and two engines totalling 50 hp. Her dimensions were 136.2ft x 14.1ft x 7ft and on her first passage trip, she crossed from Ryde to Southsea pier in $16\frac{3}{4}$ minutes. This was considered more than satisfactory but apart from the cost of her building, £3,950, the United paid extra for her speed. It was claimed: '. . . superbly-fitted saloons with mirrors and crimson velvet seats . . . these and machinery which will gain a few

163

seconds between Ryde and Portsmouth are not the principal qualifications requisite in these steam packets. A dry deck and freedom from rolling being far greater desiderata. . . .' Her lack of stability and consequent tendency to heavy rolling were only remedied after a considerable number of experiments had been carried out with the aid of ballast.

While the *Edinborough* was settling into service, her sister ship, the *Princess Alice,* was launched from the same yard on 20 June 1869 by 'Miss Clarke, daughter of Mr George Clarke of the Hard, Portsmouth'. The *Princess Alice* differed from the *Edinborough* only in having a 'three-quarter woman' head. Her arrival on station and her commencement on passage appears to have aroused little comment in the local press, which was more concerned about this time with the misbehaviour of one of the older steamers :

> *Her Majesty* was converted into a steam ram by her Captain and a ram taken at Ryde Pier railings with considerable force and damage on coming into the west angle of the Pier head. The railings were cracked like matchwood by the bowsprit of the steamer which flew up with the concussion and left the remaining force of the impetus to fall upon the figurehead of Our Sovereign Lady, which was also ruefully damaged!

In January 1873 an opposition company was formed to challenge the established monopoly of the United. This was the Southsea and Isle of Wight Steam Ferry Co, sometimes referred to as the 'Ryde & Southsea Steam Ferry Co'. In the course of the year four wooden-hulled, single-masted screw steamers—the *Shanklin* (53.04 tons gross), the *Ventnor* (50.95 tons gross), the *Ryde* (59.15 tons gross) and the *Southsea* (70.53 tons gross) were placed on the Ryde station. All four were built by John White at East Cowes and engined by Plenty & Co of Newbury, Berkshire. The *Shanklin* (99.2ft x 16.4ft x 7.1ft) and the *Ventnor* (90ft x 16.1ft x 7.3ft), were both sloop-rigged with an elliptical stern and had single engines developing 30 and 20 hp respectively. The *Ryde* (99.4ft x 16.7ft x 7.1ft) was cutter-rigged with two high-pressure condensing engines totalling 30 hp, while the *Southsea* (97ft x 15.8ft x 6.8ft), also cutter-rigged and with an elliptical stern, had two inverted, direct-acting engines totalling 35 hp.

The United company replied to the challenge of these new screw steamers on the Ryde station by the introduction of two considerably larger ones of their own, both built by Lewis & Stockwell at Blackwall. The first was the iron-hulled *Princess Louise* of 110.97 tons gross, launched in July 1873. Single-masted and cutter-rigged, with an elliptical stern and 'scroll' head, her two engines supplied by J. A. Blythe & Co totalled 40 hp and her dimensions were: 103.6ft x 17ft x 6.6ft. Her sister-ship, the *Princess Beatrice* of 99.38 tons gross, followed on 4 May 1874, sloop-rigged with a round stern, a 'shield' head and two engines totalling 44 hp. Apparently, neither vessel proved successful for the *Beatrice* was sold within weeks of acceptance and later went to Martinique, while the *Louise* went to Grimsby in December 1874 and was renamed the *Jennie*.

The war which then developed was fought between the four new screw steamers and the United's fleet comprising *Her Majesty*, the *Prince of Wales*, the *Prince Consort*, the *Duke of Edinborough*, the *Princess Alice*, the *Princess of Wales* and the *Princess Royal*. The United's vessels, however, old as some of them were, had a distinct advantage over the rival screw boats inasmuch as the former's paddle wheels and sponsons made them decidedly more comfortable in a seaway—all the Ryde steamers having a narrow beam. The United then gained a further advantage when they acquired a much larger and faster paddle steamer than had previously been on the Ryde station. This was the iron steamer *Heather Belle* (of 267.61 tons gross), which went into service in April 1876. Originally built by Blackwood & Gordon of Glasgow for the Ardrossan to Arran services, the *Heather Belle* (207.7ft x 21ft x 8.8ft) was single-masted and smack-rigged with a square stern and two engines totalling 150 hp. Her arrival at Portsmouth evoked the comment: '. . . she

165

and the larger Southampton steamers make the insignificance of the other little "Cock boats", "Blue bottle craft", more palpable . . .'. But by this time the opposition war had already stopped the United's dividends, while the new company was unable to cover its working expenses. The quarrels that developed led to an inquiry before the Railway Commissioners in the House of Lords, the rolling of the screw boats being the main cause of complaint, though the traffic manager of the L&SWR took advantage of the opportunity to state a case for the establishment of railway-owned steam boats on the Ryde passage. The commissioners' findings, however, were favourable to the United company.

The war ended in June 1876 with the defeat of the Southsea & Isle of Wight Steam Ferry Co by the United but the resultant merger or takeover does not seem to have produced any startling results by way of improvement to the service. In May 1878 it was being asked why these steamers, 'belonging to a company having the monopoly of traffic on this station', were continually breaking down. All of them, it was suggested—with the exception of the *Heather Belle* which was employed mainly on excursion work—contrasted sadly with the Southampton steamers. The directors and shareholders of both the Ryde Pier and the steamer companies were also warned that they would see the error of their ways too late—prophetic words indeed for within less than two years the United company had foundered ignominiously, despite a desperate last-minute acquisition of two new large vessels.

The first was the iron steamer *Albert Edward*, of 268.86 tons gross, built and engined by Oswald Mordaunt of Woolston, Southampton, in July 1878. Single-masted and cutter-rigged, her dimensions were 169.4ft x 20.5ft x 9ft and her two engines totalled 120 hp. The second, which joined her the following year, was the 235-ton *Alexandra* (171ft x 20.2ft x 8.5ft), also single-masted and cutter-rigged and fitted with two engines total-

166

ling 120 hp. Her builders were Scott & Co of Greenock.

Three of United's older paddle steamers were then disposed of. The *Prince of Wales* and the *Princess Royal* were sold for breaking-up in 1878 and *Her Majesty* met with the same fate in 1879. The four small screw steamers were also sold and dispersed around the coast.

But all these measures proved unavailing and the end of The Port of Portsmouth & Ryde United Steam Packet Co came in March 1880, when its vessels and assets were acquired jointly by the London & South Western Railway Co and the London, Brighton & South Coast Railway Co, United shareholders receiving from the liquidators £3 for each £10 share. The vessels taken over, however, did not remain long under railway ownership. The *Princess Alice* and the *Prince Consort* were broken-up in 1882, the *Duke of Edinborough* in 1884, and the *Princess of Wales* was sold and hulked in 1889. The *Albert Edward* lasted a little longer, being sold to David McBrayne in October 1893, and the *Heather Belle* was sold to the South Coast & Continental Co of London in 1900, being broken up in 1903. The last of the line, the *Alexandra,* was sold in 1913 to the Bembridge & Seaview Steam Packet Co and, in 1915, to Cozens & Co of Weymouth. She ended her days somewhat ignominiously as a show boat on the Thames.

The joint railway company replaced the old fleet with their three famous 'double-enders', with a pointed stern and bow rudder to facilitate manoeuvring astern, all built by Aitken & Mansel of Glasgow.

The first, the steel-hulled *Victoria* of 361.46 tons gross (191.9ft x 25.1ft x 8.6ft), was two-masted and schooner-rigged with two 'compound direct-acting oscillating engines' totalling 160 hp supplied by David Rowan of Glasgow. Her two funnels were conventionally placed fore and aft, whereas the second and third steamers, built in 1884, had their funnels athwartships, or side by side. These were the *Duchess of Edinburgh* of 342.9 tons gross (190.6ft x 26ft x 8.8ft), two-masted and schooner-rigged, with two 'compound direct-acting diagonal engines' totalling 200 hp supplied by John & James Thompson of Glasgow, and her almost identical sister-ship, the *Duchess of Connaught*.

The *Victoria* was ultimately sold to Holland in 1899 for breaking-up, and the *Edinburgh* and the *Connaught* shared the same fate the following year.

The ownership of the joint railway companies' fleet passed to the Southern Railway Co in 1923.

CHAPTER FIVE

LYMINGTON AND YARMOUTH STEAMERS

LYMINGTON, REPUTEDLY known to and used by the Phoenicians and later occupied by the Romans, is mentioned in Domesday Book as 'Lentune'. The Lymington river was originally navigable as far as Ampress, having been deeper, wider and longer than at present. It now leads to the Boldre ('Full river') but only as a mere stream. Its importance as a port, dating from the time of Henry II (1154-89), began to decline when the increasing size and draft of vessels obliged them to seek deeper ports with wider approaches. Yacht and shipbuilding flourished, vessels up to 60 tons, including revenue cutters and many famous yachts having been built there, although the staple trade of the town was salt manufacturing. Salt had been produced at Lymington since the twelfth century, and in the early part of the nineteenth century about 6,000 tons were produced annually. But by 1865 the last salt works had closed down, victim of competition from Cheshire and the commercial importance of the town then declined.

The prominent sea mark of Lymington has for centuries been the tower of the parish church of St Thomas the Apostle, considerably altered since it was built in 1250 and the tower added in 1670. The railway pier, opened in May 1884, replaced an earlier jetty constructed in June 1861.

Six and a half miles to the east of Lymington, lies the small village of Beaulieu at the head of the Beaulieu river. The Abbey there was founded in 1204 by King John and destroyed in 1539 by Henry VIII. Two miles from Beaulieu, on the west bank of the river, is Bucklers Hard, and from this tiny hard, particularly from 1743 onwards under the direction of the Master Builder Henry Adams, came many famous men-o-war, including the *Agamemnon* (Nelson's favourite ship), the *Bellerophon*, the *Illustrious* and the *Euryalus*.

Also concerned with this chapter, is the Isle of Wight town of Yarmouth, situated at the entrance to the Yar river. Mentioned in the Domesday Book as 'Eremud', it received its first charter in 1135 from Baldwin de Redvers, Lord of the Island (1107-56).

The harbour was formerly larger than at present and more exposed, as the breakwater, commenced in 1843, was not completed until 1847. Prior to the opening of the Yar bridge in 1876, the crossing from Yarmouth to Norton Sands was maintained by small boats. And to accommodate travellers, a shelter house, similar to that at Crosshouse, Southampton (a small round building of stone, divided into four and fitted with seats) was erected on the west shore by Sir Andrew Snape Hammond.

THE LYMINGTON AND YARMOUTH STEAMERS

Until 1830, the 3½-mile passage between Lymington and Yarmouth, Isle of Wight, had been made by boats under oars or sail and at times this could be a rough or tedious crossing, lying as it does across the main tidal stream of the West Solent and almost at right-angles to the prevailing south-westerly winds.

Sailing vessels from these ports also maintained a passage to Portsmouth, calling at Cowes and Ryde, and despite the tedium or discomfort the voyage might involve, travellers from the Lymington and Poole districts, bound for Portsmouth, generally preferred it to the overland journey. The latter, due to an inadequate stage coach service and the dreadful state of the unsurfaced, rutted roads, frequently proved a feat of endurance for even the hardiest of travellers.

There was, therefore, great jubilation locally in 1829 when it was announced that a steamer was to be introduced on the Lymington, Yarmouth and Portsmouth passages. The *Duke of Buccleugh* was then being built at Cowes for this purpose but, instead, she was placed on the Cowes to Southampton station in opposition to the *Emerald*, and it was finally a Lymington-owned steamer, the *Glasgow*, that started the Lymington steamer service.

The *Glasgow*, a wooden-hulled steamer of only 17 tons register, built in 1828 by Stephen Wood of Newcastle, was bought from her Newcastle owners in March 1830 by three enterprising Lymington business men, Charles and Samuel St Barbe, bankers and salt-factory owners, and Edward Hicks, a banker. Her master was Capt Robert Dore, late master of the Cowes-registered, 23-ton sailing vessel *Charlotte*, who was to command the *Glasgow* for eighteen years, until his death in 1848.[1] The *Glasgow*'s dimensions were: 52ft 10in x 13ft 4in x 7ft 4in and she had a bowsprit, a 'billet' head, one striking mast, a square stern and quarter badges.[2]

Her trials proving satisfactory—she made the passage from Lymington to Yarmouth in thirty minutes 'with only half her power on'—the *Glasgow* went into service on 5 April 1830. She sailed between Lymington and Portsmouth, calling at Yarmouth, Cowes and Ryde, for three days each week; and between Lymington and Southampton calling at Yarmouth and Cowes, on the other three days. On Sundays, she maintained the Lymington to Yarmouth passage only. During her lays-up, or when she was out of service and under repair, her place on station was taken by the *Duke of Buccleugh*.

The *Glasgow*'s passage work was generally uneventful although in April 1835 she had a narrow escape when, lying at moorings in Cowes during a gale one night, she was run into by

171

LYMINGTON AND YARMOUTH STEAMERS

THE GLASGOW

PASSAGE

TO AND FROM

LYMINGTON,

YARMOUTH,

AND

C O W E S.

PASSENGERS Booked and **PARCELS** received
AT THIS HOUSE,
and all Information given respecting the Departure and Arrival of the
STEAM BOAT.

Poster for the *Glasgow's* service, c1830

172

the *George IV* and had her mast brought down about the ears of a surprised and no doubt indignant crew.

Local boatmen and wherrymen, however, were not entirely displaced by the advent of this steamer. The death of one was reported in 1837 as: 'John Rodgers, many years a boatman between Lymington and Yarmouth, who during the early part of his life, held a very respectable station in society . . .'—perhaps the blacksheep of some distinguished local family. Even better known was the mailboat man, M. Webster, of Yarmouth, whose 23ft wherry capsized during a squall in April 1837, spilling the twelve occupants into the West Solent, ten of whom, including women and children, were drowned. Webster was complimented on retaining the mailbag until he was rescued and for having held a child in his arms until she died. He himself died in November 1844 at the age of seventy-six, 'leaving six children to lament his loss.' In 1800, he had been awarded the mail contract of £10 per year to make a daily mail passage in his hoy which was embellished with the King's Arms and flew the Post Office flag. In 1821, he owned a vessel, a wherry, and a light four oared boat. He held the mail contract until 1841 sharing it with the P.S. *Glasgow*, during the summer months (1830–41). British Rail eventually secured the contract and it was not until 1967 that mails ceased to go by this route.

Passengers on board the *Glasgow* were enabled to enjoy a little more of her much advertised 'commodious' deck space when, in May 1836, tow boats were introduced for the conveyance of horses, cattle and carriages—a practice which was to continue on this station until the 1930s. And in June 1841, the pressure on her boilers was eased slightly when she was joined on passage by the iron-built steamer *Solent* and the Solent Sea Co was formed to accommodate '. . . the large influx of visitors expected with the arrival of the railway'.

Slightly larger than the *Glasgow*, the *Solent*, of 61 'full tons' and 34 tons register, was built at Northam by Summers, Groves

173

& Day, and launched on 18 May 1841 by W. Squires, a shareholder of and later secretary to the Solent Sea Co. With an overall length of 84ft, she was single-masted and sloop-rigged, with a fixed bowsprit and one engine of 15 hp. She was rapturously received by an admiring public, her saloon being especially commended for its panelling upon which were portrayed various views of the neighbourhood, 'the *tout ensemble* being the most complete we have seen'. (Picture, p144.)

Both steamers were now referred to as 'Royal Mail' steam packets, the *Glasgow* maintaining the Lymington to Yarmouth service and the *Solent* maintaining the Lymington to Portsmouth and Lymington to Southampton service. The *Glasgow* sailed from Lymington for Yarmouth on weekdays at 9.0 am, 12 noon, and 4.0 pm, returning at 10.0 am, 1.0 pm, and 6.0 pm. On Sundays, she made two crossings from Lymington, at 9.0 am and 3.0 pm, returning at 10.0 am and 4.0 pm, tow boats not being available on this day. The *Solent* maintained a service on Mondays, Wednesdays and Fridays from Lymington to Portsmouth, calling at Yarmouth, Cowes and Ryde, 'up and down'; and on Tuesdays, Thursdays and Saturdays, from Lymington to Southampton, calling at Yarmouth and Cowes, also 'up and down'.

A no doubt welcome break from routine was enjoyed by the *Glasgow* in April 1842, when she was taken off passage to make excursions to Totland Bay, carrying hundreds of sightseers to view a dead whale, 71ft long, that had been washed onto the beach. The carcase was eventually bought by a Mr William Kingswell at an Admiralty auction and towed to Gurnard where the skeleton was removed. Later, it was reconstructed and placed on show at Blackgang Chine—admittance 1s per head—in a large, slate-roofed shed and is still on view to this day.

Two years after the *Glasgow*'s whale excursions, her engineer was nearly drowned during a stormy crossing. He was seen tending some part of the machinery on deck when a sudden heave of the vessel threw him backwards over the bulwarks and he vanished from sight, only suddenly to reappear clambering over the bulwark and as dry as a bone. By a lucky chance, he had landed on the sponson outboard and so saved his life.

The *Solent*'s passage work was also occasionally eventful, as when it was discovered that her mooring ropes had been cut through as she lay at Lymington. It transpired that a retired crew member, described as 'An old Solent Sea Dog', had crossed to Lymington to collect his pension and, returning on board four sheets in the wind, had caused so much trouble that he had been charged for his passage. His indignant retaliation led to his appearance before the local magistrates and payment of a nominal fine.

When the novelty of the steamer service had worn off, passengers soon began complaining, one particular irritation being that the steamers were often taken out of service in order to tow other vessels in and out of harbour. Another complaint was that sailing departure times were frequently delayed while tow boats considerably reduced the speed of the steamers while on passage. But, on the other hand, when tow boats were not in use—and heavy weather sometimes resulted in their cancellation—complaints were even louder because passengers had to share the limited deck space with sheep, horses, pigs and other farmstock. The resultant noise, confusion and atmosphere is perhaps best left to the imagination of anyone inclined to sea-sickness!

Matters presumably grew worse in September 1849, because the *Solent* was then obliged to maintain the passages single-handed, the old *Glasgow* having been offered for sale, 'adapted as a tug'. Apparently she found no buyer, as she remained the property of the Solent Sea Co until she was broken-up in October 1852.

In June 1852 the *Solent* achieved modest fame when she was instrumental in the rescue of seven survivors from the French brig *St Barbe* which had foundered off the Needles, later landing them at Cowes. The *St. Barbe* (Captain Hay) of Bordeaux, was bound from Newcastle to Algiers. In May of the following year, however, she was involved in a less fortunate incident. She was off Portsmouth platform one afternoon when a small skiff nearby was swamped, spilling the occupants—three men and a five-year-old girl—into the water. Two of the men, after struggling for several minutes, went down in front of hundreds of spectators who were lining the shore. The third man, who kept hold of the little girl, still managed to cling to the waterlogged boat and these two were rescued—the man by means of a rope thrown to him by a seaman in the *Solent*, which had meanwhile manoeuvred along-side; and the girl by the *Solent*'s master, Capt Edward Webster, who '. . . with great dexterity and personal risk, suspended him-self from the bulwark with one hand and foot and with the other, caught the little girl by her fingers . . .'. The subsequent inquest found that although the *Solent*'s wash had swamped the skiff, it had obviously been unseaworthy owing to its 'trumpery' con-struction.

In addition to her passage work, the *Solent* made excursions during the summer months, mainly to the Needles or Alum Bay, and it was on such an excursion in 1857 that she salvaged a mysterious-looking object found floating in the West Solent. It proved to be a serviceable cart, minus horse, driver or cargo, though what the Receiver of Wrecks made of this prize is, un-fortunately, not recorded.

In June 1858, in anticipation of an increase in passenger traffic to the Isle of Wight following the opening of the Brockenhurst to Lymington Railway in the following month, another steamer was placed in service to assist the *Solent*. This was the wooden-hulled steamer *Red Lion* of 54.34 tons gross (13.74 net) built in 1856 by Thorburn & Alman of N. Shields. Single-masted and sloop-rigged, she had a round stern and one engine of 29 hp. Dimensions were 76.8ft x 15.7ft x 8.3ft. Her arrival in Lyming-ton, however, was almost ignored and the kindest remark recorded concerning her was, 'She is a tight little boat'. The *Red Lion*, nevertheless, performed her duties efficiently and for two years maintained the Lymington service single-handed following the withdrawal from service of the *Solent* in 1861 after twenty years on this station.

The next steamer to operate out of Lymington was the *Solent* (II), a wooden-hulled steamer of 61 tons gross (32.9 net), launched from the Lymington yard of G. & I. Inman in October 1863. Slightly larger than her predecessor—85.4ft x 15.6ft x 7.1ft—she was single-masted and smack-rigged, with a square stern and an engine of 32 hp. Under the command of Capt J. H. Cribb, she made her first voyage in November 1863—an excursion to Stokes Bay with a party of directors and their friends—and averaged, it was claimed, a speed of twelve knots. But there was a marked lack of interest when she went into service shortly afterwards, '. . . The Rifle Bugle Band which was expected did not appear and no curiosity was elicitated in her by the public . . .'

The *Solent* (II), which, incidentally, made excursions around the island in 1864 and 1865, and the *Red Lion* were joined in July 1866 by another steamer, the 69 tons gross iron-hulled *Mayflower*, built by Marshall Bros, Wellington Quay, Newcastle. Capt J. H. Cribb was appointed master when she arrived at Lymington on 12 July. With a length of 98.3ft, a beam of 15.7ft and a moulded depth of 6.8ft, she was driven by two oscillating engines totalling 40 hp and was single-masted and sloop-rigged, with a round stern. She was considered a first-class steamer as regards her accommodation. In the large after saloon, situated below deck level and next to the ladies' cabin, the seats were arranged around the sides leaving a clear space in the centre. The fireplace was let into the bulkhead 'so that the chimney is out of sight of the people'—which implies that other similar vessels were provided with only a primitive bogey-stove. This saloon was lit by stained-glass skylights, and a 'good

177

L

sized' fore saloon was provided forward, together with a smaller cabin for the use of the crew and ship stores. The construction of the *Mayflower* had been supervised by the chief engineer of the Solent Sea Co, Charles Hayball, late engineer of the *Red Lion*, who must have been a man of some versatility as, in 1863, he had built a steam road carriage, weighing two tons and fitted with a 6 hp engine which, it was claimed, could carry twenty people and attain a speed of 20 mph on a good road.

The *Red Lion* was finally transferred to South Shields in August 1880 and the two steamers remaining on the Lymington station, the *Solent* (II) and the *Mayflower*, were acquired by the South Western Railway in July 1884 for the sum of £2,750. The former was sold to Holland in 1901 for breaking-up and the latter was broken-up in 1912.

This chapter is concluded, perhaps not inappropriately, with a reference to one of Alfred Lord Tennyson's greatest works, 'Crossing the Bar'. Tennyson (1809-92) composed this in October 1889, while crossing from Lymington to Yarmouth in one of these small paddle steamers on a visit to his old home at Farringford.

CHAPTER SIX

HYTHE STEAMERS

HYTHE, SITUATED on the shore bordering the New Forest at the head of Southampton Water, was originally part of the Fawley and Dibden parishes. During the early nineteenth century, Hythe was little more than a small fishing hamlet, although boats, merchant vessels—and during the French Wars and the War of American Independence, men-o-war—were built there.

Because the inadequate roads and predominance of marshland made overland travel in this area a feat of endurance, it is understandable that travellers passing between the New Forest and Southampton, should have favoured the faster and more comfortable route—by wherry across the river Test to Southampton. The earliest record of a ferry service is a reference found on Saxon's Map of 1575 to 'Hitheferye'.

THE HYTHE STEAMERS

Of all the early Southampton steamers, none caused so much consternation and frustration as the first Hythe steamer, the *Emerald,* and because of this and despite the fact that she was in service for only three years, perhaps more is known of her exploits than those of any other local steamer.

Her story began in 1828 when a 'spirited' company, led by W. C. Westlake, was formed to build and operate a steamboat service between Southampton and Hythe, presumably much to the chagrin of the Hythe boatmen whose livelihoods were thus threatened.

The *Emerald,* a wooden-hulled paddle steamer of 22 tons register, was built by John Rubie of Cross House, Itchen and launched in the winter of 1829. Her dimensions were: 63ft x 10ft x 7ft and she was single-masted, with a rounded stern. Her single engine developed a modest 10 hp. She carried out trials in February 1830 and, we are assured, astounded the local populace with a crossing time, between Southampton and Hythe, of eleven minutes and furthermore, '... in fourteen against the tide!'

She went into service in March 1830, sailing between Southampton and Hythe during the mornings and afternoons but at mid-day, much to the disgust of fuming, would-be passengers waiting at either Southampton or Hythe, the *Emerald* made a return passage to Cowes. Fares between Southampton and Hythe were 6d and 3d single and, between Southampton and Cowes, 3s single in the after cabin and 1s 6d in the fore cabin.

Complaints from disgruntled passengers, however, appear to have made little impression on the astute Mr Westlake, who continued to neglect the Hythe service on the least pretext. The enterprising individual he had chosen to command the *Emerald* was J. B. Humphries, engineer and one-time factory owner, who had also supervised the building of this vessel, his first command. The following year, the *Emerald* was the first steamer to make one-hour excursions on Southampton Water, and the first to offer towage services—to and from Eling, Redbridge, Northam, Bursledon and Beaulieu.

In 1832 the *Emerald* was stationed in Cowes and was making a 9.0 am passage daily to Southampton, where she engaged in towage work or excursions or maintained the Hythe passage. Inconvenienced Hythe passengers could only complain but the island steamer proprietors, into whose domain the *Emerald* had dared to enter, could and indeed did do more. They placed the steamer, *Duke of Buccleugh,* in opposition on the same passage,

COWES & SOUTHAMPTON.

THE "EMERALD,"
STEAM-PACKET,

WILL resume her Station on **TUESDAY**, the 10th of **APRIL**, leaving **COWES** precisely at **NINE** in the Morning, and **SOUTHAMPTON** at **FIVE** in the Afternoon (Sundays excepted).—This excellent little Sea-boat is now calculated to afford every comfort and satisfaction to Passengers, and may be hired by private Parties, from Eleven till Four o'Clock daily.

N.B.—An excellent BOAT, belonging to her, 22 Feet long Copper fastened, is for Sale.

Announcement of the *Emerald's* return to service

whereupon Mr Westlake prudently transferred his steamer to Southampton. The competition, however, continued, leading the *Emerald* to reduce her fares by one-third and, later, to be advertised under the defiant title of 'The Matchless Little Steam Packet *Emerald*'. She was now sailing from Southampton at 10.0 am for Cowes and Ryde, returning from Ryde at 2.30 pm —'The hours at which this swift and comfortable packet leaves and returns to Southampton, enables pleasure parties in the vicinity to visit the Isle of Wight, or take a delightful water excursion at little expenses. . . .' Single fares were now down to:

181

Southampton-Cowes, 2s and 1s; Southampton-Ryde, 2s 6d and 1s 6d; Cowes-Ryde, 1s 6d and 1s, after cabin and fore cabin respectively. The *Duke of Buccleugh* was not slow to follow suit and to reduce her fares correspondingly. Recriminations soon followed and, as was the fashion in those days, the contestants chose to make their rival claims in the local newspapers. Mr Westlake took considerable space to caution the public against 'the dark hints and base fabrications engendered against the *Emerald,* in the vain hope of driving her away from the I.O.W. passage. . . .' These had included assertions that her engine had no safety valve and that her boilers were unsafe. He pointed out that she not only had two safety valves but furnished an affidavit, signed by Samuel Marshall, boiler maker, to the effect that the boiler had no equal in strength or quality, and furthermore, he placed on show at the office of Mr N. M. Priaulx, 78 High Street, Southampton, a specimen of iron cut out of the boiler during the preceding winter. Westlake also claimed that the *Emerald* had not only carried many hundreds of satisfied passengers—on one occasion she took seventy on one passage to Cowes—but that she was an 'overmatch' for the *Duke of Buccleugh.* And, finally, because he asserted that men of the 'I.O.W. steamer company' had actually deterred several passengers from embarking in the *Emerald* at Cowes by saying she was unsafe, and that one of her crew had been ordered off the Fountain Quay on pain of trespass, Westlake reduced his fares yet again between Southampton and Cowes to a phenomenal low: 1s and 6d single, aft and forward.

The island steamer proprietors, however, remained unrepentant and replied with the exhortation:

> Examine and Judge for Yourselves! Don't Be Cajoled or Induced to Travel in a Boat, WHEN YOU CAN BE ACCOMMODATED IN THIS VERY SUPERIOR VESSEL, 'THE DUKE OF BUCCLEUGH'. She is clean, comfortable and commodious, and is, in every respect, superior to other vessels of her class.

And her fares were brought down to match the *Emerald's.*

In September 1833, the contestants, presumably having had enough 'opposition warfare', managed to effect a compromise whereby the fares of the *Emerald* and the *Duke of Buccleugh* were, by agreement, raised to more economic level. These then became: Southampton to Cowes, 3s and 2s; Cowes to Ryde, 2s and 1s; Southampton to Ryde, 3s and 2s. But at the end of the season, Mr Westlake played his trump card—asking to be bought out, '. . . If not sold, she will be placed on passage again very early in the Spring'. In the event, the island steamer proprietors decided to buy, much to the fury and indignation of Capt Humphries at having his ship sold from under his feet. The subsequent exchanges in local papers between the captain and the shipowner, indeed, made the previous year's slanging appear almost gentlemanly by comparison. Capt Humphries complained that the owner had ignored his earlier offer to buy the *Emerald* for £700 and sail out of another port, and had then sold out to the opposition without even having consulted him. Westlake, he stated, had put the steamer up for auction, bought her for £325 and had then promptly sold her to the 'I.O.W. Company' (sic) for £1,200. The captain added that he had worked on a commission basis, sharing in the profits with the owner, and that at times, especially during the 'opposition', his earnings had been less than a guinea a week. He finally quoted letters from the owner, promising to 'remember' the captain should the vessel be sold—and now he was to be cut off without even the proverbial shilling!

Westlake's reply was equally blunt. He criticised the captain for publishing confidential letters and suggested that the captain was lucky to have had his weekly wage because the owner had actually lost money. He called on a friend, Edward Thompson, to witness that the captain had already been considering taking up employment in London; had left the *Emerald* for days at a time, leaving the engineer, George Blaker, in sole charge; had worked in the steamer *Lord Beresford* whilst receiving payment from him; and, lastly, had demanded a £50 loan from the owner under threat of airing his grievances in the local newspaper.

The captain's reply, published a week later, closed the correspondence. He explained that his London job-hunting had been done after he had heard from the 'opposition' that the *Emerald* was to be sold from under him. He conceded having asked Westlake for a loan but only because of his reduced circumstances and emphatically denied having made any threats. He closed with the magnificent suggestion, that Mr Thompson be referred to the 13th chapter of the 1st Corinthians.[1]

The *Emerald* then vanished temporarily from the records. Westlake devoted himself to his other business enterprises; the island steam proprietors, relieved at long last of an irritating opposition, resumed their passage work a little more peacably; and the *Emerald's* intrepid commander set about restoring his depleted fortunes. Within a few years, he was supervising the building of the steamer *Rio Doce* and went in her to South America.

Eight years passed, then, in 1841, the *Emerald's* name came into the news once again when three small boys were charged at Southampton magistrates' court with having stolen some copper piping from this '. . . derelict little steamer, laying on the mud at Northam'. Her epitaph was written in the subsequent report:

> The *Emerald* was built about ten years ago by J. B. Humphries and was the property of the late Mr W. C. Westlake. The boat did not answer the expectations of its proprietor and was found so annoying to the proprietors of the other steam boats on station that they bought it off. She lay on the mud at Northam and was often plundered but the late Capt J. H. Knight (Superintendent of the I.O.W. Steam Navigation Co) viewed her with such disgust that nothing was done. . . .

The later I.O.W. Steam Packet Co, however, must have thought more kindly of her memory because, in 1857, they perpetuated her name with the launching of another 'elegant and clipper-looking' steamer of the same name.

Three years elapsed before a replacement was found for the old *Emerald*, during which time passengers had to be content with small boats on a passage then described as 'lengthy and occasionally dangerous'. And they might well have gone on doing so had it not been for the initiative of Day, Summers & Co who, in June 1835, announced they were building an iron paddle steamer to improve communications between Southampton and Hythe. They added that they had no wish to become steam-boat proprietors, and offered the steamer for sale on completion.

The new steamer was ultimately bought by Capt J. H. Knight Snr and Messrs Smith & Co, owners of two local trading sloops. Named the *Forester* and built at Millbrook in 1836, she was the first iron steamer to be built south of the Thames. Of 20 tons register, her dimensions were: 65.4ft x 10ft x 5.9ft and she had a 6 hp Boulton & Watt engine. She went into service in July 1836 under the command of Capt George Robert Mason, maintaining an hourly service between the Royal Pier and the gravel hard at Hythe, sometimes carrying between sixty and seventy passengers per trip. During the summer months she also made excursions to Beaulieu and Lymington. Capt Mason, incidentally, was also landlord of the Wheatsheaf Inn, Southampton, which, built in 1824, is still in business in East Street.

A tragedy occurred in February 1837 when the 17-year-old engineer, James Heath, and his 17-year-old friend, Thomas Crocker, a cabinet maker, attempted to board the *Forester* late one night as she lay at moorings off Hythe. Their boat foundered within a few feet of the steamer in sight of the only person on board, the 12-year-old stoker, Samuel Eastman. He managed to pass a rope to the young men in the water, which they caught, but he was not strong enough to haul them up nor could they clamber up under the counter stern: '. . . so after a fearful struggle, they resigned themselves to their fate and sank to rise no more. . . .'

Public support for the steamer service, however, proved insufficient and during the winter lay-up the proprietors appealed to the public to favour the service during the 'summer months also', implying that passengers were deserting the steamer in good weather for more pleasant and leisurely trips in boats under oars or sail. As an inducement, a stove was fitted in the main cabin but this innovation was presumably no more successful than the owners' appeal because, in March 1838, a warning was issued that unless the steamer received more patronage the owner would quit, having already lost money. Public support was forthcoming and the *Forester* maintained the Hythe passage during the summer months of 1839 but the response during the early part of the 1840 season was again so poor that, in August, the owners announced, with regret, the complete cessation of the steamer service, stating that the *Forester* would instead operate on a station between Exeter and Exmouth. But this transfer did not take place because in October 1840 it was recorded that the *Forester* towed *The Pride of The Waters* (renamed *Ruby*) from Itchen to Millbrook. It is possible that she ended her days as a tug, for she is not mentioned again on the Hythe passage.

The *Forester* appeared in the news for the last time in March 1844 when two boys, aged nine and twelve, were charged at Southampton magistrates' court with having stolen a copper from her as she lay at Crab Niton, Itchen. Luckily for them, the case was dropped because the witnesses had refused to attend, but the magistrate warned the elder boy, who had been convicted before, that had the case gone to quarter sessions he would most probably have been transported for life.

And so, the *Forester*, like her predecessor, the *Emerald*, was left to disintegrate in the mud at Northam, not very long after her launching.

Despite the failure of both the *Emerald* and the *Forester*, a number of Sotonians were confident that the Hythe steamer service could be operated economically and, in 1845, they placed another steam vessel on this station. Their paddle steamer, the iron-hulled *Gipsy*, of 20.5 tons register, was launched on 5 July 1846 at the Northam yard of Summers, Day & Baldock and christened by Miss Emily Clarke, daughter of one of the steamboat proprietors. Driven by a 16 hp engine, she was flush-decked with a break and had a rounded stern. Her dimensions were: 73.8ft x 11.1ft x 5.1ft and she had a draught of 14in. This 'light and elegant steamer' made her maiden voyage on 20 August, on an excursion from Southampton to Beaulieu with the directors and their friends on board. After landing at Beaulieu Bridge to visit the ruins of the abbey, they dined on board and, on the return journey to Southampton, called in at Cowes at the request of the ladies in the party.

The *Gipsy* entered service on 25 August 1845 under the command of Capt G. R. Mason, using the new Hythe 'pier', or landing, which had been built the preceding year. It was not held in high esteem, however, being unapproachable at low water and, furthermore, the 1d increase in fares to pay for this facility was considered firstly, extortionate—'A halfpenny would have been ample for the mere substitution of stone for gravel', and then 'Unjust', because only the fore cabin passengers were required to bear the increase. The *Gipsy* ran an hourly service from Hythe from 8.15 am until 6.15 pm and from Southampton from 8.45 am until 6.45 pm. Average passage time was 12min and fares 6d best cabin and 4d fore cabin.

The *Gipsy*, however, proved no more successful than her predecessors and within two years, in May 1847, the owners found it necessary to warn that unless more support was forthcoming, the winter passage, if not the entire service, would cease. But this went unheeded. Possibly the passengers were susceptible to the blandishments of the boatmen who could more easily 'pick-a-back' passengers over the muddy and sometimes flooded hard at Hythe. At the end of the summer season of 1847 it was reported that only two-fifths of people making the crossing went by steamer. In a last desperate attempt to keep the service going, the proprietors called a public meeting at Hythe on 11 December 1847, to propose the formation of a larger company and the acquisition of another steamer. But so few people attended and those who did gave such little support that the owners terminated the service that day. Three years after her withdrawal from the Hythe station, the *Gipsy* was transferred to London, and in 1855 to Plymouth, where she was broken up in 1870.

In April 1855—after a lapse of nearly seven and a half years—it was proposed to re-open the Hythe steamer service yet again, 'to meet with the hurrying habits of our times'. Certainly there was room for improvement, since the passage, under oars and against the wind and tide, could take up to one hour!

A joint stock company—the Hythe & Southampton Steam Ferry Co—was formed in June 1855, under the leadership of A. R. Drummond of Cadland with the Duke of Buccleugh and Mr Sloane Stanley listed among the shareholders. By 23 July, a capital of £2,500 had been raised and the secretary, Mr Goater, informed shareholders that two screw steamers had been ordered from Payne of Bristol. When, after some considerable time, these failed to materialise the company was obliged instead to accept a tender for a paddle steamer from Day, Summers & Co who, while admitting the cost was greater than that of a screw boat, maintained that the station was 'unsuited' for screw vessels or high-pressure engines. Delivery of this vessel was also delayed by a strike of shipwrights at Northam, who claimed their pay of 5s a day compared unfavourably with the London rate of 9s to 10s. They stood out for some time for a modest 6s a day, but they met with an equally determined resistance and the strike eventually petered out.

Meanwhile, the ferry company had acquired an ex-London river paddle steamer, the 10-year-old, wooden-hulled *Prince Alfred*, of 30.5 tons gross (19.24 net), and on 26 February 1856 she made her local maiden voyage—yet another excursion to Beaulieu with a party of directors, shareholders and their friends.

Built at Frindsbury, Kent, ten years earlier, the *Prince Alfred* had no mast, a square stern and two engines totalling 20 hp. Her dimensions were: 70.4ft x 11.7ft x 5.4ft. Within one month of her going into service, it was commented that 'she plies with a punctuality and convenience of accommodation which is very satisfactory'—though no doubt much to the chagrin of the Hythe boatmen whose rough manners, objectionable touting and often exorbitant fares had earned them scant sympathy from the travelling public.

The company's second steamer was launched from the Northam yard of Day, Summers & Co in December 1856, and then sailed to Hythe where she was christened *Lady Elizabeth* by Lady Elizabeth Drummond who, after inspecting her namesake, adjourned with other guests to the Drummond Arms for a celebration dinner and to drink success to the Hythe Steam Ferry. Larger than the *Prince Alfred,* the *Lady Elizabeth* (98ft x 13.9ft x 6.5ft) was 58 tons gross (36.92 tons net) and mastless, with a rounded stern and two engines totalling 28 hp.

Despite this addition to the service, passengers were far from satisfied with the landing at Hythe which was still unapproachable at low water, while the town quay also suffered from the same disadvantage. However, barely twenty months after her launching, having presumably proved too large and unwieldy for the Hythe passage, the *Lady Elizabeth* was transferred to the river Orwell and her place taken by the smaller *Louisa*. Built in December 1858 by Joseph Hodgkinson, Cross House Hard, Itchen—builder of the second Itchen floating bridge—the *Louisa* (79.8ft x 12.4ft x 5.6ft) was 36.76 tons gross (23.16 tons net) with a single mast and rounded stern. Her designed speed, with two oscillating engines totalling 20 hp, was eleven knots. An innovation at this time, she had a bow rudder in addition to the usual rudder aft, to enable her more easily to manoeuvre in and out of the creek at Hythe.

In addition to their passage work, the *Prince Alfred* and the

Louisa made summer excursions, mainly to Beaulieu and occasionally to Spithead to attend the Fleet Reviews. In 1863, the *Prince Alfred* was sold for breaking-up and her place was taken by the iron-hulled *Frederica*, 34.53 tons gross, 21 tons net, built in February 1863 at the Northam yard of Day, Summers & Co. Mastless and with an angular stern, her dimensions were: 80.4ft x 12.1ft x 5.6ft and her two engines totalled 16 hp.

Prominent individuals associated at this time with the Hythe steamer service included E. N. Harvey of Fawley, W. Winkworth and Frederick Fry of Hythe, and members of the distinguished Percy family whose close connection with this ferry service continues to this day.

The *Louisa* and the *Frederica* were acquired by the present company on its formation in December 1874 under the title of the Hythe Pier & Hythe & Southampton Steam Ferry Co. In 1923, this was divided into two companies, the Hythe Pier Co owning the pier and railway, and the General Estates Co Ltd owning the vessels. This service, so gallantly pioneered by the 'Matchless Little Steam Packet *Emerald*' in 1830, continues today.

CHAPTER SEVEN

SOLENT TUGS

The first steam paddle-wheel tug to be built and employed locally was the *Earl of Egremont,* launched at Milton on 20 December 1820 for the Portsmouth & Arundel Canal Co, to tow barges from Portsmouth to the harbour lock at Milton and to Dell Quay. Of 17 tons net and fitted with Maudslay engines of 24 hp, she underwent trials in April 1821.

In the Solent area, many references are found to cross-Channel and island steamers undertaking towage duties while, more specifically, in 1825, Ryde steamers offered tows to vessels '. . . prevented by wind from entering or leaving harbour'. In 1831, the Hythe steamer *Emerald* was employed towing vessels to and from Eling, Redbridge, Northam, Bursledon and Beaulieu, and the second Hythe steamer, the *Forester* is also mentioned as being engaged in towage in 1840. In 1839 it was recorded that the cross-Channel steamer *Monarch* towed the schooner *Brilliant* from Southampton to Portsmouth to have her masts stepped.

The first steam tug, built as such, to be employed in Southampton was the 28-ton *John Lee,* owned by the Southampton Dock Co and placed in service under the command of Capt Treadwell in February 1845. Only a week before her arrival, however, it was noted that the island steamer *Medina* had towed a 'mud engine' from Portsmouth to Cowes to dredge the entrance to White's new steam frigate dock. The *John Lee* (90.2ft x 17ft x 9ft) was built by Andrew Woodhouse of South Shields for London River service. She returned to London in 1850, and was renamed the *Saucy Jack*. During her service in Southampton, the *John Lee*'s towing service charges were moderate[1], though in 1848, passengers at Lymington were complaining that the service there was being continually interrupted because the Lymington steamers were being used to tow vessels in and out of harbour.

The screw tug *Mary* of Southampton (78ft x 8ft; 6 hp), built in 1851 by Tod & MacGregor of Glasgow for Andrew Lamb of the P & O Company, was the first vessel to enter Southampton's inner dock at the ceremonial opening in November 1851, followed by the P & O's *Madrid*, the East Indiaman *Hampshire*, and the South Western Co's *South Western, Dispatch* and *Atalanta*. The same year, the 21-ton tug *Trimdom Grange* (78.2ft x 14ft x 7ft) was stationed at Cowes. Two-masted and schooner-rigged, with engines developing 40 hp, she was built at Newcastle in 1848 and owned by Edward Phillips of Cowes. She was sold to Joseph Redman, also of Cowes, in 1852 and, in the following year, to Swansea owners for use as a 'passage boat'.

Money, Wigram & Co, of Northam, launched the tug *Surprise* in June 1852, the christening being followed by a celebration dinner at the Castle Inn. At this time, the Southampton island steamers were advertising their towage services. In September 1853, the government tug *Echo* of Portsmouth salvaged the American sailing vessel *Eliz. A. Cochrane*, stranded on the Shingles, West Solent, but only after the *Ruby* had made an earlier but unsuccessful attempt, parting her hawser in the process.

Towage did not become big business in Southampton until July 1853 when the Southampton Steam Towing Co was formed with a capital of £10,000. One of their first tugs was the *Aid* (84.8ft x 17.3ft x 9.7ft and 45 hp), a wooden-hulled paddle steamer of 82.9 tons gross (27.99net) built at North Shields in 1852.[2] In 1854 the company acquired the *Phoenix* (72.9ft x 19.6ft

192

x 7.9ft and 40 hp), another wooden paddle steamer of 70.62 tons gross (30.08 net) built at Northam by Money, Wigram & Co. The company's fleet of tugs also included the iron-hulled *Monarch* (95ft 4in x 17ft 5in x 9ft 7in and 80 hp) of 122 tons gross, built in 1854, and the *Belmont.*[3]

The *Belmont* was known as the 'runaway tug' following an incident which occurred in January 1854. Whilst towing the *Walter Hood* in Southampton Water, the little *Belmont* was rammed by her charge and pushed over onto her beam ends, losing her mast and funnel in the process. The crew of the stricken tug scrambled on board the *Walter Hood* when, to their astonishment, the *Belmont* slowly righted herself and, mastless and funnel-less, steamed gaily off down Southampton Water. The mortified crew, as soon as they could, gave chase in a rowing boat, finally catching up with her off Calshot, where she had been boarded by the crew of the light vessel. Five months later, the *Belmont,* while making an excursion to the Spithead naval review, was rammed by the Union Steam Collier Co's *Saxon* and, although crew and passengers were safely got off, the little *Belmont* slowly filled and sank. However, she was soon raised and put back into service.

In 1870 the company was renamed the Southampton New Steam Towing Co, and one of their first new vessels was the iron screw steamer *Alexandria* (110ft x 19.1ft x 8.9ft), built by Day, Summers & Co. Of 120.7 tons gross (62.49 net), the *Alexandria* was single-masted and cutter-rigged, with an elliptical stern and two 'compound inverted surface condensing engines' totalling 60 hp. Finally, in 1884, the company's three tugs and a barge were acquired by the present Southampton, Isle of Wight & South of England Royal Mail Steam Packet Co Ltd, which remains, today, the principal towage company on the South Coast.

M

CHAPTER EIGHT

SOLENT EXCURSION STEAMERS: 1823-60

> Hark, the merry bugle's sounding,
> See the steam boat's under weigh,
> Pleasure's group on board are bounding,
> Haste to join our holiday.
>
> —*Southampton Herald*, 10.7.1826

> A band of music was taken with them and they enjoyed the pleasures of Terpsichore without the drawbacks of Sea Nymphs. The entire party arrived back full of pleasurable feelings towards the worthy lessee of the Royal Pier and the Commander, Captain D. Corke Jnr.
>
> —Report of an excursion round the Isle of Wight in the *Medina. Hants Advertiser*, 14.8.1852

The *Medina* made the first two recorded (53 mile) steamer excursions around the Isle of Wight in September 1823 and, within a year, similar trips were being made by the *Ariadne,* the *Camilla* and the *Lord Beresford.* The island steamer *George IV* was no sooner launched in 1826 when she, too, was paddling around the island, an example quickly copied by the Ryde steamers *Union, Arrow* and *Lord Yarborough.*

Excursions were also made from Southampton to Brighton, 'accompanying yacht races', for launchings, Fleet reviews, 'to view

194

the burning cliff at Halworth' in 1827, and in 1830 to see the 'Cowes fireworks'. The larger cross-Channel vessels carried up to 300 passengers and sometimes a 'full band of music'. Fares varied from 3s to 6s with 'cold collations' available at times for an extra 2s. Stewardesses were provided by larger vessels and their services were no doubt appreciated at the back of the island during bad weather by ladies who had not acquired their sea-legs.

The early excursions around the island took from 6 to 7½ hours and, the comparatively small vessels of this period having a light draught, were made close inshore and were quite leisurely outings. By 1834, a Southampton steamer was making an excursion round the island every Monday throughout the summer months. Similar excursions were also made by the General Steam Navigation Co's *Superb* (Capt Wm Major) in 1831; the *Monarch* and the *Atalanta* in 1837; the *Lady de Saumarez* in 1840; the *Calpe* in 1841; the *Princess Victoria* in 1842; and the *Ruby* in 1843. The 1,670-ton P & O steamer *Oriental* was to have made one in 1840, with Lord Minto, First Lord of the Admiralty, on board but bad weather prevented the mail steamer from venturing past the Needles. By way of contrast, the Hythe steamer *Emerald* made one-hour excursions from Southampton in 1831, while in 1836 the *Forester* made excursions from Southampton to Beaulieu. In 1841, excursions were made from Southampton to Brighton and also to Swanage, the fares being the same, single, 7s forward, and 10s aft.

The popularity of sea excursions increased still further following the advent of the railway and the subsequent rush of holidaymakers to Southampton and the South Coast. One of the earliest 'specials' was in September 1841 when, by arrangement with the South Western Railway and the General Steam Navigation Co, the *Grand Turk* made a round-the-island excursion with 'holiday folk' from London. The return trip, a distance of approximately 222 miles, was completed in 14½ hours and cost the passengers £1 each. In 1843 the *Monarch* made a similar excursion in conjunction with the South Western Railway, the trains arriving at Southampton with up to 600 passengers each, to return within four days at one-third normal fares.

Landing cruises or picnic excursions began in the 1830s and, in the absence of piers or jetties, passengers were put on shore and re-embarked in boats, an indication of the leisurely nature of these outings. In 1842 the *Edinborough Castle* made a cruise, with a 'band of music' on board, to land people at Alum Bay and Hurst Point. The fares from Southampton were 5s and 4s. The following month, a 'Pic-Nic' excursion was made by the same vessel from Southampton to Beaulieu, calling at Cowes, out and home, for the same money.

The *Medina* was the first steamer to put into Ventnor while on excursion. On Tuesday, 29 September 1843, she anchored in the harbour under a salute of thirteen guns from the 'hotel battery'. She had left Cowes at 11 o'clock the same morning with 200 passengers and a band on board, and most of the company remained on shore at Ventnor for just one and a half hours. The same month, the *Ruby* (Capt Samuel Summers) left the Royal Pier at 9.0 am and Fountain Pier at 10.0 am and put her passengers out at Alum Bay, allowing them two or three hours on shore, and returning to Cowes at 5.0 pm. Fares were 4s and 3s, and refreshments were available on board at 'moderate prices'. The same fares were charged for her later trips around the island.

On 16 August 1844 the 'powerful and efficient' *Lord Yarborough* was chartered by George Knight of the Wellington Tavern, Portsmouth, for an excursion to view Netley Abbey and the Southampton Regatta, joining the Southampton steamers engaged in the same work. The following month, fares in the *Ruby* for her trip round the island were 3s 6d and 2s 6d. In October, both she and the *Monarch* took sightseers from Southampton to Portsmouth to witness the departure of the French king, Louis Phillipe, but they were disappointed because his sailing had been postponed.

196

Excursions became even more fashionable after the Royal Family joined in. Queen Caroline, the Queen Mother, made a trip round the island in the royal yacht *Princess Alice* in July 1845, and in September 1848 Queen Victoria made an excursion in the royal yacht *Fairy* from East Cowes to Beaulieu. The Royal Family made yet another 'round the island' trip in July 1849, in the *Victoria and Albert*.

An excursion with a difference was made in September 1845, when the *Atalanta* went around the island with a Mr W. Crook on board, who lectured his fellow passengers on geology, with particular reference to the strata of the Isle of Wight.

During the summer of 1846, three or four local steamers were making a weekly trip around the island, and some were not without incident. On one occasion the *Lady de Saumarez* went aground on Ryde Sands while returning from the back of the island, having previously witnessed the departure of the 'Experimental Squadron' from Spithead. Capt J. Goodridge Jnr, the master, had gone below for his dinner when the mate, Mr Stone, hauled her too close to the westward and the *Lady de Saumarez* struck, one paddle wheel becoming firmly embedded in the sand. The outlook appeared anything but cheerful because the tide was ebbing and all attempts to get her off were unsuccessful. It was some time before the passengers were taken off by one of the Ryde steamers—which, adding insult to injury, charged each passenger the considerable sum of 5s for 'services rendered'. The *Lady de Saumarez* was finally towed off Ryde Sands by the *Transit*.

In 1848, excursions could not be started early enough for some Sotonians who complained, in May, that there were no excursion boats to take sightseers to see the laying of the last stone of the new steam-boat basin at Portsmouth. However, two months later, the *Prince Albert*, sailing from Portsea and Gosport, began her weekly 'round the island' trip every Wednesday and Saturday, and maintained it for the rest of the summer

197

season, charging 3s each—children and servants half-price'.

The first excursion in 1849, from Southampton to Swanage, was made by the *Ruby* with 183 passengers, who each paid 2s for the privilege. They had three hours on shore, most of which was spent inspecting the quarries. Even the vagaries of the English weather failed to deter the excursionists, and on Coronation Day 1850, despite torrential rain, crowds of holiday-makers made their way along the Royal Pier to embark in the *Atalanta*, bound for Brighton. Some 400 managed to squeeze on board, a number of whom sheltered in the engine-room, while a further 100 were obliged to forego the trip for 'want of room'.

At Portsmouth, the following month, similar hordes bore down to the piers, heading towards the *Earl Spencer* and the *Prince of Wales* bound 'round the island'. The latter vessel had nearly 300 passengers on board and completed her trip around the island in 4hr 38min. On one occasion she made two excursions in one day, starting from Ryde Pier at 9.30 am and returning in 4hr 33min. She left again at 2.45 pm with nearly 200 passengers on board and was back within about five hours. On each trip she carried a band.

Private excursions were also undertaken, as in August 1850 when Sir A. E. Cockburn, MP for Southampton (later Lord Chief Justice), invited a party of 120 on board the *Gem*. It proved a lively occasion. Dancing took place on deck, fireworks were discharged on board and a large quantity of champagne was consumed. And to round off the proceedings, as the revellers were disembarking at the Royal Pier, a young woman fell over the side. She was eventually hauled back on board when, to everyone's astonishment, another person was found to be clinging to her skirts. He was a friend who had gone to her rescue unobserved.

The same month, the Ryde steamer *Lindsey* made an excursion from Portsmouth and Ryde to Dodner, near Newport, with 400 passengers. The following months, while bound for Cherbourg in company with the *Lord Yarborough* and the *Prince*

198

Albert, she broke down some six miles off St Catherine's Point. Repairs proving unsuccessful, a passenger was rowed ashore and, as soon as he could procure a carriage, made his way to Ryde to report the accident. The *Princess Royal* was despatched to take the no doubt thoroughly disgruntled passengers on to Cherbourg, while the *Prince of Wales* set off to tow the *Lindsey* into Portsmouth, where she arrived at 4 o'clock the following morning. As a result of the rivalry which then existed between the two Ryde steamer companies, the excursion season of 1850 continued until mid-October.

In 1851, a race around the island took place between *Her Majesty* and the *Prince Albert*. The former vessel, carrying 300 passengers, won the race in 4hr 14min against the latter's $5\frac{1}{2}$hr with 200 passengers. Indeed, throughout the 1850s, the steamers of all the local companies formed a veritable excursion fleet during the summer months.

Another excursion with a difference was made in July 1851, when the *Ruby* took members of the staff of Queen Victoria's Osborne estate from Trinity Pier, East Cowes, to Southampton, on their way to visit the Great Exhibition. Of these 142 men, women and children, it was said that 121 of them had never before left the island.

The *Prince of Wales* made a trip to Swanage on 23 July 1851, calling at Ryde and Cowes, out and home. She left Ryde Pier at 10.0 am and returned at 9.0 pm, having landed her passengers for a period of three hours. A 'delightful band' was on board. The following day she went around the island with 100 passengers and took five hours on passage.

The *Medina II* (ex-*Times*) began her long and eventful excursion career in June 1852 with a Coronation Day excursion to Poole. Her second was a trip to Weymouth with 280 passengers —'filled to the full number allowed by law' (an Act of Parliament restricting overloading was passed in 1851). Upon her return, passing up Southampton Water, she overtook and 'passed with ease' the then fast *South Western*, and on another occasion she paddled her way from Weymouth to the Needles in only two and and a half hours.

On 8 August 1853, the *Medina* was involved in a tragic accident, the first of its kind throughout the thirty-three years the island steamers had been in service. She had sailed that morning from Southampton and, after calling at Cowes and Ryde for more passengers and passing through the Fleet at Spithead, had stopped off Shanklin for two hours to land her holiday-makers. It was a clear sunny afternoon when she finally left for her trip around the island and, after clearing Ventnor, she set course westwards towards the Needles. Shortly afterwards, while making about $9\frac{1}{2}$ knots, she had the misfortune to run down a yawl off Atherfield in which were two men and a boy, all members of the local Warne family. The boat and occupants went directly under one of the paddle wheels, one man being killed instantly while the other two, after struggling for several seconds in the sea, disappeared. A boat had been launched from the steamer as soon as possible but no trace of the men or boy could be found.

At the subsequent inquest before the Shorwell jury, some interesting facts came to light. The *Medina* had had a complement of nine—master, mate, two seamen, an engineer, a stoker, a steward and a boy. A pilot/helmsman, John Light, who had been engaged at Cowes, was also on board. Several witnesses, however, created something of a sensation in court when they claimed that, at the time of the accident, Capt Corke, who had been seated on the bridge facing aft, was throwing handfuls of nuts to the passengers below, who were scrambling after them. But other witnesses, including Capt Corke, were adamant in declaring that no such incident had taken place.

John Light stated that he had remained at the helm throughout the entire voyage. 'I have charge of the compass'. Of Capt Corke, he said, 'He is a very young man but there is not a more careful captain anywhere.' He further added that, in steering, he relied entirely upon the assistance of a lookout stationed forward. (In these early, flush-decked steamers, the helmsman, standing right aft, had his forward visibility considerably restricted by the position of the mast, paddle boxes and passengers promenading the decks. This necessitated the services of a lookout who was stationed forward in the bows of the vessel.)

Another member of the crew, seaman William Harris, of French Street, Southampton, with 'ten years in the company', stated:

> I partly look to the passengers and attend them if they are sick, or if they want anything to drink.... Before the accident, I and the boys were busy getting the ashes up.... Captain Corke always gives us plenty of hard work in cleaning the ship. He is rather strict in his discipline and likes to see that everybody does his duty.

Then, presumably gaining more confidence, '... I don't think we had hands enough, the vessel being a very heavy one, and we are obliged to be up at 4 o'clock in the morning.' He added that he had told the boy, John Bezen, aged sixteen, to keep a look-out but, presumably because of his age and lack of experience, the boy was not questioned at any length.

The mate, John Saunders of French Street, with '... fourteen years in the company', appeared worried: '...I have not eaten or hardly slept since the accident'. He spoke well of Capt Corke:

> I have known the Captain from a child and have sailed with him ten or eleven years. I never knew him injure anybody or anything, except such as running against a pier, unshipping a bowsprit, or capsizing a figurehead or two. He is very good at handling a steamer, plenty of nerve and all that sort of thing. Generally, he is pretty careful and skilful. I don't think there is anyone in the company his equal as regards skill or care, or his better. He is rather hasty, of course. I am very mild myself, or I should not have stayed so long with him, for it is sometimes almost more than I can manage....'

The mate admitted being on the foredeck immediately prior to

201

the collision, but maintained that the boy had been told to keep a lookout. Only after a series of penetrating questions did he eventually concede that, in his opinion, Capt Corke was to blame for the accident.

Finally, Capt Corke, with 'ten years in the company', gave evidence. He stoutly denied that the 'nut throwing' had occurred. Then, supported by arguments put forward by his father, Capt D. Corke, Snr, superintendent of the Isle of Wight Co, he claimed that on many occasions the master was exempt from responsibility towards his vessel, such as '. . . when he presided at the dinner table with the passengers or was below deck or *otherwise engaged*'. And, further, 'All on board are expected to keep a lookout'.

The whole of the evidence indicated that there was much to be desired regarding lookout duties in the *Medina*. Apparently there were no standing orders concerning this duty, which was often passed on from one crew member to another, without a word being spoken. To seamen, therefore, it seemed that only one conclusion could be drawn and the Shorwell jury, presumably including seamen in their number and possibly influenced by the deaths of their neighbours, decided that Capt Corke Jnr was responsible for the accident and brought in a verdict of 'Guilty of manslaughter'.

The unfortunate captain was then released on a bond of £1,500, secured by his father and the 'Isle of Wight Company' (sic) and had to wait many months for his trial at the next assizes. This took place in February 1854, when he was charged with 'Feloniously killing and slaying William, Jacob and George Warne' and forced to defend himself for the second time. On this occasion, however, he was more fortunate because, after a short retirement, the jury returned a verdict of 'Not Guilty'. Capt David Corke Jnr was soon back in harness and on Coronation Day in June 1854, he commanded the *Medina* on her excursion to Poole.

The fine weather which lasted throughout the summer of 1854 led to numerous excursions taking place. The Ryde steamers were making a daily excursion around the island and it was commented: 'A greater treat than which can scarcely be found in the whole catalogue of steam boats either in this country or on the Continent'. During the first week of September 1854, the *Prince of Wales* made a trip to Shanklin, '... to see the rowing, sailing and the pole dance etc'. On Friday of the same week she visited Bonchurch, '... to view the Flower Show held in the grounds of Dr Leeson' and on the Saturday she made an excursion to Alum Bay. The Ryde steamers charged 3s 6d and 2s 6d for their 'round the island' voyages, which were completed in an average of five hours. Excursions to Alum Bay, the Needles and thence to Swanage were 4s 6d and 3s 6d. In addition, cheap cruises were available: 'Evening cruises through the Fleet at Spithead: main deck 6d; fore deck 4d.'

The Ryde steamers began their excursion season early in 1855, taking sightseers to Spithead in March to witness the departure of the 'Flying Squadron' for the Baltic, and although fares were necessarily increased the boats were well patronised. The steamers from Southampton started excursions in June, offering the prospective passenger: 'A view of the whole coast of the Isle of Wight WHILE ROUNDING THE ISLAND and Also a part of Dorsetshire, with a sojourn at Shanklin'. A first-rate band and the usual cold collations and other refreshments were provided, the fares being 3s and 2s. By this time, the first trip of the season was considered something special, and it was recorded of the *Medina* that: 'A very numerous and respectable party was on board including many of the fair sex who presented the worthy Captain Corke with a magnificent bouquet of the choicest flowers in season.' The same vessel made several excursions to Branksea (sic) Island, near Poole, at 4s 6d return fare, to view the castle, and similar excursions were made to Poole, leaving Southampton at 9.30 am and arriving at Poole at noon, allowing passengers up to three-and-a-half hours on shore.

A veritable armada of pleasure steamers opened the excursion season of 1856 in April and raced to Spithead to see the 'Grand Naval Review', the assembled fleet comprising four squadrons, totalling 160 warships. The excursion vessels included the French *Le Nord*, the *Victoria*, the screw collier *Saxon*, the tugs *Aid* and *Belmont*, and the *Ruby*, the *Gem* and the *Earl of Malmesbury*—passengers being crammed into the latter vessels at 12s 6d a head. A similarly large number of excursion steamers bore down on Netley in May 1856, when Queen Victoria laid the foundation stone of the Royal Victoria Hospital, Netley (demolished in 1967, with the exception of the main tower and chapel below). The Southampton civic dignitaries who attended the stone-laying ceremony later dined on board the *Medina*.

In the July of 1856, Capt D. Corke Jnr was again the victim of misfortune while on excursion in the *Medina*. He had landed a party of 300 at Shanklin when the weather began to thicken during the afternoon and although 5.30 was the sailing time, waiting for stragglers delayed the departure for an hour. No sooner had the *Medina* got under way than the fog closed down and within several minutes, owing to the compass 'being faulty', she ran on to one of the edges of the Culver Rocks, just below the cliffs of the same name. There was no sudden jerk but a low grinding noise which brought the vessel up abruptly, and alarm was further increased when, soon afterwards, the fog cleared a little and the cliffs of Culver could be seen towering overhead. It was decided not to use the one available boat to land the passengers lest it should be overloaded and swamped, added to which the nearby cliffs were almost perpendicular, and therefore, impossible to climb. Attempts to back the vessel off the rocks proved unsuccessful and prospects looked grim until, suddenly, the fog cleared and the *Medina* was sighted by a pilot boat, No 91, which put a pilot on board and stood by until the rising tide enabled the *Medina* to get off the ledge. This was not until 10.0

pm and it was 2.30 in the morning before the *Medina* arrived back at the Royal Pier, Southampton. Subsequent reports referred to 'slight damage', the boiler and engines having been lifted some three inches. Nevertheless, Capt Corke continued in command and was again paddling round the island the following year in the *Medina*.

In June 1858 the tugs *Aid* and *Phoenix* made short excursions from Southampton Town Quay to Hamble, the fare being 1s 6d. The following month, the Ryde steamer *Her Majesty* also nearly came to grief when she ran aground on Ryde Sands while homeward bound with 300 passengers on board. The more timid ones got off in the boats which flocked to the scene and were landed at Ryde and Seaview, but their abandonment was premature because the rising tide soon had *Her Majesty* afloat again. Other excursions the same year included those of the *Solent* from Lymington and Yarmouth to the Needles, and a cross-Channel trip to Cherbourg by the pilot boats *Ranger* from Ryde and *Traveller* from Cowes. Also, the *Atalanta* made an excursion from Southampton to Brighton. During the 1858 season, the Ryde steamers alone made thirty-six trips around the island, the average takings being £15 6s 8d per excursion.

The *Prince of Wales* caused great consternation during an excursion in June 1859 when she went racing callously past the crowded decks of the *Gem* into Cowes Harbour with the decomposing body of a man suspended over her bows. The *Prince* had picked up the corpse off Peel Bank on her way from Ryde.

In July 1859 the *Sir Francis Drake* from Plymouth made several trips round the island from Southampton, and the following month the Hythe steamer *Louisa* joined the excursion fleet which descended on Spithead to see the 'Magnificent Fleets of England and the Russian Empire'. The same day, the South Western steamer *Courrier* sailed to Portland and Weymouth.

A special excursion was made by the *Gem* under the command of Capt Muston in July 1859 when, after calling at Cowes, Ryde and Portsmouth, and steaming through the Channel Fleet which was under sail, she anchored in Stokes Bay opposite the seat of the Baring family. The grounds had been opened for this occasion and the band of the Tipperary Militia was placed at the disposal of the excursionists, who were landed in boats under the supervision of Capt Muston and members of the Stokes Bay Coast Guard. It proved a pleasant outing for everyone, we are assured, apart from the loss of Mr Cifton's 'well-stocked hamper' which fell off the Royal Pier before the trip had begun. The complete absence of smoke from the *Gem*'s funnel throughout the day was said to be the result of the careful application of 'Mr O'Regan's Patent' to her furnaces.

By September 1860 it might seem that pleasure trips had reached the height of popularity, for it was stated that : 'Excursions by water have become part of "Ye manners of the English" ' yet their popularity was to increase still further throughout the Victorian and Edwardian eras, culminating in the peak pre-Second World War period. These steam vessel excursions round the island, which had started in 1823 when the *Medina* had paddled valiantly around, '. . . crowded with fashionable persons of both sexes . . .', virtually ceased in 1968 and the 145-year-old cry which had resounded along the piers and quays of Southampton, Portsmouth, Lymington and the Isle of Wight during the summer months, 'Any more for round the island?' is heard no more. Occasional excursions round the Isle of Wight have since been made during the summer months, mainly by the MV *Balmoral*, on charter to P. & A. Campbell of Bristol.

CHAPTER NINE

LOCAL STEAMER OWNERS
AND MASTERS

SOUTHAMPTON TO COWES STEAMERS

THE STEAMER service began in 1820 when George Ward and William Fitzhugh placed the *Prince of Cobourg* on passage, followed soon afterwards by the *Medina* and the *Earl of Malmesbury*. Control of these vessels which carried the mails during the summer months, passed to Fitzhugh following Ward's death in 1829. This 'Cowes Line' became known as the Isle of Wight Royal Steam Packet Co.

Meanwhile, in 1826, Sotonians had placed the *George IV* in opposition on the same passage and this 'Southampton Line' was referred to as the Isle of Wight Steam Packet Co. In 1828, however, the two companies began sharing a common timetable, and this 'union of interests' was presumably further strengthened in 1840 when Capt David Corke of the Southampton Line became superintendent of the Cowes Line, the monopoly of the two companies being then threatened by the establishment of the newly-formed but short-lived South Western & Isle of Wight Co. A close union was again suggested in 1857 when the *Emerald* was built 'under the superintendency of both companies'; and in 1858 when the two companies took a lease of the pier at Cowes as a 'United Company'.

It was not until 1861, when the opposition Southampton, Isle of Wight & Portsmouth Improved Steam Boat Co was formed, that the two older companies merged. A committee of management of the two companies was formed on 9 April 1861, but ceased to exist on 10 September 1861, when the new company came into being as the Southampton, Isle of Wight & South of England Royal Mail Steam Packet Co. The combined fleet numbered seven vessels, the *Ruby*, the *Pearl*, the *Queen*, the *Medina*, the *Gem*, the *Emerald*, and the *Sapphire*.

The rival Improved Steam Boat Co, nevertheless, lived up to its title. The new *Lord of the Isles* and *Lady of the Lake* were larger, faster and more comfortable than the steamers of the older companies. The Improved Co, furthermore, intended to dispense with the time-delaying and sometimes dangerous tow boats, replacing them with the *American*, a large beamy vessel specially built for the conveyance of cattle and carriages etc. Floating pontoons were also provided at Southampton and Cowes to facilitate landing and embarkation.

Despite these commendable innovations, however, the new company was unable to weather the competition it had so deliberately sought and within twelve months bankruptcy proceedings had been instigated, the principal creditor being the Thames Iron Works & Shipbuilding Co. The end of the Improved Co came in 1865 when its vessels and assets were acquired by the Southampton, Isle of Wight, & South of England Royal Mail Steam Packet Co, which also bought the West to East Cowes steam ferry *Precursor* in 1867, the Cowes floating bridge in 1868, and East Cowes Pier in 1887.

George Ward (1751-1829), of Northwood House, Cowes, principal owner of the first island steamers, was a London merchant of 'great eminence' when he took up residence in the Isle of Wight in 1793. (Picture, p54.) He was the son of John Ward, who settled in England in 1782 after many years as a merchant in Spain.[1]

Following the death of George Ward in 1829, control of the island steamers passed to William Fitzhugh (1757-1842) of Bannisters Court, Southampton, son of Valentine Fitzhugh who had retired from the Levant Company and settled at Bitterne, Southampton, in 1763.[2] William Fitzhugh was in the service of the East India Company from 1775 to 1791. (Picture, p54.) He was MP for Tiverton from 1804 to 1819; a member of the London & Southampton Branch Railway Committee of 1830; and with George Ward instigated the building of the Royal Pier, Southampton, in 1833. His surviving daughter, Emily (1801-59), launched the *Princess Victoria* in 1833; and his surviving son, William Anthony Fitzhugh (1793-1881),[3] following the death of the father in 1842, became the principal owner of the Southampton steamers and remained as such until 1861 when the present company was formed. He then held the second largest number of shares, the principal shareholder being a local banker, Henry Stanley Robert Pearce of Maddison & Pearce, 172 High Street, Southampton, who had conducted the finances of the Fitzhugh family since the 1820s.

CROSS-CHANNEL STEAMERS

After eleven years of intense rivalry on the Channel passage, the owners of the *Ariadne* and the *Camilla* were forced to unite because the rapidly expanding railway companies, backed by tremendous capital, were spreading their lines across the country and towards the South Coast, seeking, ultimately, steamship ownership. Thus, in 1835, the South of England Steam Navigation Co was formed, its fleet including the *Ariadne*, the *Camilla* —and later the *Monarch* and the *Atalanta*—while shares were also held in the island steamer *George IV*. These vessels were to trade between Southampton, the Isle of Wight, France and the Channel Islands.

A similar company, the British & Foreign Steam Navigation Co, was formed in London in October 1835 but with wider

N

interests—to trade between London and other important ports of the United Kingdom to France, the Channel Islands, Spain, Portugal and the Mediterranean. But this company, whose vessels included the *Calpe*, the *Byron*, the *Watersprite*, the *City of Glasgow*, and *Lady de Saumarez*, was taken over in September 1837 by the Commercial Steam Navigation Co, whose vessels using Southampton included the *Grand Turk*, the *Transit*, the *William IV*, the *Kent*, the *Edinborough Castle*, and the *Robert Burns*. This company lasted less than five years, being 'broken' by railway interests in March 1842 and divided into two new companies—the Commercial Steam Navigation Co with London as its principal port, and the South Western Steam Packet Co based on Southampton. W. J. Chaplin, chairman of the South Western Railway and other directors were on the board of the latter company.

Railway ownership of Southampton cross-Channel services had been sought in order to improve these services and, by competing effectively with those at Dover and Folkestone, to prevent losses on the South Western Line. It was also planned to establish a link across the Channel with the French Railways.[4]

To facilitate this, the South Western Railway loaned £5,000 to the South Western Steam Packet Co in March 1842 and in August 1842 made a further loan of £46,000. The company then added two new ships to its fleet, the *South Western* and the *Wonder*, and set about defeating the rival South of England Co's fleet. It triumphed in November 1844, 'amalgamating' with the South of England Co, and in July 1846 acquired the latter's fleet when the South Western Steam Packet Co was re-formed under the title of the New South Western Steam Packet Co, the board comprising at least ten directors of the South Western Railway.

In August 1848, despite the opposition of steamship owners, the London & South Western Railway obtained Parliamentary permission to hire, buy and build steam vessels for a period of fourteen years and to operate in and out of Weymouth, Poole,

210

Lymington, Southampton, Portsmouth, Gosport, the Channel Islands and Havre and French ports adjacent. And from 1 January 1849, the London & South Western Railway acquired a $13\frac{1}{2}$-year lease of the steam vessels of the New South Western Steam Packet Co.

Finally, in July 1862, following repeal of the Act of Parliament prohibiting railway proprietors from owning steamships and termination of the lease of the New South Western Co's vessels, the latter company, together with its vessels and assets, were acquired by the London & South Western Railway.

The principal owner of the *Camilla* and the *Ariadne* of 1824, and the island steamer *George IV* of 1826, was William Chamberlayne (1761-1829) of Cranbury Park, Winchester and of Weston Grove, Southampton.[5] (Picture, p108.) Originally of Coley Park, Berkshire, he had been given Cranbury Park by a close friend, Thomas Dummer, MP, who died childless in 1791.

PORTSMOUTH STEAMERS

The Portsmouth & Ryde Steam Packet Co was formed in 1825 and by 1850 had placed six steamers in service, the *Arrow*, the *Union*, the *Lord Yarborough*, the *Earl Spencer*, the *Prince Albert* and *Her Majesty*. An opposition company, the Portsmouth & Ryde New Steam Packet Co, known also as the Portsea, Portsmouth & Isle of Wight Steam Boat Co, then began competing on this passage with three steamers, the new *Prince of Wales* and *Princess Royal* and the old *Lindsey*. A brief but bloody 'war' lasted until June 1851, when the new company was taken over by the old under the title of The Port of Portsmouth & Ryde United Steam Packet Co and the fleet increased by the addition of four more vessels, the *Prince Consort*, the *Princess of Wales*, the *Duke of Edinborough* and the *Princess Alice*.

A second war of opposition developed on this passage in 1873 when the Southsea & Isle of Wight Steam Ferry Co was formed, placing four new screw steamers in service, the *Ryde*, the

Shanklin, the *Ventnor* and the *Southsea*. The 'United' replied with two new screw steamers, the *Princess Louise* and the *Princess Beatrice*, and although these were in use for only a brief period, they finally defeated the rival company in 1876, and acquired its four steamers, which were later sold and dispersed around the coast.

However, despite the 'United's' efforts to keep up with the times—including buying the large but old *Heather Belle* in 1876 and building the *Albert Edward* in 1878 and the *Alexandra* in 1879—the service failed to meet the requirements of an ever increasing and demanding public and in 1880 it was acquired jointly by the London & South Western Railway and the London, Brighton & South Coast Railway. This 'joint' fleet was taken over by the Southern Railway in 1923.

One of the earliest pioneers among Ryde steamer owners was George Player of Ryde House, who died in 1843.[6] (Picture, p108.) His youngest daughter, Marie Jane, christened the *Earl Spencer* in 1833, and his sister, Elizabeth Lydia, married John Lind, MD, of Ryde. Their son, John Player Lind, MD, was a registered owner of the *Prince Albert* of 1847, and chairman of the Portsmouth & Ryde Steam Packet Co in 1850.

Another pioneer was Richard William Ford (1822-1900), 'honorary secretary of the 'New' company in 1850, and a prominent citizen of Portsmouth.[7] The second son of Henry Ford of Portsmouth and Waterlooville, he became a solicitor in 1843, entering into a partnership with his elder brother, Henry. He played an important part in the development of the 'United' company, being its solicitor and secretary for almost thirty years, until its acquisition in 1880 by the joint railway companies.

LYMINGTON TO YARMOUTH STEAMERS

Charles St Barbe,[8] (1776-1848), Lymington banker and salt-factory owner (picture, p108), was the principal owner of the first Lymington steamer, the *Glasgow*, which commenced in service in June 1830. This vessel was joined by the *Solent* in 1840, when the Solent Sea Co was formed to deal with the expected increase in passenger traffic brought about by the development of railway services to the South Coast. The Solent Sea Co placed the *Red Lion* on the Lymington passage from 1858 to 1880, the *Solent* (II) in 1863, and the *Mayflower* in 1866. The latter two vessels were acquired by the London & South Western Railway in 1884, which then operated the Lymington to Yarmouth service.

HYTHE STEAMERS

The first Hythe steamer, the *Emerald*, was placed on station in 1830 by William Colson Westlake[9] and though the service proved uneconomic, her nuisance value on passage work between Southampton and the Isle of Wight was such that the established steamboat proprietors were obliged to buy her out in 1833.

Capt James Hoskins Knight Snr was the principal owner of the second Hythe steamer, the *Forester* of 1836. But the service was again discontinued as uneconomic in 1840. The third Hythe steamer, the *Gipsy*, was similarly unsuccessful, being in service only from 1845 to 1847.

The first Hythe Steam Ferry Co was formed in 1855, placing the old *Prince Alfred* and the new *Lady Elizabeth* in service. The present company, then known as the Hythe Pier & Hythe and Southampton Steam Ferry Co, was formed in 1874.

STEAMER MASTERS

Capt James Hoskins Knight (1777-1838), who had proposed the introduction of steam vessels on the Southampton to Cowes passage in 1820, was a man of Cowes and master and part-owner of several sailing passage vessels, including the mail packets. He commanded the first two local steamers, the *Prince of Cobourg* and the *Medina* and was master of the latter vessel during her historic voyage to the Channel Islands in 1823. He became superintendent of the Isle of Wight Royal Mail Steam Packet

Co and a director of the South of England Steam Navigation Co. His son, James Hoskins Knight Jnr (1798-1840), also commanded several of the early steamers and succeeded his father as superintendent in 1838.[10]

The third superintendent was Capt David Corke (1797-1866), who was born at Cowes, one of nine children of Capt Edward Corke, the chief harbour pilot of Cowes. David Corke was landlord of the Red Lion Inn, High Street, Cowes (now an off-licence) in the early 1820s and was appointed master of the *George IV* in 1828. He became superintendent of the 'Royal Mail' company in 1840 and, in 1844, was appointed one of the three sub-commissioners of pilotage for Trinity House. Finally, in 1861, when the present Southampton, Isle of Wight, & South of England Royal Mail Steam Packet Co was formed, he became their marine manager. He died in 1866 and in his obituary it was said that 'Whoever writes the biography of Captain David Corke will give the history of local steam navigation.' (Picture, p54)[11] He was succeeded as marine manager by his son, Capt David Corke Jnr (1822-77).

Capt James Corke, brother of David Corke Snr, was formerly landlord of the now defunct Pilot Inn, Cowes High Street. He commanded steamers of the Isle of Wight Steam Packet Co and was a member of the Cowes Local Board until his death in 1873.

Capt James Beazley of Portsmouth, who died in 1833, was one of the principal proprietors of the Portsmouth and Ryde sailing packets. His son, Capt George Beazley, commanded both sail and steam vessels on the Ryde passage during the 1820s. The grandson, Capt George Beazley Jnr, likewise commanded steamers on this passage and in the late 1860s transferred to the Southampton steamers, becoming master of the *Lord of the Isles*. His son, Capt John Beazley, served in the Southampton company and retired in 1914 after forty-three years of service.

Capt John Bazin, the eldest of fourteen children, was born at St Peter's Port, Guernsey, on 7 March 1780 and went to sea at the age of nine with his father, master of the cutter *Three Friends*, trading to France. At the age of eighteen, he commanded the *Agenoria* of 55 tons, and later the cutter *Harry*, his father being part-owner of both vessels. In 1806 he commanded the *Active* and the *Speedy* packets on government service for Sir John Doyle, Lieutenant-General of Guernsey. During his service in the latter vessel, Capt Bazin became extremely religious and in all the vessels he subsequently commanded, swearing, gambling and drinking were not tolerated, sermons, lectures and the distribution of religious tracts being the order of the day. His subsequent interest in steam navigation culminated in his acceptance in 1824 of command of the *Ariadne*. In 1836 he was appointed to superintend the building of the *Atalanta* steam packet at White's yard, Cowes, for the South of England Steam Navigation Co, but he did not live to witness her launching. He died on 12 February 1836 in his fifty-sixth year while attending a temperance meeting at East Cowes.[12] (Picture, p108.)

Capt James Goodridge Snr (1785c-1855), was a descendant —presumably a grandson—of Capt John Goodridge (1710-81c), commander of one His Majesty's packets stationed at Falmouth. Whilst commanding the sailing cutter *Cracker*, trading between Southampton and the Channel Islands during the French Wars, he was captured by the French and suffered a period of imprisonment. He was mate of the *Lord Beresford* in 1824 and master in 1828; later commanding the *Lady de Saumarez* and the *South Western*. His three sons were all seafarers. Capt John Goodridge and Capt William Goodridge each commanded vessels of the South Western Steam Packet Co and the cross-Channel steamers *Morlaix* and *Argyle*. Capt James Goodridge Jnr (1810c-76), however, had the most distinguished career.[13] He commanded the *Liverpool* in 1835, the *Transit* in 1839, and subsequently, the famous *Wonder*, and other steamers of the South Western and New South Western Steam Packet companies.

CHAPTER TEN

SOME SOLENT SHIPBUILDERS

THROUGHOUT the nineteenth century, Southampton's principal shipbuilding firm was that of Day, Summers & Co which had originated in November 1831, when Capt Nathaniel Ogle (inventor and builder of steam carriages and locomotives) and William Alltoft Summers bought the Millbrook Iron Foundry from Alexander Fletcher and John Young. In October 1834 the foundry came under the ownership of Summer, Groves & Day, and in May 1840 the boiler-making and iron-shipbuilding department was moved to a site just below Northam bridge, having a 500ft frontage onto the river Itchen. The engineering and foundry departments, however, remained at Millbrook until June 1849 when the firm, now Summers, Day & Baldock, enlarged and modernised the premises at Northam, '... demolishing that queer, old public house, the Ship and Anchor' but replacing it by a new one of the same name, which remains today.

Summer, Groves & Day built the first iron steamer to be built south of the Thames, the Hythe steamer *Forester* in 1836, about which information is available, but two more built by the same firm, the *Viratio* and the *Rio Doce* have so far escaped the notice of the historian.

The *Viratio*, launched in March 1839, was of 120 tons builder's measure, 113ft overall length and had a hold depth of 7ft. Driven by one 25 hp engine, she was built for ferry work on

216

the Tagus, where she arrived on 12 July 1839. The *Rio Doce,* launched in May 1839, was of 230 tons burthen (136ft x 18ft 6in x 9ft 6in), three-masted and schooner-rigged. Her two engines totalled 60 hp and her paddle wheels were 16½ft in diameter. The *Rio Doce* was built for a company of that name operating sawmills on the Rio Doce in Brazil and reached her destination in August 1840, under the command of Capt John Barnett Humphries, the former master of the 'Matchless Little Steam Packet' *Emerald.*

Charles Day, formerly of the East India Company, who had financed the firm of Summer, Groves & Day, died in 1849 and was succeeded by his son, Charles Arthur Day (1803-92). Charles, however, does not appear to have taken an active interest in the firm, being celebrated instead for his frequent visits to the yard dressed in hunting pink.

W. A. Summers was the hardest-working member of the board and during the 1840s and 1850s particularly, working in conjunction with Andrew Lamb, engineer superintendent of the P & O line, invented, constructed and improved upon, marine engines, boilers and auxiliary equipment, some of which were supplied to vessels of the P & O and the Royal West India Mail Steam Packet Co, later known as the Royal Mail Line.

Many large vessels were built in the Day, Summers yard including, in 1865, the *Allemania* of 2,484 tons for the Hambourg America line. The firm also manufactured and exported many traversing tripod shears with a lifting capacity of up to 180 tons—a form of shear legs with a powerful screw incorporated in the rear leg which had been invented by Metcher, the yard foreman.

A. J. Day, the last member of this family to have control of the company, died in 1923 and three years later, the yards and assets of Day, Summers & Co were acquired by John I. Thornycroft & Co. Charles Day's great-grandson, Group Captain Harry

Melville Arbuthnot Day, G.C., D.S.O., O.B.E., R.A.F. (ret'd) or 'Wings Day' was a leading planner behind the mass breakout of the World War II prison camp, Stalag Luft III, Germany. His great-uncle, Capt George Fiott Day, V.C., C.B., R.N., was awarded his V.C. in the Crimea War.

COWES SHIPBUILDERS

Although the first two steam vessels built in Cowes were built by Lynn Ratsey—he died in August 1830 and was succeeded by his son, Michael—the principal local shipbuilder during the early part of the nineteenth century was Thomas White (died 1859). He had already established a considerable reputation as a builder of fast sailing craft at Kent prior to his acquisition of Nye's yard, Cowes in 1803. His son by his first marriage, Joseph, acquired a yard at East Cowes but he was adjudged bankrupt in 1854 and his yard was taken over by his half-brothers, John and Robert, already ensconced at their father's yard.

Early records of this family's shipbuilding activities have not survived the years, with the possible exception of those which, together with some coins and several copies of the Isle of Wight magazine, *The Wanderer,* were buried under the foundation stone of the steam frigate dock, opened in July 1844. This dock was extended in 1853 and filled in during 1889.

From 1803 onwards an immense variety of craft came down the slipways of White's yard: small trading vessels and yachts, West and East Indiamen, naval brigs and clippers, large steam vessels for the Turkish Navy and mail steamers for the P & O and Royal Mail lines. The famous lifeboat designed by Andrew Lamb and John & Robert White in the 1850s was, however, the key to the later success of the company, John Samuel White Ltd, for this was the forerunner from which developed the fast and manoeuvrable torpedo-boats and destroyers of the two world wars which made the name of Whites famous among the navies of the world. A silver model of the Lamb & White lifeboat is on exhibition in Cowes Maritime Museum. In 1965, after almost 162 years of shipbuilding, the yards of J. Samuel White Ltd were closed down.

APPENDIX 1: SOLENT STEAMER FLEET RECORDS

NOTE: *Ships are listed in chronological order of their arrival in the Solent*

SOUTHAMPTON-COWES STEAMERS

Built Acq'd Disp'd	Name	Builders & Engines	Type	Length-Beam-Depth	Tons	H.P.	Remarks
1817 1820 1826	*Prince of Cobourg*	Gainsbro' Lincs	Wood P.S.	76′ 11″ × 14′ 4½″ × 5′ 10″	52 & 58/94	24	1826 off passage. 'Hulked' in Southampton.
1814 1821 1821	*Thames* ex-*Argyle*	Glasgow	Wood P.S.	76′ 6″ × 14′ 5″ × 6′ 6″	49 & 67/94	14	1821 summer season only. So'ton/ Cowes/Portsm'th.
1822 1822 1848c	*Medina* O.N. 4696	L. Ratsey Cowes Millbrook?	Wood P.S.	85′ 9″ × 18′ 9″ × 9′ 10½″	84 & 58/94 (1842.42.8 Reg)	36	1823 1st steamer into Guernsey. 1st S.P. Round the Island. Occ'l So'ton/Havre. 1852 to Liverpool. 1873 to Ardrossan. Converted to sail. 1880 lost at sea.
1825 1825 1856	*Earl of Malmesbury* O.N. 13361	L. Ratsey Cowes Millbrook?	Wood P.S.	77′ 9″ × 17′ × 9′ 10″	64 & 84/94 (1842.48.6 Reg)	36	1856 sold Plymouth. 1858 50 hp (2 engs). 1885 'No trace'. (Scroll Figue & 50 hp in1856)
1826 1826 1853	*George IV*	W. Evans Rotherhithe, London	Wood P.S.	95′ × 16′ × 8′ 3″ 100′ (1843)	60 & 11/94 (1843 : 47 Reg)	56	Occ'l So'ton/Havre. 1853 broken up. (One engine.)
1830	*Duke of*	J. White	Wood	72′ 4″ × 12′ 10″ × 8′	38 &	15	1859 to Falmouth—tug.

Years	Name / O.N.	Builder	Type	Dimensions	Tonnage	H.P.	History
1855 1844	*Victoria*	Day, Summers			30 ton		1850 broken up.
1840 1840 1883	*Gem* O.N. 25119	T. White Cowes Day, Summers	Wood P.S.	99.7×14.9×8.2 (1851.+9') Draft 6ft	47.1 Reg 87.0 Gr	42	1861 to I.O.W. Co. (1866. On cargo) 1883 to Pollock and Brown. (£236.) 1884 to Middlesbro'. 1889 broken up.
1840 1841 1872	*Ruby* ex-*Pride of the Waters* O.N. 13862	Day, Summers Southampton " "	Iron P.S.	114.9×16.4×8.1 Draft 4ft 2in	49.5 Reg 103.0 Gr	44	1861 to I.O.W. Co. Last service-cargo. 10.5.1872 sold. £260. 1872 broken up.
1844 1844 1867	*Pearl* O.N. 13863	" "	Iron P.S.	89.8×13.3×7.9 Draft 5ft 6in	32.7 Reg 64.0 Gr	26	1861 to I.O.W. Co. 1867 to Bournemouth— £150. 1872 broken up.
1848 1848 1876	*Queen* O.N. 13865	" "	Iron P.S.	117.1×14×7.5 Draft 5ft 8in	56.2 Reg 93.5 Gr	40	1861 to I.O.W. Co. 1876 sold. £227 10s. 1876 broken up.
1851 1852 1882	*Medina* (2) ex-*Times* O.N. 13860	T. White Cowes Day, Summers	Wood P.S.	120.8×14.9×8.6 Draft 6ft 4in	55.34 Reg 103.5 Gr	56	1861 to I.O.W. Co. 1882 sold. £206. 1883 broken up.
1857 1857 1871	*Emerald* O.N. 22523	Day, Summers Southampton " "	Iron P.S.	105×14.1×8.1 Draft 5ft	43 Reg 69 Gr o.s.c.	32	1861 to I.O.W. Co. 1871 sold. £1,000. 1871 to Spain.
1860 1860 1873	*Sapphire* O.N. 29130	" "	Iron P.S.	120.3×14.5×7.5 Draft 5ft 6in	51 Reg 82 Gr	40	1861 to I.O.W. Co. 1873 sold. £1,600. 1873 to Spain.

Built Acq'd Disp'd	Name	Builders & Engines	Type	Length–Beam–Depth	Tons	H.P.	Remarks
1861 1861 1889	*Lord of The Isles* O.N.29100	Thames Iron Works J. Stewart	Iron P.S.	135.5×18×7 Draft 4ft 6in	91.5 Reg 123 Gr	60	Improved S.B. Co. 1865 to I.O.W. Co. Oct 1883 cargo. Oct 1889 sold. £115 10s
1861 1861 1887	*Lady of The Lake* O.N. 43772	Thames Iron Works J. Stewart	Iron P.S.	147.6×17.9×7.6 Draft 4ft 6in	104 Reg 142 Gr	60	Improved S.B. Co 1865 to I.O.W. Co. Dec. 1882 cargo. Oct. 1887 sold. £103.
1861 1861 1868	*American* O.N. 29885	Muntze, Millbrook ,, ,,	Iron P.S.	130.3×25.5×8.5	173.7 Gr	80	Improved S.B. Co. 1868 sold. To London. 1870, sold foreign.
1866 1866 1911	*Vectis* O.N. 56125	J. White, Cowes	Wood P.S.	140.7×18.2×8.2 (Draft 5ft 9in laden.)	122 Gr	60	I.O.W. Co. 1st steamer built for company. 1887 re-engined by Day, Summers & Co. 1887 cargo. 1910 sold to Pollock & Brown for breaking (1911).

(Comp diagonal engines. 24″ & 40″–36″ stroke.)

SOLENT CROSS-CHANNEL STEAMERS

Built Acq'd Disp'd	Name	Builders & Engines	Type	Length–Beam–Depth	Tons	H.P.	Remarks
1822 1823	*Medina* O.N. 4696	L. Ratsey Cowes Millbrook ?	Wood P.S.	85′9″×18′9″×9′10½″	64 & 58/94	40	I.O.W. Steamer. 1st st.vl. into Guernsey, June 1823 May 1824, So'ton/Havre
1824 1824 1853	*Camilla*	W. Evans Rotherhithe	Wood P.S.	107′10″×17′10″×10′ (120′6″ in 1833) (122&17/94T. in 1833)	101 & 68/94 Full 172 tons	60	1824 Chamberlayne & Co 1836 S.O.E. Co. 1846 New S.W. S.P. Co. 1853 broken up.

Dates	Name	Builder	Hull	Dimensions	Tonnage	History
1852c				(138&6/94T. in 1832)	Full 197 tons; 70	1847 New S.W. S.P. Co. 1852c broken up.
1824 1824 1843	*Lord Beresford* O.N. 3942	W. Scott & Sons, Bristol	Wood P.S.	100'×18' 2"×11' 9" (117'11" in 1832) (117 Tons in 1832)	81 & 17/94	1824 Jersey-owned. 1843 to Bristol. 1863 broken up.
18?? 1824	*Earl of Liverpool*		Wood P.S.			1824 Gen. Steam Nav. Co. So'ton to Chan. Islands.
1823 1826 1862	*Sir Francis Drake*	Plymouth	Wood P.S.	103' 8"×18' 8"×11' (1836) 113·2×16·8×10·9 (1848) 124×16·8×10·9	118 & 100 93; 70	1826 Plymouth-Portsmouth-Channel Islands. 1862 sold London.
1822 1827 1827	*St David*	Liverpool	Wood P.S.	78' 11"×15' 6"×7' 4"	180; 76	1827 only, James Weeks & Co. So'ton-Havre. 1860 converted sail. 1872 foundered.
1822 1828 1830	*George IV*	Hilhouse & Sons. Bristol	Wood P.S.	109' 6"×20' 4"×11' 2"	180; Reg 126 tons; 64	1828 from Bristol. S'ton-Havre; Jas. Weeks & Co. 1830 to Bristol. 1839 broken up.
1823 1829 1830	*Bristol*	Bristol	Wood P.S.	90' 2"×16' 2"×9' 7" (1828) 100' 7"	130; 60	Ex-Bristol & Glamorgan S.P. Co. So'ton-Channel Is. 1830 to Bristol.
1825 1825 1827	*Brunswick*	Rotherhithe	Wood P.S.	128' 6"×21'×10' 6"	218; 100	1826 Plymth/Portsmth. 1856 Liverpool. 1857 sold foreign.
1831 1831 1833	*Lord of The Isles*		Wood P.S.	145' 6"×22'×12' 11"	345; 120	London Jersey&G'nsy S.P. Co. London-Chan. Is. So'ton-Chan. Is. 1833, to Portugal.

Built Acq'd Disp'd	Name	Builders & Engines	Type	Length-Beam-Depth	Tons	H.P.	Remarks
1823 1831 1831	Superb		Wood P.S.		350	100	G.S.N. Co. So'ton/Chan Is. So'ton-Plymouth-Bordeaux.
1832 1834 1835	Apollo	Hunter & Dow Glasgow	Wood P.S.	131' 2" × 16' 1½" × 9' 1"	104 & 37/94	100	Ex-Glasgow. 1834 Apollo S.P. Co.; 1835 to London; 1836 Brit. & For. Co.; 1837 Comm. Co.; 1837 snk, Thames.
18?? 1835	Isle of Guernsey		Wood P.S.		500	180	London-Chan. Is. So'ton-Chan. Is. 1835 only.
1830 1835 1835	Liverpool	R. Steel & Co.	Wood P.S.	136' × 22' × 14' 8"	500	180	Ex-Glasgow S.P. Co. 1835. So'ton-Chan. Is. 1835, to P.&.O.?
18?? 1835 1837	Lord Byron		Wood P.S.				1835 British & Foreign Co. So'ton-Chan. Is. Comm. Co.
1835 1835 1849c	Lady de Saumarez (Samaurez)	H. Wimshurst Millwall Seaward	Wood P.S.	127.2 × 20 × 12.8	Reg 157.1 Full 254	90	Brit. & Foreign Co. 1837 Comm. Co.; 1846 New S.W. Co.; 1849c broken up.
1836 1836 1864c	Atalanta O.N. 13805	White, Cowes, Maudslay	Wood P.S.	142 × 22.4 × 12.7 (160 in 1851)	Full 311 Reg 161.9	120	S.O.E. Co.; 1846 New S.W. Co.; August 1869 'hulked' in Jersey; 1893c broken up.
1837 1837	Monarch O.N. 13975	Rubie & Blaker, So'ton.	Wood P.S.	142 × 23.8 × 11.7	Full 314	120	S.O.E. Co.; 1846 Nw S.W. Co.; 1849 converted 'sail' to New

Dates	Name	Builder	Type	Dimensions	Tonnage	Notes
1837 1869	O.N.13813	...n & Mare Maudslay	P.S.		Reg. 160.	Comm. Co.; 1846 disposed; (Orig. London-Gibraltar.) 1855 hulked Southampton. 1869 broken up.
1832 1837 1842	*City of Glasgow*	J. Scott & Sons Greenock	Wood P.S.	120×20·5×11·2	218 120	Brit. & For. Co.; 1837 Comm. Co.; So'ton-Chan. Is; So'ton-London. '8 knots, laden—when calm'
1835 1837 1849c	*Calpe*	McGhie & Hawks Rotherhithe	Wood P.S.	125·4×19·5×12·8	Full 259 120 Reg 157	Brit. & For. Co.; 1837 Comm. Co.; New S.W. S.P. Co.; Weymouth & So'ton—Havre. (Orig. London-Gib.)
1837 1837 1856	*Grand Turk*	R. Duncan & Co. Greenock Murdoch Aiken & Co.	Wood P.S.	135·3×20·2×13	Full 369 150 Reg 243	Comm. Co.; New S.W. Co.; 1849 to Mediterranean. 1851 So'ton-Havre. 1856 broken up.
1835 1837 1846	*Robert Burns*	R. Duncan & Co. D. Napier	Wood P.S.	132·1×19·4×10·5	Full 309·4 80 Reg 184·7	Ex-Largo, Millport & Ayr service. Comm. Co; S.W. Co; 1853 broken up
1842 1842	*Duchess of Kent*		Wood P.S.			S.W. Co.; So'ton-Chan. Islands.
1842 1842 ?	*Prince of Wales*		Wood P.S.		Full '700' 260	S.W. Co.;So'ton-Havre. 'Similar to L'pool-Glasgow *Princess Royal*'
1835 1842 1843	*Princess Victoria*	Blackwall	Wood P.S.		100	S.W. Co.; So'ton-Bordeaux. 1843 sold.

O

SOLENT CROSS-CHANNEL STEAMERS

Built Acq'd Disp'd	Name	Builders & Engines	Type	Length-Beam-Depth	Tons	H.P.	Remarks
1843 1843 1863	South Western O.N. 13839	Ditchburn & Mare Seaward	Iron	145·4 × 18·7 × 9·8	Full 204 Reg 132	80	S.W. Co.; So'ton–Havre; So'ton–Chan. Is.; 1865 sold Shanghai—paddles removed—sailed out. 1866–67. Employed on Hong Kong–China coast–Manila passage.
1844 1844 1874	Wonder O.N. 13825	Ditchburn & Mare Seaward & Capel	Iron P.S.	158 × 20·6 × 10·1	Reg 168·5 Full 350	140	9.1.1874 broken up.
1847 1847 1859	Express	Ditchburn & Mare Maudslay	Iron P.S.	159 × 21·4 × 10·4 Two funnels	Reg 170 Full 378	180	On lines of the Wonder. 1859 wrecked, S.W. Jersey coast.
1847 1847 1874	Courier O.N. 13814	Ditchburn & Mare Maudslay	Iron P.S.	167 × 22·5 × 10·8 Two funnels	Reg 147 Full 423	200	11.2.1875 broken up.
1847 1847 1885	Dispatch O.N. 13819	Ditchburn & Mare Maudslay	Iron P.S.	166·7 × 22·1 × 11·6 Two funnels	Gross 423 Reg 149·2	200	'Sister to Courier'. 1885 'hulked'. 1890 broken up.
1855 1855	Alliance O.N. 25115	Ditchburn & Mare	Iron P.S.	175·5 × 23·7 × 14·6 Two funnels	Gross 473	225	1878 re-engined by Day, Summer & Co.; re-boilered

				Dimensions (Keel 171' 2¼")	Tonnage	H.P.	Remarks
1875		Seaward			Net Reg 200		Channel Is.
1860 1860 1888	*Southampton* O.N. 28109	Palmer Bros Newcastle	Iron P.S.	215.5×25.4×12.9 (236.1 in 1880) Orig two funnels	Gross 650 200 Net Reg 299 (250)		1890 re-engined by Day, Summers & Co.; sold Holland 1898.

PORTSMOUTH-RYDE STEAMERS

					Tonnage	H.P.	Remarks
1822 1825 1857	*Union*	W. Evans Rotherhithe	Wood P.S.	76×12' 2"×8'	36 & 29/94	16	Originally registered in Dover. 1857 converted to sail, 3-masted schooner. 1863 broken up.
1823 1825 1833	*Arrow*	J. Lang of Dumbarton	Wood P.S.	92' 8"×11' 11"×7' 7"	46 & 29/94	30	1833 broken up.
1826 1826 1852	*Lord Yarborough* O.N. 5669	D. List Fishbourne I.O.W.	Wood P.S.	81' 7"×14' 4"×9' 5"	47 & 14/94	30	1852 sold to Robert Vivian, coal merchant, Plymouth. 1863 broken up.
1833 1833 1853	*Earl Spencer*	B. Denham Ryde	Wood P.S.	77'×13' 8"×8'	37 & 67/94	24	1855 sold to Liverpool.
1847 1847 1871	*Prince Albert* O.N. 19685	G. & J. Inman of Lymington	Wood P.S.	96'×12' 4"×8'	46 & 9/3500	20	1871 broken up. (Oscillating engines.)
1850 1850 1878	*Prince of Wales* O.N. 19684	J. White Cowes Summers & Co.	Wood P.S.	107·6×13·2×8·3	57	40	New company. 1851 to the United Co. 1878 broken up.

Built Acq'd Disp'd	Name	Builders & Engines	Type	Length-Beam-Depth	Tons	H.P.	Remarks
1850 1850 1878	*Princess Royal* O.N. 19687	J. White Cowes Summers & Co.	Wood P.S.	„ „ „	„	„	„ „
18?? 1850 1850	*Lindsey*	?	Wood P.S.	?	?	?	New company. In service for brief spell only.
1850 1850 1879	*Her Majesty* O.N. 19683	Robinson & Russel, Millwall	Iron P.S.	129·1 × 14 × 7.2	66 & 1424/ 3500	50	Old company. 1879 broken up.
1859 1859 1882	*Prince Consort* O.N. 27721	J. Scott Russel, Millwall	Iron P.S.	154·5 × 15·1 × 6·7	103·77 Gross	60	1880 to 'Joint' Fleet. 1882 broken up.
1865 1865 1889	*Princess of Wales* O.N. 48894	Lewis & Stockwell, London J. Watt, Birmingham	Iron P.S.	140 × 16 × 6·9 (152 in 1870)	100·47 Gross	50 osc	1880 to 'Joint' Fleet. 1889 hulked.
1869 1869 1883	*Duke of Edinborough* O.N. 62171	Money Wigram & Co. Blackwall	Iron P.S.	136·2 × 14·1 × 7	95·24 Gross	50 osc	1880 to 'Joint' Fleet. 1884 broken up.
1869	*Princess*	„	Iron	„ „ „	94·48	50	1880 to 'Joint' Fleet.

Years	Name & O.N.	Builder	Construction	Dimensions	Tonnage	H.P.	Notes
18?3 1873 1879	Ryde O.N. 68561	J. White, Cowes Plenty & Son, Newbury, Berks.	Wood Screw	99·4×16·7×7·1	59·15 Gross	30	1876 to United Co. 1879 to Barrow-in-Furness. 1882 to Berwick. 1884 to Granton.
1873 1873 1880	Shanklin O.N.68558	„ „	Wood Screw	99·2×16·4×7·1	53·04 Gross	30	1876 to United Co. 1880 London S.B. Co. 1883 to Inverness.
1873 1873 1880	Ventnor O.N. 68557	„ „	Wood Screw	90×16·1×7·3	50·95	20	1876 to United Co. 1880 London S.B. Co. 1884 to Sunderland.
1873 1873 1879	Southsea O.N. 68568	J. White, Cowes. Plenty & Son, Newbury, Berks.	Wood Screw	97×15·8×6·8	70·53 Gross	35	1876 to United Co. 1879 to Inverness and re-named *Rosehaugh*.

PORTSMOUTH-RYDE STEAMERS

Years	Name & O.N.	Builder	Construction	Dimensions	Tonnage	H.P.	Notes
1873 1873 1874	Princess Louise O.N. 68559	Lewis & Stock- well, Blackwall. J. & A. Blythe.	Iron Screw	103·6×17×6·6	110·97 Gross	40	1874 Nov, to Grimsby and re-named *Jennie*.
1874 1874 1874	Princess Beatrice O.N. 68567	„ „	„	„ „ „	99·38 Gross	44	1874, 2 months in use, sold to A. Blyth of Harrow; thence sold to Martinique.
1871 1876 1900	Heather Belle O.N. 60624	Blackwood & Gordon, Glasgow	Iron P.S.	207·7×21×8·8	267·61 Gross	150	Ex-Ardrossan/Arran. 1880 to 'Joint' Fleet. 1900 to S. Coast & Continental Co. of London. Register closed 1903.
1878 1878 1893	Albert Edward O.N. 76914	Oswald, Mordaunt & Co., So'ton	Iron P.S.	169·4×20·5×9	268·86 Gross	120	1880 to 'Joint' Fleet. 1893 to D. MacBrayne, Glasgow. Re-named *Carabinier*.

PORTSMOUTH-RYDE STEAMERS

Built Acq'd Disp'd	Name	Builders & Engines	Type	Length-Beam-Depth	Tons	H.P.	Remarks
1879 1879 1913	Alexandra O.N. 81004	Scott & Co., Greenock	,,	171 × 20·2 × 8·5	234·74 Gross	120	1880 to 'Joint' Fleet. 1913 to Bembridge & Sea View S.S. Co. of Portsmouth. 1915 to Cosens, Weymouth. (Later Show Boat on River Thames.) 1934 broken up.
1881 1881 1899	Victoria O.N. 84238	Aitken & Mansel, Glasgow. P.S. D. Rowan ,,	Steel	191·1 × 25·1 × 8·6	361·46 Gross	160	1899 sold, Holland.
1884 1884 1910	Duchess of Edinborough O.N. 87432	Aitken & Mansel J. & J. Thompson, Glasgow	Steel P.S.	190·6 × 26 × 8·8	342·9	200	1910 sold, Holland.
1884 1884 1910	Duchess of Connaught O.N. 87437	,, ,,	Steel P.S.	190·6 × 26 × 8·8	342·9	200	1910 sold, Holland.
				LYMINGTON-YARMOUTH STEAMERS			
1828 1830 1852	Glasgow	Stephen Wood, at South Shore, Gateshead	Wood P.S.	52' 10" × 13' 4" × 7' 4" (58' 9" in 1831)	26 & 84/94 17 Reg. Net 51 Gr	16	1841 to Solent Sea Co.
1841 1841 1861	Solent O.N. 16616	Day, Summers ,, ,,	Iron P.S.	84' 4" × 13' × 7' 7¼"	34 Reg 61 Gr	15	Solent Sea Co. (Later 25 hp.)
1856	Red Lion	Thorburn &	Wood	76·8 × 15·7 × 8·3	54 Gr	29	Ex-Admiralty.

Dates	Name / O.N.	Builder	Type	Dimensions	Tonnage	H.P.	Notes
1863 1863 1901	Solent (II) O.N. 44913	Inman of Lymington. Day, Summers	Wood P.S.	83.4×13.6×7.1	61 Gr	32	Solent Sea Co. 1884 to L.S.W.R. £1,250. 1901 sold Holland.
1866 1866 **1905**	Mayflower O.N. 51300	Marshall Bros., Newcastle	Iron P.S.	98.3×15.7×6.8	69 Gr	40	Solent Sea Co. 1884 to L.S.W.R. 1905 sold to J. Constant, London. 1912 broken up.

HYTHE STEAMERS

Dates	Name / O.N.	Builder	Type	Dimensions	Tonnage	H.P.	Notes
1830 1830 1833	Emerald	J. Rubie, So'ton. Millbrook?	Wood P.S.	63×10×7	21 & 78/94	10	Occ'l So'ton/Cowes. 1833 to I.O.W. Co. 1844 broken up.
1836 1836 1840	Forester	Day, Summers ,, ,,	Iron P.S.	65.4×10×5.9	20 Reg	6	1st iron steam boat built south of Thames. 1847 broken up.
1845 1845 1847	Gipsy O.N. 5722	,, ,, ,, ,, ,, ,,	Iron P.S.	73.8×11.1×5.1	20.5 Reg	16	1850 to London. 1855 to Plymouth. (22 hp.) 1870 broken up.
1846 1856 1863	Prince Alfred O.N. 9449	Frindsbury, Near Chatham	Wood P.S.	70.4×11.7×5.4	19.25 Reg 30.53 Gr	20	Hythe Steam Ferry Co. (1st). 1863 broken up.
1856 1856 1858	Lady Elizabeth O.N. 18151	Day, Summers ,, ,,	Iron P.S.	98×13.9×6.5	36.9 Reg 58 Gr	28	Hythe Steam Ferry Co. (1st). 1858 to Ipswich.
1858 1858 1895	Louisa O.N. 22538	Hodgkinson, Cross House, So'ton	Iron P.S.	79.8×12.4×5.6	23.2 Reg 36.8 Gr	20	Hythe Steam Ferry Co. (1st). Bow rudder 11 knots. 1895 converted to barge.
1863 1863 1897	Frederica O.N. 44904	Day, Summers ,, ,,	Iron P.S.	80.4×12.1×5.6	21 Reg 24.5 Gr	16	1897 broken up.

Recorded c1875

	Wonder (1844)	*Courrier* (1847)	*Dispatch* (1847)
Holds, tons	2	3	3
Capacity	88	190	150
Draft	9·0		
Light ft	7·0	9·6	9·6
Laden ft		7·0	7·0
Height			
'Tween Dks	6·5	7·0	7·0
Lower Hold	4·2	4·8 Aft	4.8 Aft
		3·0 For'd	3.0 For'd
Coal			
Tons, Bunkers	20·0	31·0	34·0
Consumption			
(cwt/hr)	13·5	13·0	13
Knots	12·5	12·0	13
Passengers	217	265 Summer	272 Summer
		213 Winter	229 Winter
Berths, 1st	42	45	61
,, 2nd	8	14	44
St'rage	—	—	—
Accommodation			
Officers	(Mate, Forecabin)	Deck	Deck
Crew	Fo'c'sle	Fo'c'sle	Fo'c'sle
Decked	Poop	Poop	Poop
Cabins on deck	Nil	Nil	One
			9ft × 7ft
Hatches	Two—	?	Three—
	5·6 × 4.0		5 × 5
	? × 4.0		6·6 × 6·1
			6·8 × 6·0
Engines	3 atmosph (Seaward)	2 annular (Maudslay)	2 annular (Maudsla'
Cyl diam	54in	61in outside	61in outside
Stroke	3ft 6in	28¾in trunk	28¾in trunk
Paddle wheel			
diameter	18ft	18·9ft	18·9ft
R.P.M.	36	26	27½
I.H.P.	437·5	700	700
Boilers	1	1	1
Pressure	18lb psi	18lb psi	20lb psi
Donkey Eng's	1	1	1
Winches	2 common	2 common	2 steam
Water Tanks	1	2	2
Capacity	200 gallons	300 gallons	300 gallons

	Alliance (1855)	*Havre* (1856)	*Southampton* (1860)
Holds, tons	2	2	2
Capacity	208	207	242
Draft			
Light ft	11·0	11·0	11·0
Laden ft	9·6	9·6	10·0
Height			
'Tween Dks	6·8	7·0	7·1
Lower hold	6·0	6·0	7·6 Aft
			5·3 For'd
Coal			
Tons, Bunkers	27	48	50
Consumption			
(cwt/hr)	22·5	25·5	35
Knots	13·0	13·5	13·25
Passengers	360 Summer	387 Summer	420 summer
	300 Winter	320 Winter	373 winter
Berths, 1st	113	78	108
„ 2nd	36	28	33
St'rage	18	18	16
Accommodation			
Officers	Deck	Deck	Mate (Fo'c'sle)
Crew	Fo'c'sle	Fo'c'sle	Fo'c'sle
Decked	Flush	Flush	Poop
Cabins on	Two—	Three—	?
deck	8×6	8×6	
Hatches	Two—	Two—	?
	6×5·1	6·2×5·1	
	5·9×5·1	?	
Engines	3 atmosph (Seaward)	3 atmosph (Seaward)	2 oscillating
Cyl diam	62in	62in	60in (Palmer)
Stroke	4ft 6in	4ft 6in	5ft
Paddle wheel			
diameter	21·6ft	21·4ft	22·0ft
R.P.M.	27	28½	27
I.H.P.	787·5	787·5	1,000
Boilers (tublr)	1	2	4
Pressure	18lb psi	16lb psi	20lb psi
Donkey Eng's	2	2	2
Winches	2 steam	2 steam	2 steam
Water tanks	1	2	2
Capacity	500 gallons	400 gallons	400 gallons

Ivanhoe: (Capt William Comben, died at Weymouth in 1841, aged 61.) 158 tons, 60 hp; 102ft 3in x 18ft 4in x 11ft 2in. Built in 1820 by J. Scott, Greenock. Acquired in 1821 by the Government and based at Holyhead before being transferred to Weymouth in 1827. In 1837, transferred to London and renamed *Boxer*.

Watersprite: (Capt Frederick White, died at Guernsey in 1834, aged 52.) 162 tons, 60 hp. Built in 1826 at Harwich, 107ft x 17ft 6in x 11ft 8in. First steamer to carry mail from Weymouth to the Channel Islands. Renamed *Wildfire* in 1837. Broken up in 1888.

Meteor: (Capt Connor). 190 tons, 60 hp. Built in 1821 by William Evans, Rotherhithe. Wrecked at Portland, 1830.

Flamer: (Capt Liveing). 165 tons, 60 hp. Built in 1831 by Fletcher & Farnell, Limehouse, 111ft x 17ft x 11ft 4in. Renamed *Fearless* in 1837 and employed as a survey vessel. In August 1843, embarked Queen Victoria at the Royal Pier, Southampton, for transfer to the royal yacht. In 1844, employed in a survey of Southampton Water under Lieut (later, Admiral) W. L. Sherringham, RN.

Dasher: (Capt Robert White, who entered the mail-packet service in July 1817, when promoted from mate in the Admiralty cruiser *Greyhound* to command of the *Countess of Liverpool*, which was employed on the Weymouth station for seven years.) 275 tons, 100 hp; 120ft x 21ft 8in x 13ft 6in. Built in 1838 at Chatham. First steam vessel built for the Admiralty mail-packet service on the Weymouth station. In 1851, employed on Fishery Protection duties. Broken up, 1855.

Cinderella: 234 tons, 80 hp; 119ft 6in x 19ft 8in x 12ft 6in. Built in 1824 at London. Renamed *Cuckoo* in 1837. Engaged in Fishery Protection from 1847 to 1850. In May 1850 was wrecked in Jersey Harbour under the command of Capt Dumeresque, but was subsequently salvaged.

WEYMOUTH & CHANNEL ISLAND STEAM PACKET CO'S STEAMERS*

Aquila: Built 1854 by J. Henderson & Sons, Renfrew. Oscillating engines by MacNabb & Clark, Greenock. 243 tons register; 180.4ft x 21ft x 10ft 9in; two-masted and schooner-rigged; elliptical stern; 'eagle' head, 2 x 110 hp. Acquired by the Plymouth, Channel Islands & Brittany Steam Packet Co in August 1889 and based in Guernsey. In 1896, transferred to Swansea and renamed *Alexandra*. In 1897 acquired by the Hastings & St Leonards & Eastbourne Steam Ship Co and renamed *Ruby*.

Cygnus: Official No 17807. Built 1854 by J. Henderson & Sons, Renfrew. Oscillating engines by MacNabb & Clark, Greenock. 227 tons register; 182ft x 21.4ft x 9.7ft; two-masted and schooner-rigged; 'fiddle' head;

elliptical stern; 120 hp. Transferred to London in 1889; to D. MacBrayne in 1891 and renamed *Brigadier*. Later wrecked in the Hebrides.

Brighton: Official No 11918. Built and engined by Palmers of Jarrow in 1857. 269 tons register; 193·5ft x 20·9ft x 10ft; two-masted and schooner-rigged; 'shield' head. Her two oscillating engines, totalling 140 hp, were reconstructed in 1877 by the Thames Iron Works.

Railway and Other Steamers, Duckworth and Langmuir, T. Stephenson & Sons, 1968, p190.

NOTES AND REFERENCES

GENERAL

Considerable material has been drawn from the following:
Southampton Herald (1823-31), *Hampshire Advertiser* (1831-85), *Hampshire Independent* (1835-85), *Hampshire Telegraph* (1817-60), *Hampshire Chronicle* (1800-48), *Southampton Times* (1860-5), *Isle of Wight Observer* (1852-4), *Isle of Wight Times* (1869).

Other sources include: *A History of Cowes*, by E. H. Gooch; *The History of Steam Navigation*, by J. W. Kennedy; *Nautical Magazine*, 1832-49; *The Notary Book of Thomas Ridding, Southampton*; *The Early Channel Island Steamers*, by J. M. David; *English Channel Packet Boats*, by C. Grasemann and G. W. P. MacLachlan; *History of the Southern Railway*, by C. F. Dendy Marshall; *100 Years of Towage, 1833-1933*, by F. C. Bowen; *The First 100 Years*, by G. W. O'Connor; *The Birth of the Steam Boat*, by Spratt; *The London & South Western Railway*, Vol 1, by R. A. Williams; *Ryde Ventilator* 1876-8; and *The Clyde Passenger Steamer*, by Capt James Williamson (1904).

CHAPTER ONE

1. The 1st Earl of Yarborough died at Vigo in 1846 while cruising in his 96-ton yacht *Kestrel*. A conspicuous obelisk, erected by members of the Royal Yacht Squadron and dedicated to him, may be seen today on Culver Down, East Wight.
2. The Medina Hotel, East Cowes, served as a clubhouse for the Yacht Club until 1825 when the Gloster Hotel, West Cowes, was chosen. Cowes Castle was not acquired by the Royal Yacht Squadron until 1855. Prior to this date, the castle was used as a residence for Governors of the Isle of Wight.—(*Memorials of the Royal Yacht Squadron*, by Montague Guest and William B. Boulton, John Murray, 1903.)
3. J. A. Hassell, *A Tour of the Isle of Wight*, 1790.
4. Southampton's first port installations were constructed by the Romans at Bitterne, on the east bank of the river Itchen. Saxon settlements were established on the west bank of the same river, in the vicinity of St Mary's, the port facilities comprising a natural lagoon, which, however, silted up over a period of years. It was not until the ninth and tenth centuries that the new town of Hampton developed on the higher

236

ground of the east bank of the river Test. The first recorded mention of a quay refers to Castle Quay and dates from 1214. The Platform was constructed at the end of the thirteenth century; the West Quay is first mentioned in 1323; and the Water Gate Quay—forerunner of the present Town Quay—is in records dated 1411.—(*The Story of Southampton Harbour*, by E. A. Shillington, G. F. Wilson & Co, 1947; and *A Survey of Southampton and Its Region*, British Association for the Advancement of Science, 1964; and *Historical Perspectives of Southampton*, by L. A. Burgess and H. S. Faircloth, 1954.)

5. The first floating landing-stage or pontoon was erected on the east side of the pier in 1864 and was moved to roughly its present position in 1870, when the head of the pier was extended 60ft and widened 100ft to accommodate the railway station, then under construction. The pier was extensively rebuilt 1891-3 and opened in 1892 by HRH the Duke of Connaught whose mother, Queen Victoria, had opened the new pier fifty-nine years earlier. The Pier Pavilion, built in 1894, was added to in 1922. The railway ceased operating on the pier in 1914. The present pier entrance was built 1929-31.—(*Hants Advertiser*, 15.7.1833, and *Old Southampton Shores*, by J. P. M. Pannell; David & Charles, 1965.)

6. Sailing-packet charges were: Four-wheel carriage, two horses and luggage (horse boat and other boatage included), with or without family; horses above two to be paid for extra at 3s 6d each £1 9s
A family and luggage without carriage or horses.......................... 15s
A wherry or row boat with two men 12s 6d
A vessel for the day without carriage or horses, to and from Southampton £1 1s
Horses, each 4s 6d. Passengers, each 1s.—(*Skelton's Southampton Guide*, 1819.)

7. Marquis Jouffroy d'Abbans (1715-1832), eminent French inventor, mathematician and engineer, member of a distinguished family.—(*Nouvelle Biographie General*, Rosenkilde et Bagger, Copenhagen, 1967.)

8. With a cylinder bore about 2ft in diameter, and a stroke of perhaps 3 or 4ft, the engine was connected to the paddle-wheel shaft crank through side levers, operating at roughly 25-30rpm. The iron boiler was fired by coal and worked at a pressure of about 2-3lb/per sq in and frequently had to be blown out to remove salt deposits left by the steam.

9. *The Birth of the Steam Boat*, H. P. Spratt, 1958.

10. The ship-building Ratsey family is not to be confused with the Ratsey sail-making family. Lynn Ratsey (1764-1830) had a yard close to the southward of Fountain Quay, now called Dinnis's yard. He was succeeded by his son, Michel Ratsey (1797-1870) who, following the death of Thomas White in 1859, became principal yacht builder to the Royal Yacht Squadron. The yard passed out of the family during the lifetime of Michael Edward Ratsey (1831-1915).

11. *Earl of Malmesbury*, 77ft 9in x 17ft x 9ft 10in; 24 hp. In 1837, lengthened 10ft by T. White of Cowes. In 1856 she was transferred to Plymouth and in 1858 was recorded in the Plymouth Customs register as altered from 'Three to two-masted, schooner-rigged'; having two engines of 25 hp each; engine-room length 23ft, tonnage 52; 'Round house re-

moved'; tonnage altered from 83.66 to 59.43 tons; 107.4ft x 17.2ft x 9.7ft, and having a 'scroll head'.

12. A ditty of 1825 referred to Cowes as:
Of all the gay places for yielding delight,
There is none can compare with the famed Isle of Wight,
For here every visitor shortly allows,
That the cream of true pleasure flows freely from Cowes.

Time was when fair winds refusing to blow,
Our boatmen were forced from Southampton to row,
But now thanks to George Ward, although strange it may seem,
Our voyages are done, like potatoes, by steam.

But Cowes is the spot, after all, for delight,
Where 'tis very well known, they've five Days★ to one Knight★★.
May the Yacht Club still thrive and the island be full,
And Cowes never fail to attract Johnny Bull.

★A reference to a Cowes family of five brothers; ★★Master of the *Medina*.

13. *George IV*. In 1840 she received 'a handsome new bow' and in 1843 was registered as lengthened by 5ft and as being of 47.1 tons; engine-room length 35.4ft and of 42.7 tons.
14. *Southampton Herald*, 14.8.1826.
15. The *Duke of Buccleugh* was registered at Penzance in 1861 as of 48.79 tons (77.1ft x 13.3ft x 7.8ft); engine-room length 22.5ft, tonnage 20.47; and two-masted, schooner-rigged.
16. Capt J. H. Knight's house or 'family villa', situated a quarter of a mile outside Cowes, had a large lawn, shrubbery and garden, well stocked with choice trees. The house was described as substantial, having a basement, 'good' kitchen, scullery, cellar and convenient offices. On the ground floor next the entrance was a drawing-room, 18ft long and 14ft wide, communicating by folding doors with a smaller room. There was also a dining-room, breakfast parlour, butler's pantry and w.c. On the top floor were five bedrooms, the main ones having French windows which opened on to a stone terrace, offering extensive views across Cowes and the Solent. In addition, there was a detached coach-house having a stall stable and harness room, with a servants' room and large loft above. This house cannot now be identified but is believed to have been sited in the vicinity of Mill Hill.
17. The *Gem* lost her figurehead and bowsprit in 1851 and in 1853 she was registered as 107.6ft in length. Engine-room length, 38.8ft, tonnage 39.7.

CHAPTER TWO

1. *Hants. Advertiser*, 17.10.1840.
2. *Hants. Advertiser*, 14.11.1840.
3. *Hants. Chronicle*, 21.1.1844.
4. *Hants. Advertiser*, 16.12.1843.

NOTES AND REFERENCES

5. *Hants. Advertiser*, 9.6.1848; *Royal Mail 1839-1939*, by T. A. Bushell, p37.
6. *Hants. Advertiser*, 4.8.1849.
7. The *Medina's* timbers were of English oak: 'the engine beam and outer skin of mahogany; and an inner skin of fir, planked diagonally'. Her two engines, installed in an engine-room 27.6ft in length, were of the direct-acting type (cylinder diameter 32in, stroke 28½in) and drove the 12ft diameter, feathering paddle wheels at 42-44rpm. Each of the paddle wheels had twelve floats, measuring 6 x 2ft, with an immersion float of 2ft 'or just awash'. Her boilers were on the Lamb & Summers patent flue principle, which claimed a vastly reduced fuel consumption. And by way of innovation at this time, she had an auxiliary pumping engine for supplying the boilers when the main engines were stopped.—*Hants. Advertiser*, 7.8.1852.
8. Later, in 1861, it was reported that 'during the 43 years of the company's existence (sic), there has been no fatal accident, except one case when an intoxicated passenger forced himself on the engine'. But, as recorded in Chapter 8, the *Medina* is known to have run down and drowned three fishermen off Atherfield.
9. The *Sapphire* ('114 tons builders' measure' and '120 tons at displacement load line') was fitted with Morgan's patent paddle wheels, 13ft 6in in diameter. On trials, she averaged 12.4 knots with paddle wheels at 46 to 48rpm and boilers, with super-heating apparatus, at 340°.—*Hants. Advertiser*, 7.7.1860, and *Hants. Independent*, 17.8.1860.
10. The present company's house-flag, also incorporated in the cap badge worn by officers and staff—a diagonally quartered flag in red, white, green and blue—is said to symbolise the *Ruby*, the *Pearl*, the *Emerald*, and the *Sapphire*.
11. *Hants. Independent*, 12.10.1861.
12. The *Vectis* was built at the contract price of £19 10s per ton, and 5s per additional ton for copper sheathing and fastening. She was engined by Day, Summers & Co with two compound diagonal engines totalling 60 hp at a cost of £2,550.

CHAPTER THREE

1. Jersey, the largest of the Channel Islands, measures some 12 by 6 miles, lies 122 miles from Southampton and 14 miles from the coast of France. The harbour of the principal port, St Helier, situated at the southern end of the island, consisted originally of a small promontory built in 1700-51. At the close of the eighteenth century, the North Pier was added and in 1822, the South Pier. The harbour was further improved by the building of the Victoria Pier in 1846 and the Albert Pier in 1853.

Guernsey, the westernmost of the Channel Islands, measures 9½ by 6¼ miles, lies 103 miles from Southampton and 26½ miles from Jersey. The principal port and capital, St Peter's Port, situated on the east coast, was originally quite exposed and the construction of a harbour was ordered

239

by King Edward I in 1275. Further building was undertaken 1580-1780 and again in 1836 and in 1850.

2. Le Havre, 104 miles from Southampton and strategically situated at the mouth of the Seine, was formerly known as 'Havre-de-Grace' being named after the Chapel of Notre-Dame-du-Grace, founded in 1509 by Louis XII. Its importance followed its development as a naval port by Francis I to further his warlike schemes against Great Britain. Whereas the oldest dock, Bassin du Roi, dates from 1669, the principal dock of the nineteenth century was the Bassin de L'Eure, built 1846-56 and extending over fifty acres.

3. The *Ariadne* was lengthened to 124ft in 1832 and her tonnage altered to 138.

4. The *Lord Beresford* was lengthened to 117ft 11in in 1832, her tonnage altered to 117 tons, and she was fitted with three masts, schooner-rigged. In 1834 her galleries and one of her masts were removed. She was also fitted with '68 beds'.

5. The *Camilla* was lengthened to 120ft 7in in 1833, her boilers renewed and her tonnage altered to 122. In 1847 one of her three masts was removed.

6. Sailing vessels included *Watersprite* (Page), *Lady Wellington* (Fuszard), and *Nelson* (Wheeler) to Le Havre; and *Aeolus* (Priaulx), *Speedy Packet* (Bedbrook) and *Diligent* (Porter) to the Channel Islands.

7. The *Brunswick*, built in 1825 and fitted with engines developing 100 hp, remained on the south coast until 1855. For twenty of these years she was under the command of Capt Thomas Russell. His successors were Capts William Harvey and H. M. Shapcott. Her latter service was between Southampton, Torquay, Plymouth, Devonport and Falmouth; and Torquay, Plymouth and the Channel Islands.

8. *Sophia Jane*: see *West Country Passenger Steamers*, Grahame Farr, T. Stephenson & Sons, Prescot, 1967, p165.

9. *St David*: dimensions: 78ft 11in x 15ft 6in x 7ft 4in; 76 hp.

10. *George IV*: dimensions: 109ft 6in x 20ft 4in x 11ft 2in; 64 hp. She returned to Bristol in November 1830.

11. Rivalry between the government mail steamers and the privately-owned steamers had commenced after the former went into service. In August 1827 the *Ariadne*, the *Lord Beresford* and the *Sir Francis Drake* refused to vacate their berths in St Helier harbour, which had been previously allocated for the government steamer.—*Early Channel Island Steamers, 1823-1840*, J. M. David.

12. *Early Channel Island Steamers, 1823-1840*, J. M. David.

13. *Jersey Argus*, 9.2.1836.

14. The low fares tempted unsuitable individuals into the main cabin, which led to some disgraceful scenes as drink and dancing and high spirits got the better of some of the passengers in the *Liverpool*. The sleeping arrangements for a full number of passengers in the same vessel— which were probably similar in other vessels—left a lot to be desired, because when all the berths were occupied it was necessary for some individuals to lay mattresses and pillows on the deck of the cabin. This led to arguments between those wishing to sleep and others who wanted

to play cards or drink or dance to the small hours.—*Early Channel Island Steamers, 1823-1840,* J. M. David.

15. Capt Robert Forder, a Sotonian and substantial shareholder in the *Camilla.* Capt Ward, a shareholder in *Camilla* and a Southampton town councillor. W. J. Le Feuvre, mayor of Southampton and a shipping agent. N. M. Priaulx and Joseph Clarke, shipping agents of Southampton. John Rubie, a Southampton shipbuilder who built the first Hythe steamer in 1830, and the cross-Channel steamer *Monarch* in 1836. William Colson Westlake, a Southampton shipowner and grain merchant. Capt J. Bazin, master of the *Ariadne,* and Capt J. H. Knight of the Isle of Wight steamers.

16. The *Kent,* built in 1829 by Baukman of Gravesend for the Milton & Gravesend Steam Packet Co. Acquired by the Commercial Co in 1837 and wrecked in 1842.

17. The *Edinborough Castle,* built in 1838, and the *Windsor Castle* (150 tons and 80 hp) built in 1832, were owned by C. H. Frewen of Rye before being acquired by the South Western Steam Packet Co in 1843. —*Railway and Other Steamers,* C. L. D. Duckworth and G. E. Langmuir, T. Stephenson & Sons, 1968, p355.

18. The *Calpe's* summer service was the Weymouth-Cherbourg passage, maintained in conjunction with the *City of Glasgow,* a passage extended to Alderney and Guernsey by the *Kent* for three months in 1839.

19. In 1840, the *Rose* (108ft x 14.1ft x 9ft) sailed between Weymouth and Southampton, calling at Swanage, Yarmouth, Cowes and Ryde. Her later masters included Capts Thomas Francis Scriven, John Geary, Charles Garland and John Attwool. Her registered owners were: George Pearce Scott, innkeeper of Weymouth, Henry Drew of Southampton, William McNeill of Chipstead, Surrey, and Richard Danvers, ward of Chancery—all directors and trustees of the company. Her fares in 1841 between Southampton and Yarmouth were 5s and 3s; and between Southampton and Swanage, 10s and 7s.

20. The *British Queen* was built by Curling & Young, Limehouse, and should have been completed by the spring of 1838. When the *Great Western* was completed on time, the *British Queen's* owners, the British & North American Co, were obliged to charter the Irish steamer *Sirius* in 1838 in order to be first across the Atlantic. The *British Queen* first sailed from the Solent for New York on 12 July 1839 and took fifteen days on passage. In 1839 she made three round voyages, London, Motherbank and New York and in 1840, five. But like most of the early Atlantic steamers, she proved uneconomic and was sold to the Belgian Government in August 1841, being broken up in 1844. Of 1,862 tons and 500 hp, she was claimed to be: 'The largest and finest steam vessel ever built, exceeding by 36ft the length of any ship in the Royal Navy'. She measured 275ft from figurehead to taffrail; 223ft in length of keel; beam between paddle boxes 40ft 6in and overall, 64ft. She had a depth of hold of 27ft and drew, fully laden, 18ft of water. Cylinder diam 77$\frac{1}{2}$in, stroke 7ft. Her master under the British flag was Lieut Richard Roberts, who had once commanded a Royal Navy brig, 'hunting down slavers'. He had commanded the *Sirius* during her historic voyage

241

P

to New York in 1838, and was master of the steamer *President* when she disappeared without trace in the Atlantic in 1841.

21. The *Royal Adelaide* was wrecked on the Tongue Sands, Thames Estuary in 1850.

22. The *Phlegethon* distinguished herself in 1848, rounding up Chinese pirates who, while being transported to India in the *General Wood*, had mutinied, murdered some of the crew and passengers and made off with the ship. The pirates later wrecked the *General Wood* and were captured as they made their escape in small boats.

23. William James Chaplin was originally of the coaching firm of Chaplin & Horne. In 1837 he succeeded W. C. Westlake on the board of the London & Southampton Railway. He was MP for Salisbury, and chairman of the London & South Western Railway only four months before his death in January 1859.—*The London & South Western Railway*, vol 1, R. A. Williams; David & Charles, 1968, pp34, 77 and 92.

24. The *Wonder*: a second inscription reads: 'Presented to the Master Mariners' Club—1933—by Captain John Goodridge, FRAS, AINA. And in memory of Dr Woods, Bishop of Winchester, the Club's first Stowaway Cachalot'. A silver salver, suitably inscribed, was also presented to Capt James Goodridge at the same time, and is now in the possession of J. H. Goodridge, Esq, of Gloucester.

25. One of the *Wonder*'s worst passages was in January 1848 when she took all of 38 hours from Jersey and Guernsey to Southampton, having been obliged by bad weather in mid-Channel to put back into Guernsey where she anchored overnight. She redeemed herself, however, the following November when, under the command of Capt Paul, she made a record passage from Le Havre to Southampton in 6hr 45min.

26. The *Express* was wrecked in September 1859 under the command of Capt Charles Mabbs on passage from Jersey and Guernsey to Weymouth with 200 passengers. She struck on the Grunes Houilleres—a rock in the Goaler passage—and was badly holed. She was got off and steered into St Brelades Bay where it was hoped to beach her, but she struck once again and sunk close inshore with the loss of three lives.

27. The *Dispatch*'s last service was on the Jersey and Granville station. She was hulked in 1885.

28. Capt R. White was relieved of his command in 1846 on the grounds of 'mental affection'. Later, he delivered the steamers, the *Marchioness of Breadalbane* to Egypt and the *Achilles* to India. Returning to England in 1848, he jumped overboard in the Red Sea and was drowned.

29. The *Havre*'s luck finally ran out on 15 February 1875, when she was lost after striking a sunken rock, the Platte Boue, in the Russel Passage, near Guernsey, the passengers, crew and mails being got off safely.

30. The *Southampton*'s two boilers, fitted with Boden's patent superheating apparatus and fed by ten furnaces, gave her a speed of 13.064 knots on the Stokes Bay measured mile. Steam at 151lb/per sq in; paddle wheels at 28rpm, vacuum 22½-24. She was lengthened in 1880; had one funnel removed and new engines, totalling 250 hp, fitted in 1880, and was placed on the Le Havre service. Her last service was on excursion to the Jubilee Fleet Review at Spithead in 1897.

CHAPTER FOUR

1. A mid-nineteenth-century guide book.
2. In December 1817 the *Britannia* was offered for sale by auction by Mr Garnett at the Star and Garter tavern, Portsmouth, '... on Wednesday, 10th day of December, at 12 o'clock unless sooner disposed of by Private Contract,—The Capital new-built STEAM PACKET, called the *Britannia*, with all her Machinery, Tackle, etc., measuring in length about 65ft, and Registered of 50 tons Burthen. This Packet was lately employed in the Passage between Portsmouth and the Isle of Wight, for which sort of service she is admirably adapted; and is fitted in a superior style of machinery and accommodation. For other particulars apply to Mr Goodwin, Butterley Iron Works, near Derby; or the Auctioneer, Portsea, Hants.'—*Hampshire Telegraph*, 24.11.1817.
3. The *Arrow* was offered for sale on 20 July 1826. '... in very good condition; 2 years and ¾ old, goes about 9 miles an hour, fully fitted and equipped.... For inspection, apply to Mr Thomas Heather, Portsmouth.' —*Southampton Herald*, 10.7.1826.
4. Supporters of the Portsmouth & Ryde company distributed the following scurrilous pamphlet, inserted in the *Portsmouth News* of 31.8.1850:
A stands for All of the New Packet Tribe,
Who by hook, or by crook,—by threat or by bribe,
Succeeded in bringing their boats to our shores,
Which will fill every lodging with rogues and Jane Shores.
B are the Bullies who dodge round the Town,
From the Kent to the York—from the York to the Crown,
Whilst C are the Cadgers employed on the Piers,
To curse and swear in the passengers' ears.
D is old Darby, that scrape-butter bear,
With his hoppitty-kickitty fifty bob share;
And E are the engines, all shaken and torn,
From the shocking bad usage they lately have borne.
F are the Fares which the New Packet clique,
extort from the visitors, week after week;
But G are the Grumblers, all over Town,
Who find they've been done, most uncommonly brown.
H are the Hours which were passed without grub
In that Jogging and Keel crazy rotten old tub,*
which was sent off to France, helter skelter one day,
and did what they all do—break down by the way.
L are the Lies, spread the week to trepan,
By that Hen-pecked Arcadian—The Milliner man
N or must we forget, the deep tricks carried on,
By old-Owl-eyes, the cooper, called 'Gentleman John'.
P is that Porter, with visages two,
who Quacks for the Old—underhand for the New.

*A reference to the *Lindsey*.

243

R is the Righteous and Saintly Jackdaw,
who honours the Prophet But(t) lives by the Law.
And **S** are the Shareholders—who'll look very queer,
At their dividends small at the end of the year;
And **T** is the Touter (just fined shillings ten)
who had better be minding his clocks and 'amen'.
V are the vaunts of the Captain and crew
of the *Prince** and the feats she is able to do.
But **W** are the Watermen, cunning and bold,
who wish to the devil, both the New and the Old.
Y are the Yarns, lately spun by the Jew
'That the Peelers had uttered more words that were true'.
Whilst **Z** are the Zanies who will not believe us,
When we say Anti-monopoly is a cry to deceive us.
The etceteras embrace a host of small Fry,
Such as Lapstone the Life-Guard (!) and Peg-leg the Spy.
All eager to Toady those mushroom men,
—'The Dodger', their Agents and clocky Amen.
  Sgd: Brown, Jones and Robinson, their (X) Mark.

5. *Hants Independent*, 8.2.51.
6. Ryde Pier. A double line of tramway was built on the pier in 1864 for horse-drawn trains. In October 1869 small trucks or 'stout oak and iron trolleys' were introduced. These were loaded at the pier gates, carried by tram to the pierhead and lifted by crane onto the deck of the steamer. At Southsea pier, they were craned off and lowered onto trams for carriage to the station. In 1876, steam trains were in use on the pier but they proved unsuccessful. The new pier and railway opened in July 1880. Steam trains were in use from 1881 to 1884 and electric trains from 1886.
7. Ventnor harbour was built by the Ventnor Pier & Harbour Co which was formed in 1861 under the chairmanship of Thomas Willis Fleming with a capital of £20,000, in anticipation of the opening of the Island Railway, Eastern Section. Work commenced on the western arm in April 1863. This was a timber structure, filled with stone taken from Collins Point, a natural groyne, but bad weather prolonged building operations, which lasted two years. Vessels, nevertheless, used the harbour during this period. A Portsmouth steamer was the first vessel to enter the harbour, on 29 June 1863. Unfortunately, removal of stone from Collins Point had left the esplanade exposed to easterly winds with the result that the sea wall was undermined. The harbour arms were also damaged by heavy weather and this, together with a lack of funds, led finally, in May 1867, to the Ventnor Pier & Harbour Co auctioning off the remains of the piers. £400 was realised and the structures were dismantled and taken away by horse and cart.—*The Isle of Wight Mercury*, 27.5.1955.

Ventnor Pier was re-built 1871–72; demolished during a storm in November 1881; and re-built in 1885.

*The *Prince of Wales*.

8. The *Antagonist* was sold foreign in 1867 for the sum of £2,300 after service on the Stokes Bay route.

CHAPTER FIVE

1. Capt Dore: the memorial stone marking his grave in St James' church-yard, I.O.W., overlooking the West Solent, is inscribed: 'Sacred to the memory of Captain Robert Dore, who departed this life May 12, 1848, aged 59. He was 18 years Commander of the *Glasgow* steam packet.'
2. In May 1831, the *Glasgow* was lengthened by 6ft and, during the following August, fitted with 'Mr Rutter's Patent Fuel Arrangement'. The extent of benefit derived from this undoubted improvement is not recorded.

CHAPTER SIX

1. 'Though I speak with the tongue of angels and have not charity, I become as sounding brass, or a tinkling cymbal.'—*1st Corinthians, ch 13.*

CHAPTER SEVEN

1. Towage charges. JOHN LEE. March 1845.

	Under 100 tons	100 to 250	250 to 400	500 to 500	500 to 700	700 to 1,000
In or out of So'ton docks, or the river Itchen, from or to So'ton Water, at the entrance of the Itchen	£1	£1 5	£1 10	£2	£2 10	£4 0
From entrance of Itchen, in So'ton Water, to or from Calshot Castle	£1 10	£2	£2 10	£3	£5	£7
From Calshot Castle to the Needles or vice versa	£5	£7	£8	£9	£10	£14
From Calshot Castle to Cowes or Motherbank or vice versa	£3	£4	£6	£7	£8	£10
From Calshot Castle to Spithead or vice versa	£5	£6	£7	£8	£10	£12
For any distance above the Itchen to Eling or Redbridge or the upper part of So'ton Water or vice versa	£1 10	£2	£2 10	£3	£5	£7

—*Hants Independent*, 1.3.1845

2. The *Aid* was broken up 1878. The *Phoenix*, converted to barge in 1878, was broken up in 1912.
3. Other Southampton tugs included the *Pioneer*, built in 1859 and owned by John Hodgkinson; wood; 52 tons gross, 13 net; 75ft 3in x 15ft 5in x 8ft 1in; 24 hp; and the *Rose Diamond*, built in 1860 and owned by G. H. Ackers; iron screw; 30 tons gross, 6 net; 76ft 1in x 10ft 4in x 6ft 5in; 20 hp; Southampton's first iron screw tug after Lamb's *Mary*.

1. In 1784, George Ward married Mary Woodfall (died 1813) and had six sons and five daughters. He had a brother and two sisters, one of whom, Charity, married Dr William Saunders, Physician to the Prince, and their daughter, Mary, married her first cousin, George Henry Ward (born 1785). George Henry died childless in 1849 and the estate passed to William George Ward, whose descendants now reside at Cowes. The Ward family seat, Northwood House, built in 1837, replaced a smaller mansion damaged by fire the same year. It was given to the people of Cowes by the late Capt H. J. Ward and now accommodates the town hall and council offices, the grounds serving as a public park.

2. William Fitzhugh, one of three children of Valentine and Elizabeth (*nee* Palmentier), was educated at Winchester College (1770-4) and in 1792 married Charlotte, daughter of Archdeacon Hamilton, Vicar of St Martin-in-the-Fields. Two of their four children died at an early age.

3. William Anthony Fitzhugh was educated at Winchester College (1806-9), Christchurch, Oxford and Trinity College, Cambridge, obtaining his BA degree in 1818. He took Holy Orders, became deacon in 1817 and, in the same year, priest at North Baddesley Church, Hampshire. In 1820 he married Mary Anne, youngest daughter of Thomas Lane of Bradbourne Place, near Sevenoaks.

4. The Rouen-Paris railway line opened in May 1843, and the Havre-Rouen line in March 1847.

5. William Chamberlayne was noted for his benevolence to the people of Southampton and was the prime mover in the establishment of the gasworks in Southampton in 1819. He presented the town with gas-lamp standards, and in 1822, in their turn, local worthies replied with a large column surmounted by a gas light which was dedicated to Chamberlayne and sited at Houndswell and later, 1829-65, on the Town Quay. Now unlighted, it graces the centre of Houndswell roundabout, Southampton. He was a great patron of the arts and his magnificent collection of pictures and furniture remain still in Cranbury Park. He died childless in 1829 at the age of sixty-eight and was buried in Peartree churchyard, Woolston. The estate then passed to his cousin, Thomas Chamberlayne of Charlton, Kent, who owned the famous yachts *Quiver* and *Arrow*. His son—who owned Netley Abbey and gave Netley village its recreation ground—and the grandson each maintained the family's keen participation in yachting.

6. George Player came of a distinguished local family whose ancestors took up residence in the Isle of Wight in 1705 when Henry Player of Alverstoke bought Ryde House from Sir John Dillington. Until the death of George Player, the Players were Lords of the Manor and considerably influenced the development of Ryde and Ashley. St Thomas Church, Ryde, which was erected by George Player in 1827, replaced a small chapel built by Thomas Player in 1719, the then Lord of the Manor. The Player arms appear on the west front of the present church. George Player was survived by two daughters, and Ryde House passed

to the descendants of the second daughter, Elizabeth Lydia, who married Capt Thomas Robert Brigstocke, RN. The Brigstockes remained Lords of the Manor and owners of Ryde House until the death of George Robert Brigstocke in 1956. His two sons having died without issue during the World War II, this branch of the family then ceased. Ryde House is now a private residence.

7. Mrs R. W. Ford launched the *Prince Consort* in 1859, and the *Princess of Wales* was launched in 1865 by Miss Ford, presumably a daughter. In 1852, R. W. Ford was a town councillor for St Thomas's Ward; guardian from 1858 to 1869; and mayor of Portsmouth, 1864 to 1865. He resigned from the council in 1880 and became a Clerk of the Peace, not missing a sitting until his death, twenty years later. He left five sons of whom two were members of the legal profession, one an architect, one a medical practitioner and one an Army surgeon.

8. Charles St Barbe was mayor of Lymington in 1835-40-43-46 and 48, and was also an eminently successful banker, for while other banks were continually failing, his survived and presumably prospered. He was a member of the Whiteparish branch of the St Barbe family who acquired the Broadlands estate in 1586 and retained it until its acquisition by Lord Palmerston.

9. W. C. Westlake (1791-1837), principal owner of the *Emerald*, was a prominent local businessman, grain merchant and, in 1831, a director of the Southampton & London Branch Railway & Dock Co. He built Southampton's principal grain store in 1829 on a site at Chapel Quay close to the iron shop of Pollock & Brown.

10. Capt J. H. Knight Snr died on 14 January 1838 at the age of sixty-one and was buried in St Mary's churchyard, Cowes, alongside the grave of his youngest son, Edward Knight, who died on 18 June 1826. His eldest son, Capt J. H. Knight Jnr, died on 7 December 1840, aged forty-two.

11. David Corke Snr died at his home, 3 Terminus Terrace, Southampton, on 9 March 1866, aged sixty-nine, and was buried in St Mary's churchyard, Southampton.

12. See also, *An Account of the Life and Experiences of Captain John Bazin*, by James Crabb, John Mason, London, 1837.

13. Capt James Goodridge had three daughters in addition to his three sons. One daughter married and moved to London; Thyrsa, born 1815, married into the Bascombe family which was connected with Capt Hardy of the *Victory*; and Eudosia, born 1819, became the central figure of an unfortunate court case in July 1840. Capt Goodridge was ultimately awarded £400 damages against young Terry Brooks for having 'seduced' Eudosia while the widower captain was at sea and the two daughters remained unchaperoned in the house.—*Hants Independent*, 4.7.1840.

Capts James Goodridge Snr and Jnr both received numerous testimonials and awards, which were distributed among the family following the death of J. Goodridge Jnr in 1876 at Swanage. The whereabouts of several pieces are known: a silver snuffbox, presented to Goodridge Snr by the Bishop of Winchester, dated 29 August 1843 and engraved '... in remembrance of a fog off Alderney...' is in the possession of Mrs M. Knight of Lymington. A claret jug, in silver, presented to

247

Goodridge Jnr by the ladies of Jersey in 1858, and inscribed, '... in commemoration of the People's Banquet to celebrate the inauguration of the electric Telegraph...', is in possession of Mr A. G. Lanham, of Starcross, Devon. A silver hot-water jug, presented to Goodridge Snr by the inhabitants of Guernsey and inscribed '... testimonial of esteem and record of his professional and private qualities...' is in possession of Mr D. Crofts, of Bristol. A telescope, presented to J. Goodridge Jnr by the directors of the South Western Steam Packet Co and inscribed '... in commemoration of their visit on board the *Courrier* at the Naval Review at Spithead, August 11th, 1853...', is in possession of Mr J. H. Goodridge, of Bristol. He also has a silver snuffbox, presented to Goodridge Jnr by the inhabitants of Alderney in 1842, and the silver salver, presented to Goodridge Jnr for his part in the great storm of 1847. The companion piece to this *Wonder* salver, a silver speaking trumpet, is now on display in the Master Mariners' Club, Southampton.

ACKNOWLEDGEMENTS

The author would like gratefully to record his indebtedness to the following for the kind advice and assistance which helped to make this book possible:

The late J. Attwood, of Portswood, Southampton

D. E. L. Archdeacon, Secretary, S., I.O.W. & S.O.E. R.M.S.P. Co

The Hon Commissioners of Customs & Excise

The late G. Finlay, Secretary, Hythe Steam Ferry Co

T. V. H. Fitzhugh, of Ottershaw, Surrey

J. H. Goodridge, FICE, MIMunE, MIWE, of Gloucester

T. W. Graham and the Staff of the Central Library, Southampton

Dr R. Hope, OBE, MA, DPhil, Director, Seafarers' Education Service

Dr J. Mackett, of Wootton Bridge

W. Mitchell, formerly Chairman, World Ship Society (Southampton Branch)

The late J. P. M. Pannel, MBE, MICE, MIMechE, of Southampton

The late C. W. Payne, TD, Managing Director, S., I.O.W. & S.O.E. R.M.S.P. Co

E. D. G. Payne, of Ryde, I.O.W.

P. Raynes, Librarian, Southern Newspapers, Southampton

The Registrar General of Shipping & Seamen, Cardiff

H. Sargeant, FLA, City Curator and Librarian, Portsmouth

Capt G. Thomas, of Rocomb, Lyme Regis

A. H. Waites, Curator; and G. A. Osbon, of the National Maritime Museum, Greenwich

The late Capt H. J. Ward and W. Ward, of Egypt House, Cowes

E. A. Westlake, of Droxford, Hants

Those who kindly furnished illustrations which are individually acknowledged.

The author also wishes to acknowledge the valuable help of Mr Malcolm Pinhorn who generously spent a considerable time assisting him with the preliminary revision of the text of this book.

And finally, Professor and Mrs P. B. Morice, without whose kindly encouragement and assistance this book would not have seen the light of day.

INDEX

Page numbers in bold type refer to illustrations

251